INVENTING THE NATION

General Editor: Keith Robbins

China

Henrietta Harrison
Lecturer in Chinese, University of Leeds

Hodder Arnold

A MEMBER OF THE HODDER HEADLINE GROUP

First published in Great Britain in 2001 by
Hodder Arnold, an imprint of Hodder Education
and a member of the Hodder Headline Group,
an Hachette Livre UK Company,
338 Euston Road, London NW1 3BH

www.hoddereducation.co.uk

The advice and information in this book are believed to be true and
accurate at the date of going to press, but neither the author nor the publisher
can accept any legal responsibility for any errors or omissions.

British Library Cataloguing in Publication Data
A catalogue record for this book is available from the British Library

Library of Congress Cataloging-in-Publication Data
A catalog record for this book is available from the Library of Congress

ISBN 978 0 340 74134 4

4 5 6 7 8 9 10

Typeset in 10/12 pt Sabon by Phonex Photosetting, Chatham, Kent
Printed and bound in India by Replika Press Pvt. Ltd.

What do you think about this book? Or any other Hodder Education title?
Please send your comments to www.hoddereducation.co.uk

Contents

List of illustrations

General editor's preface

The contemporary world is both repelled and attracted by the existence of the nation. Talk of globalisation sometimes presumes that the nation will fade away as organisations and individuals build for themselves new networks which by-pass the commonalities and loyalties expressed in the idea of the nation. Nationalism, too, whenever it is that various writers have supposed it to have 'risen', has been held to have been an unmitigated disaster, at least when it has been accompanied, as it not infrequently has been, by virulent xenophobia and intolerance. In the twentieth century there were significant attempts to restrain or circumvent the influence of nationalism by creating international or supranational structures and agencies.

On the other hand, it is apparent that the nation has not in fact faded away and, despite the surge of new nations, or at least new states, in the second half of that century, there remain across the contemporary world communities which feel themselves to be nations, or are in the process of becoming nations, and who see in the attainment of statehood a legitimate, desirable and beneficial goal. In other contexts, too, old nations reaffirm themselves as necessary carriers of individuality and distinctiveness in a world threatened by homogeneity. It is asserted that the nation remains the essential building block in the structure of the contemporary world. Nationalism need not be vicious. Nations can and do speak peace unto nations.

It becomes clear, however, reading references of 'narrow nationalism' on the one hand or 'national liberation' on the other, that how particular nations come to exist or be defined remains obscure and contentious. This series revisits these issues in the light of extensive debates about national identity which have been conducted over recent decades by historians, anthropologists, political scientists and sociologists in particular. To speak of 'Inventing the Nation' picks up one of the interpretations which has gained favour, or at least excited interest. Influential writers have seen 'invention' taking place in Europe in the 'springtime of the nations' at the dawn of 'modern' history, though their explanations have varied. Others, however, have regarded 'invention' with some suspicion and identify a medieval if not primordial 'nation'. Problems of definition and location clearly abound.

In these circumstances, it is pertinent to revisit the history of particular countries with these concepts and issues firmly in mind, though individual authors are not restricted or restrained in their interpretations by the series title. The case of China, however, presents a special challenge. Rarely have historians brought to the study of China's history those questions about nation-building and national identity that have become central to the concerns of historians of European countries. For some, the long history of China as a unitary state undermines the notion that nationalism is necessarily a phenomenon of modernity. For others, to cite the example of China does not discount this view. China, it is said, is merely the exception that proves the rule. In any case, for others, it is the very size and scale of China (to be compared with Europe as a whole rather than any single European nation) that makes it 'different' and difficult, if not impossible, to be compared with the history of practically any other country.

In reality, despite the confident deployment of 'the case of China' by one side or the other in this debate, few general theorists of nationalism have had sufficient specific knowledge of how Chinese history has evolved for their statements to be convincing, one way or the other. Henrietta Harrison, however, comes to these matters from the perspective of a Chinese historian. The merit of her book, in the context of this series and more generally, is that it tackles the issues of nationality, ethnicity and identity in Chinese history as being quite fundamental to any understanding of that history. It is a 'national' history that merits attention for its own sake, not merely because China may supposedly constitute, in a global context, an awkward exception to which Eurocentric writers on nationalism feel obliged to make some puzzled references in footnotes, and then pass on. They will have no excuse for doing so in the future.

Keith Robbins
Vice-Chancellor
University of Wales, Lampeter

Acknowledgements

The author and publishers would like to thank the following for permission to use copyright material in this book:

The Palace Museum, Beijing, for 'The Qianlong emperor as a Tibetan bodhisattva' (Fig. 2.1); The British Museum for 'Qing troops victorious over the foreigners with the aid of the Boxers' (Fig. 3.2); The No. 2 Archives, Nanjing, for 'Formal dress as specified by law in 1912' (Fig. 6.1) and 'The young Chiang Kaishek' (Fig. 6.5); Kwong Sang Hong for 'Kwong Sang Hong advertising calendar, 1930' (Fig. 6.7); The Bodleian Library, Oxford, for 'Political tutelage according to the party leader's teaching' (Fig. 8.1).

Every effort has been made to contact all copyright holders. Any rights not acknowledged here will be acknowledged in subsequent printings if notice is given to the publisher.

Chronology

1881	Establishment of a national telegraph system
1884	War with France over Vietnam
1895	War with Japan over Korea; Taiwan ceded to Japan
	Sun Yatsen's first revolutionary uprising in Guangzhou
1898	Hundred Days' Reforms
1900	Boxer Uprising
1904	Japan defeats Russia in a war for dominance over Manchuria
1905	Abolition of the examination system
1908–11	*Xuantong emperor*
1911	Revolution
	Mongolia declares independence
1912	**Establishment of the Republic of China**
	Presidency of Sun Yatsen
1912–16	*Presidency of Yuan Shikai*
1913	Dalai Lama declares Tibet independent
	Conference on the Unification of Pronunciation
1914	Japan enters WWI and captures the German treaty port of Qingdao
1919	May 4th Movement
1920	Sun Yatsen establishes the Nationalist Party
	Chinese Communist Party founded
1921	Soviet Russian forces establish a constitutional monarchy in Mongolia
1925	Death of Sun Yatsen
1926-28	Northern Expedition
1928	Nationalist Party government established
1931	Japan invades Manchuria and attacks Shanghai
1933	Japanese troops enter north China
1936	Xian incident
1937–45	War of resistance against Japan
1945–49	Civil war
1947	Government of the Republic of China moved to Taiwan
1949	**Establishment of the People's Republic of China**
1950–53	Korean War
1956	Hundred Flowers Movement and Anti-rightist Movement
1958	Great Leap Forward
1959	Revolt in Tibet. Dalai Lama flees to India
1966–69	Cultural Revolution
1976	Death of Mao Zedong
1980	Deng Xiaoping becomes premier and initiates reforms
1986	Martial law lifted in Taiwan
1988	*River Elegy* television series
1989	Tiananmen Square protests
1997	Hong Kong returned to China

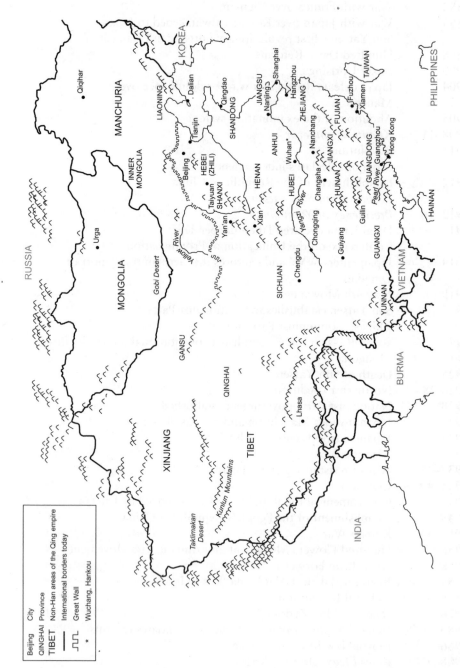

A map of China showing places referred to in the text

Introduction

The idea of China as an invented nation is of interest to historians for two reasons: first, because it is important to our understanding of how nations are constructed, and second, because Chinese nationalism is a vital ingredient in the contemporary political situation of the People's Republic of China.

Historians such as Anderson, Gellner and Hobsbawm have argued that the idea of the nation state was a new ideology of government which emerged in Europe from about the eighteenth century and replaced other, quite different, conceptions of government. More recently there has been considerable debate as to the extent to which certain 'historic nations' may or may not have had a shared sense of identity before this period. In all these arguments China is frequently cited. China is a huge country with a long history as a unitary state. Moreover, the ideology of nationalism played a central role in China's twentieth-century history. Clearly, China could well be depicted as a major exception to the argument for nations as the product of eighteenth-century nationalism. The authors of the literature on nationalism, however, cite China only tentatively and in passing. The reason for this is not hard to understand: China's history has far too often been regarded as so exceptional and different from that of other countries that comparisons have been seen as irrelevant or unhelpful. Thus, while the sweeping scale of the theories of nationalism means that their authors feel a need to consider China as an example, there has been very little literature through which the reader outside the specialist realm of Chinese history can attempt to assess its contribution. This book is intended to redress that balance.

It is only by looking at the way in which the nation was constructed that we can understand the way in which nationalism operates in China's international relations today and the power relationships it encodes within the state. After the American bombing of the Chinese embassy in Yugoslavia in the summer of 1999 feelings ran high in China. Demonstrations at the American and British embassies in the capital were described by the foreign press as 'orchestrated' and were undoubtedly used by the government both to increase nationalist feeling at home and to demonstrate Chinese anger at the bombings to a world audience. However, there is also plenty of evidence of strong popular feeling, with many resident foreigners reporting (quite unorchestrated) displays of hostility. These events show the power of the nationalist narrative of history which provides a framework through which current events can be interpreted and understood. Where news stories appear to fit into this narrative their importance is magnified and they can become powerful symbols. Prior to the bombing the presence of NATO troops in Yugoslavia was already, to many Chinese eyes, reminiscent of the gunboat diplomacy of the western powers in China in the nineteenth century. The Western bombing of a Chinese embassy not only recalled the era of the opium wars and unequal treaties, but also seemed to illustrate the hypocrisy of Western treatments of diplomatic privilege. Used to interpret the present, the narrative of China's national humiliation and resistance to imperialism comes to shape contemporary events.

On the issue of Taiwan, nationalist feeling in China plays an important role on the international stage. Most observers agree that the majority of Chinese in the People's Republic of China support their government's claim that because the inhabitants of Taiwan are culturally Chinese and the island was part of the Qing empire it should be part of a single Chinese state. In an environment where nationalism is central to government legitimacy, and where factions within the state may compete to gain a reputation for nationalism, such beliefs exacerbate regional instability. In Taiwan people fear that nationalist feeling on the mainland combined with a growing role for the military in the state might be enough to spark an invasion. Whether or not this is the case, the fear itself plays a major role in Taiwan's domestic politics and in international perceptions of the stability or otherwise of the Taiwan Straits.

It is easy to question the rather simplistic narrative of modern Chinese history put forward by nationalists, but in fact historians have proposed China as an exception to the idea of the invented nation. There are two main lines of argument that suggest this conclusion. The first is that premodern China already had the features of a nation state. If we define the nation state as having a common language, a common culture and a single bureaucracy whose members could serve in any part of the state, then (with the qualification that the common language concerned was written rather than spoken) the area that the Chinese referred to as 'the 18 provinces' can already be seen as a nation state before the arrival of the Western sea powers in the eighteenth century. However, although China was, to use Anderson's term, an imagined community, that community was not coterminous with the state. Moreover, the common culture developed only gradually in what had originally been a much more regionally and socially diverse society, probably reaching its height in the nineteenth century. The first chapter of this book describes how by that time the textually based cultural tradition of the elite had permeated the lives of even the lowest social classes. However, from the seventeenth century China had become part of a Manchu empire that included Tibet, Mongolia, Manchuria itself and part of Muslim central Asia. The Manchu emperors who ruled China from Beijing governed each of these areas according to its own language and traditions. Government documents were written in both the Manchu and Chinese languages and Chinese officials were restricted to positions within the 18 provinces. The shared written language and culture of the people of China proper continued to provide them with a sense of identity, but this had to be accommodated to fit with an empire that included, and was ruled by, large groups who did not share that culture.

The second argument for China being an exception to the processes through which nations have been invented and constructed is based on the idea of China as a civilisation rather than a state. According to this view, most famously set out by Joseph Levenson, Chinese identity was based on a worldview in which China was, quite simply, the centre of civilisation. Thus loyalty to China was not an attachment to any particular state, but a commitment to humane and civilised values. Indeed, the territories beyond China were seen as being made up not of alternative civilisations but of tributary states, who paid allegiance to the superior virtue of the Chinese emperor and beyond them wild savages. Following this line of argument, Chinese identity was not 'invented' after contact with the Western powers but merely transformed, a transformation Levenson describes as being from 'culturalism' to nationalism. Again the weakness of the argument is its failure to take account of the Manchu empire. For at the heart of the civilised world sat a Manchu emperor whose commitment to Chinese values was combined with a determination to preserve a separate Manchu culture. Indeed, it now seems likely that the commitment to China as the centre of civilised values was, in part, the product of rule by this culturally alien group. Acceptance of Manchu rule by the bureaucratic elite and loyalty to the new dynasty required that the state be reenvisioned in a way that would remove the focus from cultural or ethnic identity. Thus loyalty to civilised values legitimised Manchu rule even as it created an image of the state that obscured the Manchu empire.

In this book I will argue that China as it exists today was invented through the construction of a modern state, in very much the same way as many of the European nation states. From the late nineteenth century we see the development of a new culture closely linked to efforts to build a modern nation state. The idea of the nation state was imported alongside other aspects of modernisation and its advocates were the radical modernisers of the time. The debate began with the question of how China should respond to Western imperialism. The introduction and rapid spread of Western-style newspapers not only increased the number of people who felt themselves to be active participants in the debate, but also created a sense of community among them. There has been much disagreement among scholars about the growth of a public sphere in China. However, it is clear that the idea that it was right and proper for those outside the government to discuss issues of state was a product of the last years of the nineteenth century. With the creation of a republic in 1911 members of this community began to identify themselves as patriotic citizens through certain new customs and practices. They wore their hair short, adopted elements of Western clothing and celebrated holidays commemorating events of the Republic on dates calculated by the new solar calendar. As these practices spread so did the modern nationalism that went with them. The importance of the modern nationalist movement in shaping the Chinese government's response to Japanese invasion in the 1930s and 1940s illustrates how powerful and influential it was by that point. After the establishment of the People's Republic in 1949 vigorous state-building efforts spread what had previously been a primarily urban national culture to the countryside while also creating for the first time both a single bureaucracy covering the whole country and a national spoken language.

This process of interaction between modern state-building and the creation of a national culture is similar to that through which other nations have been invented; China's peculiarity lies in the role played by the structures of empires in the creation of the modern nation. The role of Western imperialism in the formation of nations in the non-western world has long been realised. The Western imperial powers not only supplied the ideology of the nation state, but in many cases also created the boundaries of the new nations. The elites who took part in the invention of modern national cultures did so in response to Western ideologies and the threat of Western power. However, in China's case, while Western imperialism supplied the ideology and many of the forms of modern nationhood, the territory of the new state was inherited from the Manchu Qing empire. From the first days of the Republic in 1912 it was obvious that the creation of a Chinese nation state out of the Qing empire would be deeply problematic for the vast areas of the empire that did not share the Chinese culture or language and had previously been ruled by a Manchu, not Chinese, bureaucracy. Mongolia declared independence in 1912 and Outer Mongolia has subsequently become an independent nation state. Tibet, Inner Mongolia and Chinese Central Asia, on the other hand, have been incorporated within the People's Republic of China. The desire to include these areas within the Chinese nation state has inevitably affected the way that Chinese nationhood has been constructed.

Modern nationalists who have ruled China since the fall of the Qing have used various means to try to solve the paradox of a nation state which is also an empire. Central to all of these has been an attempt to equate Chinese identity with modernity. Since the standards of modernity were adopted as a result of Western imperialist pressures in the nineteenth century, this has often had the effect of identifying what is Chinese with Western practices. Thus, for example, the queue, a nomadic hairstyle forcibly adopted by the

Chinese after the seventeenth-century Manchu conquest, had by the nineteenth century become an accepted marker of Chinese identity both in China and abroad. When republican revolutionaries demanded in 1911 that men cut off their queues they told patriotic Chinese to replace this 'foreign' hairstyle not with the Ming dynasty topknot but with Western men's hairstyles. Moreover the same sartorial transformation was demanded of the Mongols, who had never seen the queue as a Manchu imposition. The abolition of the queue is only one example of a process through which the modern nationalists rejected almost all the symbols of China's pre-modern identity. The common written language, now known as classical Chinese, was attacked in the early years of the twentieth century and had effectively ceased to exist as a living language by the 1950s. The young men and women who attacked the written form of the Chinese language did so because they knew that it embodied the cultural values of the imperial state. For them the building of the nation state demanded the replacement of traditional cultural practices and values with an entirely new modern culture. The result was a form of nationalism that was, and continues to be, the exclusive property of those groups and classes committed to modernisation.

As in other countries, nationalism has been tied to the existence of certain social classes who have benefited from the nation state. Alongside the history of nation-building, this book will also trace the interactions between popular and elite nationalism and the ways in which nationalism has been used to encode inequalities of power. Since the fall of the Qing in 1911 there have been shifts in the social background of China's ruling elite, but the commitment to the forms of Western-style modernity as a definition of nationalism has never been shaken. Because nationalist feeling has been widely seen as a prerequisite for full participation in the state, the identification of nationalism with Western-style modernity has had the effect of excluding large portions of the population. The beginnings of this exclusion are seen well before the fall of the Qing in the bitter debate over official support for the Boxer movement in 1900. The Boxers were based in rural north China and their patriotism involved the active rejection of Western influence. Since that time lifestyles and values influenced by the West have spread beyond the treaty ports and into the interior and rural areas. Widespread support for the leadership given by modernising political groups, especially the Communist Party, during World War II helped to reduce the division between traditional forms of identity and modern nationalism. Moreover, during the early years of the People's Republic of China many of the outer forms of modern nationalism, such as the wearing of Western-style dress and the rejection of traditional religion, were forcibly imposed on much of the population. Nevertheless, members of the rural population who adhere to the forms of traditional identity have continued to be regarded as less nationalist and patriotic than committed modernisers.

The view of the ethnic Chinese members of the nation state as exemplars of modernity has also resulted in the exclusion of members of non-Chinese groups within the state. If nationalism is defined as conformity to a Chinese image of modernity then members of non-Chinese groups face a stark choice between assimilating to Chinese ways or being regarded as both backward and unpatriotic. Thus the contemporary Chinese state has recreated the Qing dynasty dichotomy between a civilised China and uncivilised savages. Civilisation is monopolised by the Chinese state, while those who do not conform to its norms are dismissed as savages whose proper role is to be civilised and transformed into holders of Chinese values. During the Qing dynasty this ideology was used to legitimate the rule of a non-Chinese dynasty; today it functions to confirm Chinese rule in those non-Chinese regions of the Manchu empire that the People's Republic has inherited. The growth of Tibetan and Uyghur nationalist movements bears witness to the problems of trying to include these non-Chinese groups within a Chinese nation state. Moreover, the adoption of a nationality policy based on early twentieth-century Western views of race and heredity means that even those members of China's 'ethnic minorities' who do assimilate will continue to bear the label of their non-Chinese status. The attempt to elide Chinese identity with modernity has, as yet, failed to solve the dilemma created by the construction of a Chinese nation state from the ruins of the Qing empire.

I argue in this book that China has not been an exception to the process of the invention of nations. This is not to deny the importance of China's ancient cultural and political heritage in the making of the modern nation, but to suggest that we need to be constantly aware of the ways in which that heritage has been manipulated and in part destroyed by modern nationalists. In this respect China has much in common with those European states, such as England and France, which have been put forward as examples of 'historical nations'. Where China is different is in the exceptional complexity of the relationship between nation and empire. Chinese nationalism grew out of the collision between traditional views of the world and the expansionist empires of Europe. But the role of imperialism was not limited to European empires: the Manchu Qing empire played quite as great a role in the construction of the modern Chinese nation state as did the ideologies that followed the maritime empires of the European nations. Chinese nationalists have been torn between defining the Chinese nation in opposition to imperialism and maintaining the territory of their own empire, a contradiction that has been at the heart of the shaping of the modern Chinese nation.

PART

I

PRE-MODERN CHINESE IDENTITY

1

A common culture

Eighteenth-century Chinese lived in a state the size of Europe. The languages, customs and economic conditions of the different regions varied greatly. People in Shanxi in the northwest spoke dialects of Mandarin, ate wheat and millet as their staple diet, burned coal to heat their houses in the bitter winters and traded livestock and furs with the peoples of the central Asian steppe to the north. In Guangdong in the far south people spoke dialects of Cantonese, ate rice and sweet potatoes, feared the torrential tropical storms that destroyed houses and villages, and traded tea, silks and porcelains with merchants from southeast Asia and Europe. However, despite the differences that separated them, people in Shanxi and in Guangdong shared a perception of themselves as having not only a common political system but also a common cultural heritage.

That common cultural heritage was based on the history of a unified state at the heart of the area we now call China. Eighteenth-century Chinese would have traced this state back to the earliest emperors, mythical culture-heroes who taught the people to domesticate animals, farm and trade. However that may be, it is clear that by the time the first emperor of the Qin dynasty conquered the other warring states in 221 BC there had long been a common culture and aspirations to political unity. From then on there were many periods of disunity but ideas of political unity were never entirely lost and for many centuries there was indeed a unified state. Eighteenth-century Chinese, like many today, told China's history as the story of an unbroken line of dynasties ruling a gradually expanding area of land. While this story tends to obscure the histories of the lands that were conquered during the expansion, it does nevertheless suggest the importance of the centralised state in the creation of a sense of Chinese identity.

Structures of the Chinese state

Language

History was dominated by the Chinese cultural area in great part because it was written in Chinese characters. The earliest examples of written characters date from the sixteenth century BC. These very early examples of writing were discovered in archaeological excavations of the twentieth century; eighteenth-century readers were acquainted with a volume of literature that stretched back to at least the fifth century BC. The widespread use of a common written language was the product of the structures through which the state was governed. In the eighteenth-century boys in frontier towns in newly conquered areas of northwest China were learning to read in Chinese as well as the Arabic their fathers had read because it was the ability to read and write in Chinese that gave access to the Chinese state.

The unity of the written language was particularly important because of the great differences between the Chinese dialects spoken in different parts of the country. These so-called dialects have a degree of difference comparable to that between European languages. However, in the eighteenth century the grammar and vocabulary of the most commonly used written forms of Chinese bore little relation to those of any dialect. Moreover, the ideographic nature of the characters meant that there was little restriction on the way in which they could be pronounced. The result was that the written language could be used across the country by people whose speech was mutually incomprehensible: readers simply pronounced the written characters in their own dialects. Indeed the written language was also used by the elites of Korea and Japan, whose own spoken languages belong to an entirely different language family from that of the various Chinese dialects. Visitors from these countries could even conduct conversations with their hosts in writing, as did some Chinese travellers.

However, the vast majority of people, including the highly educated, never travelled outside the area in which versions of their own dialects were used. Merchants and other regular travellers would simply learn the different dialects they needed for their work. High officials who did move regularly across the whole country learnt to speak the north China dialect used at the court in Beijing. Under the label 'official language' (translated 'Mandarin' by contemporary Westerners) this became a kind of *lingua franca* for the bureaucracy, but emperors continued to fulminate against the incomprehensible speeches made by officials newly arrived from the south. The size of the country, the difference of the dialects and the nature of the written language all combined to preserve the multiplicity of dialects and Mandarin was used as a common language only by a few men at the highest levels of the bureaucracy. However, the existence of a single written language was what made possible a unified education system and thus a culture that was shared across the state.

Bureaucracy and the examination system

The existence of a national bureaucracy whose members could be sent anywhere in the country was probably the most important feature in the creation of a common sense of identity. The division of the entire state into counties ruled by magistrates appointed directly by the emperor is credited to the first emperor of the Qin dynasty in the third century BC. From at least the twelfth century these officials were chosen primarily by an examination system that tested their knowledge of classical texts and their facility with the written language.

The literature studied by candidates for the bureaucracy in the eighteenth century was primarily concerned with the creation of a moral society. The set texts for the exams were the Four Books and Five Classics and one particular set of commentaries on them that broadly defined their meaning. The Five Classics are a selection of early texts chosen around the second century BC to represent orthodox state ideology. Over the centuries Confucian thought changed, moving away from the precise ritual prescriptions and detailed records of the Five Classics and towards broader philosophical speculation. This trend was strengthened by the growing influence of Buddhist ideas (first introduced in the first century AD) and the new philosophical questions they posed. In the twelfth century the philosopher Zhu Xi made a new selection of ancient texts, which reflected the changes that had been taking place. This new set of texts was called the Four Books. The flavour of the selection is well indicated by the opening sentence of the compendium: 'The way of greater learning lies in keeping one's inborn luminous Virtue unobscured, in renewing the people, and in coming to rest in perfect goodness.'[1]

Central to the texts was the idea that only by adherence to a strict personal morality could the state be successfully governed. This is summed up in the following quotation, which follows a few lines later:

> Those of antiquity who wished that all men throughout the empire keep their inborn luminous Virtue unobscured put governing their states well first; wishing to govern their states well, they first established harmony in their households; wishing to establish harmony in their households, they first cultivated themselves; wishing to cultivate themselves, they first set their minds in the right; wishing to set their minds in the right, they first made their thoughts true; wishing to make their thoughts true, they first extended their knowledge to the utmost; the extension of knowledge lies in fully apprehending the principle of things.[2]

In addition to making his selection, Zhu Xi wrote the commentaries to the texts which later also came to be required for the exams. These commentaries controlled and limited possible interpretations of the texts to the philosophically based neo-Confucianism of which Zhu Xi was one of the leading thinkers.

In the examinations for posts in the bureaucracy candidates had to write essays and poems on passages or phrases selected from the Four Books and Five Classics. A typical examination question used in the mid-Qing read: 'The Master said to Yan Yuan, "To be used and then go, to be laid aside and then leave; only you and I have this."'[3] This is a quotation from the *Analects* of Confucius, which is one of the Four Books. ('The Master' is Confucius and Yan Yuan was his favourite disciple.) The candidate, who would have known the full text of the *Analects* by heart, was expected to identify the context of the quotation and then write an essay that explored the implications of the Master's comment for contemporary government and morality. The answer was expected to follow the broad lines of the philosophical interpretation of Zhu Xi and was also restricted in terms of literary style, structure and calligraphy. Thus candidates for official posts were trained to operate within a system that allowed freedom for individual opinion but within a format and philosophical framework that was specified and controlled by the government.

Eighteenth-century examination candidates were also expected to memorise the *Sacred Edict* of the Kangxi emperor. Indeed one of the sections of the lowest-level exams was simply to write it out from memory. This edict was a summary of Confucian doctrine in 16 points composed by the emperor in the late seventeenth century for the edification of the general public. Kangxi ordered that a copy of his edict should exist in every house in the empire and 30 million were printed and distributed. In addition he arranged for public lectures to be held on each of the points on the first and fifteenth of every month. The first part of the edict is concerned with harmony within the family and the local community, urging the reader to obey his parents, elder brothers and clansmen, be frugal and promote agriculture. The second part turns to even more explicit demands for obedience to the state: the reader should avoid heretical doctrines, obey and support the law, pay his taxes and take part in government-sponsored groupings of households. The effect of the summary is to reduce the whole of the Confucian classics to a demand for social order and obedience to the government.

Thus the examination system tested aspiring officials in a set of classical texts with a very limited philosophical and political interpretation that had been confirmed by the emperor. The degree of conformity this required was exacerbated by the ever-increasing number of candidates who competed for a very limited number of official positions. Candidates sat a series of exams and only those who reached the highest level of all were eligible for official positions. The process that led to the awarding of the first degree, which was considerably less selective than either of the higher degrees, suggests the impact the examination system was likely to have on those who took part in it. The examination was administered in the local county town. It was divided into sections spread over two weeks and for this period the students had to reside in the town. First the candidate had to attend the registration in the company of an existing degree-holder who acted as his sponsor. This had the effect of bringing into the town several local degree-holders who were paid by the candidates for their services and spent their time in each other's company. The following day before dawn the candidates gathered in the buildings where the exams were being held. Questions were given out at first light and the candidates had to compose an essay of 600 words. These were collected around 10 o'clock and a poetry exercise was handed out. Candidates who were quick might finish and leave in the afternoon but some stayed much longer as the time limit was not until midnight or the following dawn. The essays and poems were marked over the next two days and the names of those who had passed displayed on wooden boards outside the examination halls. Those who had failed, usually about half the candidates, then left for home. The process was repeated four times. By the time of the fifth and final examination 200 candidates would have been whittled down to perhaps 20 or 30. These candidates had to write another essay, a poem and a transcription of the *Sacred Edict*. When the final boards were hung the next day only perhaps four candidates out of the original 200 might have passed. These exams were merely the prelude to those held about a month later in much the same style that qualified a very few of those who had succeeded for the lowest degree.

The lowest degree did not in itself qualify the holder for any kind of office; it merely permitted the student to enter for the next level of exams. Men studying for the next degree often entered academies which provided either practice exams or, for the most advanced students, lectures and tuition on the Four Books and Five Classics and literary style, which were needed for the exams, and also in more abstruse areas such as mathematics, astronomy or textual criticism. The best academies were usually in the provincial capital, a place that might be many days' journey from the candidates' homes and one to which they had quite possibly never been before. The academies brought together students from across a province to live and work together often for several years. Students were addressed as 'Your Honour' and gained a strong sense both of their own position and of their membership of a community. The students studying at the academies were usually preparing for the next series of examinations: those for the second degree, which would give them the right to hold junior official positions. However, by the eighteenth century the increased numbers of degree-holders meant that the final or metropolitan examination held in Beijing was almost always necessary in order to obtain an official position. Those who passed this exam were given official posts both in the imperial bureaucracy in the capital and as the heads of counties, prefectures and provinces throughout the empire. The men who scored the top marks in the metropolitan exams joined the Hanlin Academy, which supplied the empire's highest officials. It usually took many years to reach this stage so that the careers of high officials often only began when they were in their forties or fifties.

The focus of the system was supposed to be on moral indoctrination rather than the acquisition of knowledge. In theory students memorised and studied the Four Books and Five Classics in the hope that by understanding from these texts what moral behaviour was they would be able to act morally themselves. In practice, generations of critics, including emperors, attacked the system for what they saw as its emphasis on essay-writing skills rather than moral content. Official corruption or incompetence was seen as proof that graduates were merely spinners of elegant phrases and had failed to assimilate the essential moral content of the texts they had studied. However, there was never any doubt that the proper goal of the system was moral indoctrination for the benefit of the state.

The system was also intended to be meritocratic, ensuring that the emperor was advised by the most morally worthy of his subjects whatever their origins. This idea was buttressed by rags-to-riches stories such as that of Liu Zhilun, a poor Sichuan peasant who had to gather and sell firewood to help the family make ends meet but later achieved the highest degree. For most families it would have been impossible to support a boy, let alone an adult man, who was not earning any income for more than a few years. Moreover, in practice it was far easier to acquire the education necessary to succeed in the higher levels of the system if one came from a wealthy background. Nevertheless, stories like that of Liu Zhilun were important in validating the system in the minds both of those who succeeded in the exams and of that huge proportion of the population who never had the opportunity to try.

Despite the fact that the sons of the majority of families had little hope of ever becoming officials, the content of the examination system dominated education. The ultimate goal of the education system was exam success and in order to pass the exams it was necessary to devote an enormous amount of time to book learning. Boys started at 7 to memorise textbooks that would introduce them to the characters. The first textbook they used was called the *Thousand Character Classic* (because it introduces a thousand different characters). It begins 'Heaven is dark, the earth is yellow, the universe is vast and barren' and goes on to cover virtues and duties, famous men and places and proper family life. Thus, from the very beginning the system was intended to improve morals and introduce philosophical and ethical ideas. From the *Thousand Character Classic* the boys went on to other similar texts and then to the Four Books. Writing and calligraphy were taught separately and nothing else was taught at all. The same texts were used by boys across the country. While reading and writing were important products of this system the primary aim of the process was to inculcate morality. Boys were expected to understand and learn from the texts they studied a set of common values that were promoted by the state and widely shared throughout the society.

This schooling was also thought worthwhile to inculcate good behaviour and literacy in children whose parents did not hope for official careers for them. By the eighteenth century literacy was increasingly important in a variety of walks of life. In country villages shopkeepers kept written records. Local ritual specialists such as Daoist priests drew part of the prestige of their craft from their use of written records. Even ordinary people prayed to deities using written petitions that were then burnt. Deeds of sale and mortgage were an important part of village life and while the contract might be drawn up by a professional clerk or use a standard printed form a clear understanding of the exact terms of the deed was of considerable importance to the signatories. Many villages also employed a schoolteacher. In towns and cities literacy was even more important. Many professions were open only to the literate: pawn-shop employees needed to be able to read and write receipts, the employees of banks and major trading houses had to be able to write contracts and keep detailed records. There was a whole cluster of literate professions around government offices, where literate men were employed as clerks or earned a living assisting litigants or others who had dealings with the government. Many urban residents also belonged to occupational or native-place associations that had complex written rules and might also print and circulate market reports for their members. Many children, especially the sons of small farmers, spent only two or three years in school. Boys whose parents planned to apprentice them to a trade requiring literacy usually finished their schooling around the age of 14 (often after completing the memorisation of the four books) before starting work. The daughters of some wealthy families also received a basic education, which was seen primarily as moral training. Educated women also added to the prestige of a family, especially in some parts of the country. Thus many children who would never become officials attended schools and their schooling meant that they understood and shared the official understanding of basic cultural texts and values.

The men who had passed the exams and held official positions formed the imperial bureaucracy. Because of their long and successful training in moral texts they saw themselves as uniquely well qualified to govern. Since they tended to come from quite similar social backgrounds and had shared the experience of taking the exams together and acted as patrons or sponsors for each other they had a strong sense of group identity. Local magistrates would have as patrons the men from the central government who had been their examiners as well as other men from their county or province who held more senior positions. This sense of the bureaucracy as a group was strengthened by the ways in which graduates were appointed to posts. Those who succeeded in the highest levels of the examination system could be posted anywhere in the country or to positions in the ministries of the central government in Beijing. Wherever they went they could be sure that their peers would share not only a moral system based on the texts they had learned to expound in the examinations, but also similar life experiences and lifestyles. Although some of the most brilliant new graduates were given positions in the ministries in Beijing, the vast majority were sent out to be county magistrates. They were sent anywhere in the country except to their native areas, often had to travel huge distances and might later be transferred or promoted to other distant posts. As Benedict Anderson has argued, the availability of elite career paths that traverse a particular state is a powerful means of creating a sense of unity. Such career paths were a characteristic feature of the eighteenth-century Chinese bureaucracy.

Elites and the literati lifestyle

The examination system, however, did not simply succeed in creating a small group of officials. The process through which officials were selected also affected the attitudes and lifestyles of a much wider section of society. Indeed the upper members of the local elite might well be competing for power with the county magistrate within their communities. Many members of the elite would have been men who held the first or second degrees but had not succeeded in passing the final metropolitan examination. The qualification gave them status in their local communities, as well as exemption from some taxes and from corporal punishment. They also considered themselves the social equals of the magistrate: writers on local government regularly warn magistrates against angering them. Worse still for the magistrate were men who had retired from the bureaucracy. This is the eighteenth-century playwright Kong Shangren describing a friend who had retired from office:

> At home in his village, he often wore his official robes when he called on his neighbours; and when the tax collector came to his door, he made him kneel, saying, 'Otherwise, I won't pay.' Yet he would meet his old colleagues casually attired, abandoning all formal greetings.[4]

The power of local elites over local officials was increased by the pervasive corruption within the system, which meant that almost any official might be dismissed if someone else in the bureaucracy impeached him.

The power of people outside the bureaucracy was increased by the economic growth that took place from the sixteenth century onwards. This began with the great age of European exploration and the export of luxury goods produced by Chinese craftsmen. Spanish and Portuguese traders based in the Philippines began to trade large quantities of Chinese silk, cotton and porcelain, which they exported from the southeastern coastal provinces of China. As a result of this trade silver from the new world flowed into China and the economy boomed. At the same time new crops were imported from the Americas: sweet potatoes, maize, peanuts and tobacco. Because land in southeast China could now be used to grow profitable cash crops, the price of land rose and big land-reclamation projects were organised. In Guangdong the muddy waters of the Pearl river delta were turned into productive paddy fields by building walls round the fields and then constructing drains. In southeast China large amounts of new and highly productive land were brought into use and many families became extremely rich on the proceeds while others were profiting from trade.

In many areas of the country wealthy people consolidated their power through the organisation of lineages. Lineages had first been promoted by the neo-Confucian reformers of the twelfth century who wanted to encourage families to follow Confucian precepts concerning the proper relationships between family members. Lineage organisations often held land that was donated to a trust for the benefit of the lineage as a whole. This was intended to fund sacrifices for the lineage's ancestors as well as lineage schools and occasional assistance to poorer members. In practice elite members of the lineage also benefited by being given the lineage holdings to manage, usually on a rotational basis, while farming members benefited from being able to rent their land from the lineage, which was a relatively benign landlord. By the eighteenth century almost all Chinese in south China and many in the north were members of a lineage. Lineages were approved by the state since their organisational goal was the strengthening of family relationships, which was a central part of the Confucian doctrine to which the state subscribed. They also confirmed the status of members of the local elite by presenting them as the heads of morally upright and officially acceptable organisations.

Economic growth and lineage organisation meant that by the eighteenth century an ever-increasing number of families could afford to educate their sons. Many of these aspirants to elite status took the examinations for bureaucratic positions, with the result that, since the quotas for officials did not rise, the exams became harder and harder to pass. Some men spent their entire lives studying for the exams and never gained more than the first degree. Others passed the provincial exams, which should have entitled them to official posts, but the bureaucracy was so clogged up with men from rich families who had purchased official posts that the degree-holders might have to wait many years before being given a job. This meant that there was a large number of educated and wealthy men who aspired to official posts while at the same time the men who had passed the exams and won official posts were the richest and most powerful members of society. Naturally others who wanted to claim status emulated them. This brought about a distinctive elite lifestyle with families spending large amounts of money on activities that would prove their literate culture: writing essays and poetry, practising their calligraphy, painting, collecting books and works of art, educating their wives and daughters, publishing ancient texts and organising poetry clubs.

The increase in wealth, and thus in social mobility, meant that from as early as the sixteenth and seventeenth centuries such elite pursuits and lifestyles became available to more people. Families who made money through trade converted that money into examination results by paying for the education of their sons. They also converted their wealth into elite status by engaging in the pursuits that marked out a certain section of the

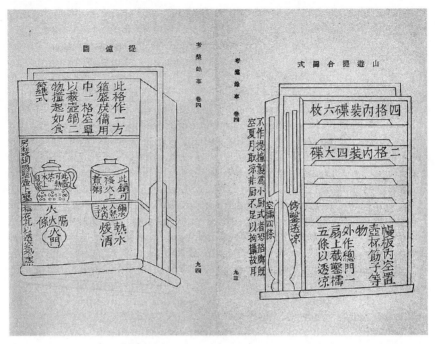

Figure 1.1   Design for a picnic box
Source: Tu Long, 'Kaopan yushi' from *Chanhuan congshu*, 1887. Shanghai:
Shangwu yinshuguan, 1937, pp. 93, 94.

population as an educated elite. The number of people who aspired to such lifestyles drove a huge expansion in the publishing industry, which in turn made the markers of elite status more available to those outside the charmed circle. Books were even written instructing the reader in how to be a gentleman: not just what he should read and think, but what he should wear and what sort of stick he should carry. Leisure pursuits were also provided for: Fig. 1.1 shows a design for a picnic box with space for a cooking pot and kettle on one side and plates and saucers on the other side. Manuals like this were not particularly expensive and the detail of their contents meant that activities that had previously been markers of the upper levels of the elite, such as a picnic to admire the view, drink tea and write poetry, were now available to anyone who was literate. People at the time were aware of the changes brought by the new wealth and lamented what they felt was a mixing of classes which should have been separate, and a disruption in the proper relations between people of different statuses.

Members of the highest levels of the elite began to look for new ways of distinguishing themselves as a group. One of the ways in which they did this was through their emotions and feelings. Elite painters painted in styles that appear to be untrained and simply expressive of the emotions, but were probably harder to achieve than the earlier more academic styles. Their paintings were created within a complex and demanding tradition with references both to earlier painting and to the yet more abstract art of calligraphy.

A similarly development occurred in the writing of poetry. When he arrived in a new city, the playwright Kong Shangren found that poetry was a way of identifying people like him. People sent poems to each other and through the emotions expressed in their poems revealed themselves as 'worthy' characters. He considered this emotional impact of the poems as much more important than their technique. For Kong Shangren emotions finely expressed through poetry were a means of identifying his own class of society, and differentiating them from the less well educated, who were dismissed as merely technically competent.

> There are many ways to find friendship but poetry is the most immediate, for it is the sound of our emotions. If we join in together chanting, we can distinguish each other's natural sensibilities. By contrast, presenting gifts of cloth to show one's esteem is as far removed from it as the momentary from the enduring. Although I have but recently made the acquaintance of gentlemen in Yangzhou, everyone communicates through poetry. Whenever a poem reaches my house, I look for the person it reveals even before considering its technique. Many are the differences between worthy and unworthy characters; were it not for poetry, how could we arrange each according to kind?[5]

Another way in which members of the upper echelons of the elite began to distinguish themselves from the new rich was the pursuit of a new type of learning known as evidential research, which was not closely related to the examination system. Scholars of this movement rejected the neo-Confucian emphasis on a personal search for morality and attempted instead to return to the original meaning of the ancient texts. Because they studied very early commentaries and texts rather than the commentaries of Zhu Xi that were set for the examinations they were to some extent distancing themselves from the examination system. Gradually, they began to move on to textual criticism of the classical texts themselves. One such scholar, a man named Yan Ruoji, collated the dates of all the events in the classics, found they were inconsistent, and argued that some of texts must have been forged at a later date. By studying the customs of ancient times in order to study the ancient sages, people were beginning to see the sages as products of their times. As with biblical research in Europe, this began a process of unravelling received authority that was ultimately to threaten the whole moral and ideological framework.

Thus, by the eighteenth century the fact that so few of those who attempted the examinations could hope ever to attain official office was already working in a paradoxical and contradictory way. On the one hand, economic growth which allowed more families to educate their sons meant that the ideas promoted by the state through the examination system were reaching an ever-wider audience. On the other hand, however, people were beginning to turn away from the system and in doing so to undermine the philosophical basis on which it was founded.

The interaction of elite and popular culture

It is interesting to note that it was a sense of historical relativity that was beginning to threaten the interweaving of the state with the moral order. For it was the absence of relativity, either historical or geographical, that created a sense of identity that was tied not to the state as such but to the preservation of civilisation. The existence of a single bureaucratic network and the examination and thus education system that led into it had created a culture that was shared by elites across the country. That culture has been described here as being specific to a certain time, place and social group. However, that was not how it was perceived by those who shared in it. They saw the values on which it was based as a universal moral code rather than one that was culturally specific. The Confucian texts they studied provided guidance not merely for eighteenth-century subjects of the Qing but for all mankind throughout history. The state structures, such as a meritocratic bureaucracy, that promoted those values meant that the Chinese state embodied civilised values. Thus the state was not merely a civilisation but was civilisation itself and the standard term for what we now refer to as China was quite simply 'all under heaven'. This view of the world, which accepted the neo-Confucian moral order and the inevitable connection of that order with the imperial state, has been described as 'culturalism'. The term culturalism as a description of Chinese identity prior to the impact of modern Western thought was first applied by Joseph Levenson in the 1950s. Levenson based his analysis on the writings of the highest levels of the national elite. It is easy to see how such people were tied in to a cultural order linked to the state. However, more recently anthropological studies have suggested that this form of identification spread far beyond the national elite and reached even the poorest and most remote villages of the empire.

The heartland of the Qing empire as it existed in the eighteenth century is easily understood by anthropologists as a single culture area. Many elements of this culture owe their origins to policies and practices of the imperial state, but by the eighteenth century they were also independent of state structures. Such practices could be used to distinguish Chinese from non-Chinese within the Qing empire and were carried overseas by emigrants. The people who subscribed to this culture are known today as the Han Chinese. At the time they used the terms 'the people' (*min*) or 'humans' (*ren*) for themselves and described others as 'savages' (*fan*) or 'barbarians' (*yi*). A quotation from a nineteenth-century British author describing one of the indigenous peoples of Taiwan gives a sense of the flavour of such terms:

> [The Kibalan] were in all respects a more intelligent and more engaging people than the Chinese of Formosa, though these latter affect superiority. Thus when I inquired of a man in the Chinese village of Sau-o, who I imagined had a dash of Kibalan in his face, if he belonged to that race, he replied 'No, I am a *man*;' (that is a *Chinese*, not a foreigner).[6]

As this brief dialogue suggests, Han Chinese culture paralleled the culturalism of the imperial state. To be Han Chinese was to be human where others were savages, to be civilised where others were barbarians. Central to this civilised culture were certain types of family structure, commercialisation, regional difference, religion and ritual.

Han Chinese culture

In their ideal form Chinese family structures were patriarchal and patrilineal in the strictest sense. A family of mother, father and children was ruled by the father. Filial piety, the foremost virtue of the Confucian moral order, demanded that children show respect and obedience to both parents, but especially to their father. According to the *Classic of Filial Piety*,

> Confucius said: 'A filial son has five duties to perform to his parents: (1) He must venerate them in daily life. (2) He must try to make them happy in every possible way, especially when the meal is served. (3) He must take extra care of them when they are sick. (4) He ought to show great sorrow for them when they are dead. (5) He must offer sacrifices to his deceased parents with the utmost solemnity. If he fulfils these duties, then he can be considered as having done what ought to be done by a son.'[7]

These duties were supposed to supersede all other obligations and ambitions. Fig. 1.2 is taken from a series of illustrations showing the famous twenty-four models of filial piety designed to accompany the text of the *Classic of Filial Piety* in a children's textbook. It shows Zhu Shoucheng, who famously abandoned high office in order to find his mother. He is seen arriving in his full official costume and hat, with his umbrella and belongings on the ground at his side. As his mother comes out of the door of the house to welcome him he kneels before her, showing the subservience of even those of the highest rank to their parents. Another story in this series tells of Lao Laizi, who when himself already well on in years would play like a child to entertain his parents. Stories of filial children, such as those who offered their own flesh to cure a parent's illness, were also the subject of folk tales and were even occasionally imitated.

Figure 1.2 'Giving up office to find one's mother'
Source: *Huitu xiaojing* (*Illustrated Classic of Filial Piety*). Shanghai: Mianzhang shuju, 1911

When children grew up marriages were arranged for the sons, and their wives came to live with the family. Marriages usually took place when the bride and groom were in their teens and since the couple lived with the groom's parents the power of the father continued. Meanwhile daughters were married out and left to live with their husbands' families. Daughters might receive large dowries but inheritance was the right of sons only. While the parents were alive sons were expected to work and eat together, pooling all their resources. However at some point, usually after the death of the father, the brothers would divide the property into equal shares and each would set up his own household with his own stove and eat separately. In practice much variation existed both between regions and between individuals, and the ideal form was seldom attained. For example, it was not uncommon in practice for the wife's widowed mother or the husband's sister to live with a couple. However the ideal of the patrilineal family with strictly equal inheritance between brothers was an important part of Han culture, and filial piety was one of the core values promoted by the state.

There was a wide variation in local customs and practices. However local customs were understood in terms of regional difference and this was co-opted into the meaning of what it was to be Han. Local gazetteers, which are formal accounts of local history and geography produced in large numbers from the eighteenth century onwards, invariably include a section on local customs and characteristics. One of the most interesting examples of variation in local customs nevertheless strengthening the sense of a unified Han identity is the case of the binding of women's feet. This custom developed during the twelfth century, and it has recently been suggested that it should be understood as part of an attempt to accentuate aspects of Chinese culture that differentiated it from the culture of the northern plains peoples who were threatening the state. Chinese men emphasised scholarship and artistry as against the martial virtues of the plains people. In order to preserve gender differences women then had to become even more delicate and feminine, while at the same time maintaining an increased segregation from men that was contrasted with the freedom of the plains women. By the eighteenth century foot binding was widespread across the country and was often used as a means of differentiating Han from non-Han. However, the practice was by no means evenly distributed. In the north, where all but the poorest women had bound feet, it appears to have been nearly universal. In Guangdong and other parts of south China foot binding was confined to the elite. One south China group, the Hakka, did not practise it at all while nevertheless defining themselves as Han. They explained that their people had migrated from north China before the practice of foot binding had been adopted. Being Han demanded, above all, a story of origin in the Chinese heartland, which the Hakka had, and local differences in customs were called upon to confirm this.

Han Chinese also shared a pantheon of deities and the way in which that pantheon was understood. Some deities, notably those promoted by the state at various points such as Guandi, the god of war, were worshipped across the country. There were also certain categories of deity that were constant: every city had a city god, every village an earth god and every home a stove god. The characteristics of some of these deities might vary (in some parts of south China the earth god was associated with a stone; in Shanxi he was often associated with a sacred tree) but there was a consistent understanding of their function. There were also many deities that were specific to certain regions, such as the goddess Mazu, who was one of the most popular deities of the southeast coast but was seldom worshipped inland. But across the country these various deities were understood as fitting into a bureaucratic framework that corresponded in many ways with that of the state. At the head of the pantheon was the Jade Emperor. Folk tales explained the relation between the Jade Emperor and the ministers of his court, such as the gods of rainfall or plague. At the local level the city god, who resided in the county seat, corresponded neatly with the county magistrate. This model of the heavenly world, which reflected the structures of the state, normalised and legitimated those structures and made them central to popular understanding of the role of the state.

Rituals and Chinese identity

Family structure, commercialisation, regional difference and religious structures have all been identified as important features of Han Chinese culture.

However eighteenth-century Chinese would have agreed with modern scholars that the most important feature that differentiated the Han Chinese from those around them was their emphasis on ritual. In an ancient phrase the Chinese referred to their country as 'the land of rituals and propriety'. For the literati elite ritual and etiquette (the Chinese term can mean both) was an essential part of what Confucius had taught. They believed that acting out proper behaviour would cause people to recognise their proper social obligations and act accordingly. Thus a son wailing aloud during the funeral rituals for his father was both expressing his feelings and simultaneously reminding himself and others of the importance of filial piety. In this case, as in many others, the meaning of the ritual (the importance of filial piety) is encoded in the actions required by the funeral, and the son is submitting to that meaning by performing the required actions.

Taking this argument further, the anthropologist James Watson has argued that it was the use of particular standard death rituals that identified a family as Han Chinese. These rituals consisted of the public notification of the funeral by wailing, the wearing of white clothes by mourners, the ritual bathing of the corpse, the transfer of food, money and goods to the deceased, the setting up of a soul tablet for the deceased, the payment of professionals to assist in the funeral, music, the sealing of the corpse in an airtight coffin and the expulsion of the coffin from the community. The wealthy could pay for more expensive versions at each stage, dressing the corpse in many layers of clothes, using a series of coffins each fitting inside the other, or providing an elaborate procession. Moreover, the rituals that accompanied the actual burial of the corpse differed regionally. However, the basic structure of the funeral rites was the same across the country and across the differences of class and wealth.

These funeral rituals, and to some extent other major lifecycle rituals, linked ordinary people to national elite culture. Members of the educated elite often acted as ritual experts, advising on exactly how the funeral or other ritual should be conducted. To do this they relied on texts and ritual manuals, and from the rise of printing in the sixteenth century it had become increasingly common for these to be printed. The texts often originated from scholars and officials who were deeply concerned with questions of the proper performance of ritual. Ritual texts were included in the original Five Classics which were central to the examination system. Long before the eighteenth century these had become very hard to understand, let alone follow, and since the second century BC dynastic governments had issued detailed instructions for rituals. Scholars independent of the government also wrote instructions and commentaries on the ritual texts. The most famous of these was the *Family Rituals* of the twelfth-century philosopher Zhu Xi. This text continued to be frequently republished through into the nineteenth century because it was written in a relatively simple style, and because Zhu Xi was so famous as one of the founders of orthodox neo-Confucianism. Many later versions revised the original text or combined it with commentaries and by the nineteenth century some of Zhu Xi's prescriptions were themselves hard to understand or used materials that were impossible to obtain. Nevertheless, the widespread use of the *Family Rituals* and other similar texts meant that the ideas of the national elite about proper rituals did come to affect popular practice.

Elements of funeral rituals that followed the recommendations of Confucian texts such as the *Family Rituals* were the ritualised wailing, the wearing of mourning garments that showed one's degree of kinship with the deceased, the placing of food and drink near the coffin until burial, the postponing of burial to prolong mourning, restrictions on social activities during deepest mourning, heavy coffins, ceremonial processions to the grave and post-burial sacrifices. These shared elements were partly the product of social continuities; rituals remained the same where they reflected unchanging patterns of social behaviour. However, they were also partly the product of the use of classical texts, which constrained the performance of funerals in certain directions. In addition ordinary people often modelled their rituals on the prestigious rituals of the elite. On the other hand, some practices that were clearly condemned in the Confucian texts, such as Buddhist services and feasts, continued as important parts of the funerals of ordinary people and were also part of the funerals of the elite. In early modern Europe attempts to reform popular culture led to a widening gap between popular and elite practices. In China this did not occur during this period: in eighteenth-century China elites were willing to legitimate most popular practices. In fact, they themselves continued to use a variety of non-orthodox practices. Meanwhile the common people imitated the elites. Funeral rituals provide a good example of the way in which a single sense of Han culture formed around the statewide elite culture.

Popular identity on China's frontiers

During the eighteenth century Han Chinese culture was gradually expanding into new territories driven by the strength of the imperial state and a renewed increase in the population. The emigrants who initiated this expansion were for the most part poor, landless labourers, far removed from the examination candidates and government officials of China's elite. They moved into south and west China, the provinces of Guangdong, Guangxi and Yunnan, and also east across the channel that separated the mainland from the island of Taiwan. By looking at the ways in which the inhabitants of these new territories adopted Chinese culture we can see both the extent to which the emigrants shared some of the attitudes of the elite, and also the ways in which Han Chinese identity could be manipulated to confirm the power and social status of particular groups. The remainder of this chapter will look first at Taiwan, where an examination of the processes of acculturation and assimilation suggests that both poor Chinese settlers and elite officials operated within a cultural model of identity that accepted that it was compliance with certain standards of behaviour that defined one as Chinese. I will then turn to the province of Guangdong, at this time far more highly assimilated than Taiwan, where Han identity was used as a marker of social class.

A CULTURAL APPROACH TO IDENTITY: TAIWAN

Before the sixteenth century the population of Taiwan consisted of peoples whose languages and archaeological remains relate them to the cultures of Austronesia. They may well have been culturally similar to the original native inhabitants of the southern Chinese mainland, but this is still the subject of considerable debate. In the sixteenth and early seventeenth centuries, when Chinese immigration was just beginning, the peoples of Taiwan lived by deer hunting and slash-and-burn agriculture, had forms of marriage that were often matrilineal or involved the husband moving into the home of the wife's parents, and were organised above the village level only for occasional alliances. There were also considerable cultural and linguistic differences between the people of the different parts of the island. In 1661 the Dutch East India Company, which had laid claim to the island, was driven out by Zheng Chenggong, a pirate leader turned Ming loyalist who escaped from the advancing Qing forces and set up a government on the island. The island did not come under the control of the Chinese mainland until 1683, when it was taken by Qing forces. Throughout the seventeenth and eighteenth centuries there was large-scale immigration to the island from the mainland, mostly from Fujian directly across the Taiwan Straits but also from northern Guangdong. The government, which feared the destabilising effect of such immigration, made repeated but unsuccessful attempts to limit it.

Thus the native peoples of Taiwan learnt Chinese ways not from the occasional educational efforts of Chinese officials but from the settlers, most of whom were poor farmers. They quickly adopted elements of Chinese culture that were immediately useful or carried a low cultural cost. Chinese muskets came into use both for hunting and for inter-village warfare. The men learnt the Chinese language of the majority Fujian population, and sometimes also that of the Hakka people who had emigrated from north Guangdong, so that they could engage in trade and local politics with the settlers. Chinese medicines and gods were also tried and sometimes adopted where they seemed useful. But above all the peoples of Taiwan took to those practices and objects that provided status in the eyes of the settler population. Huang Shujing, a Chinese official who toured the island in 1722, noticed that the people dressed partly like the Chinese, wearing trousers, hats and boots, but that elaborate Chinese embroidered robes, modelled on those of officials, were especially popular among village headmen on formal occasions. He also noted that some families had purchased Chinese-style beds, and these too were displays of wealth and status; the family continued to sleep on deerskins spread on the floor. Men were quicker to adopt Chinese customs than women since it was they who mostly interacted with the Chinese. Practices that were less obviously beneficial were much more slowly adopted: the labour-intensive agriculture practised by the Han Chinese was unpopular with the aborigines, who sometimes regarded cultivation as women's work and preferred to make a living from hunting and trading deerskins or, later, from ox-cart driving. Women had less contact with the Chinese settlers and women's dress was often slower to change than that of men: most aboriginal women never adopted the painful Han Chinese custom of foot binding.

It was the degree to which the native peoples had adopted Chinese customs that determined the way in which the Qing government classified and treated them. The Qing officials divided the aborigines into raw savages (*shengfan*) who had adopted no Chinese cultural characteristics, and the familiar or civilised savages (*shufan*) whose customs had become more similar to those of the Chinese settlers. Drawings from an album depicting Taiwan tribes who paid tribute to the Qing illustrate Chinese perceptions of the difference between these two types. The raw savage woman has her breasts and arms uncovered and is depicted walking forward, while the man is dressed in animal skins, holds a spear and a knife, and is depicted as if about to stab the spear fiercely down (Fig. 1.3). The primary characteristics

Figure 1.3 Raw savages from Danshui prefecture, Taiwan
Source: *Huang Qing zhigong tu* (Tribute-bearers of the Qing Dynasty). Taibei: Shangwu yinshuguan, 1986, vol. 3, p. 47

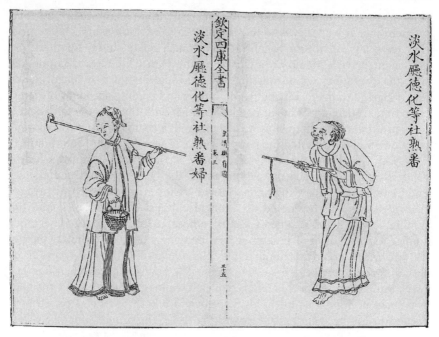

Figure 1.4 Civilised savages from Danshui prefecture, Taiwan
Source: *Huang Qing zhigong tu* (Tribute-bearers of the Qing Dynasty). Taibei:
Shangwu yinshuguan, 1986, vol. 3, p. 35

of the savages are seen to be the immodesty of the women and the ferocious behaviour of the men. Civilised aborigines of the same prefecture are shown in dress that resembles that of the Chinese (Fig. 1.4). The woman wears a long-sleeved gown over a full-length pleated skirt with a flat front panel and embroidered hems very much in the style worn by contemporary Chinese women of the upper classes. Her body and arms are fully covered like those of a respectable Chinese woman, though any contemporary observer would have noticed that her feet are bare and not bound. Over her shoulder she carries a hoe and in her hand is a basket, symbolising her engagement in agriculture rather than hunting. Her posture is gentle, static and demure. The man of her tribe also wears a costume reminiscent of that of wealthy Chinese: a long gown and over-jacket. He carries a whip, indicating that he still makes his livelihood from animals, but from herding or transport rather than hunting. Unlike the raw aborigine he is not engaged in any ferocious activity but stands slightly bent holding his whip before him in a submissive posture. His bare feet and loose hair point the difference between him and the booted, queue-wearing Chinese upper classes.

In other words, the difference between the raw and the civilised aborigines lay in the extent of their similarity to the Han Chinese. This difference influenced government approaches: civilised aborigines paid tax and had access to legal and administrative protection; raw savages paid no taxes, managed their own affairs, sometimes under a system of government-appointed chieftans, and had little access to government protection. The categories were not permanent and it was hoped that the civilising influences of the bureaucratic state would ultimately transform the aborigines from 'savages' into 'people'. Shen Qiyuan, a prefect of Taiwan in 1729, argued specifically that good government would transform Han immigrants into locals, civilised aborigines into Han and raw aborigines into civilised aborigines.

Local settlers agreed with the government that identity as Han or aborigine was primarily a matter of how one behaved. One of the most striking cases of acculturation and assimilation concerns a tribe who sold some land to Chinese settlers in the late eighteenth century. Today the descendants of the tribe still live in the area. They have a surname taken from the tribe's name, speak the Taiwanese dialect of Chinese, have customs no different from those of their Han Taiwanese neighbours, and have extensively intermarried with the Han. They are organised as a patrilineal lineage with ancestral halls and a printed genealogy. The only trace of their aboriginal origin can be found on the ancestral tablet in their lineage hall. This gives their ancestors' place of origin as Taiwan, where most Han Taiwanese would give a county on the Chinese mainland. It also identifies the ancestor who founded the lineage as an interpreter, which was an official post that only applied to aboriginal villages.

Most of the acculturation and assimilation in Taiwan was towards the Han Chinese who were now the dominant group on the island, but there are also stories about Han men who went to live in the raw aborigine areas beyond the reach of the law, adopted the aborigines' customs and were transformed into aborigines themselves and treated as such by the state. Such circumstances were not peculiar to Taiwan but were instead characteristic of many of the peripheral areas into which Han Chinese culture was spreading during the eighteenth century.

IDENTITY AND POWER: GUANGDONG

Cultural understandings of ethnicity and identity that emphasised behaviour meant that peripheral peoples could often be fully absorbed into Han culture and thus given full participation in the state. However, the same ideas could also be used to exclude outsiders and confirm hierarchies of power. Han Chinese identity was fluid but that very fluidity could be used in a variety of ways by groups with different interests. Parts of Guangdong province on the south China coast had been at the heart of Han Chinese culture for several hundred years and produced highly educated scholars who often rose to high positions in the bureaucracy. The ethnic situation in Guangdong in the eighteenth century shows how the cultural phenomena of

Han ethnicity could be produced and altered to strengthen the power and position of certain groups.

Archaeology and written references suggest that the native cultures of southeast China once constituted a single cultural area with customs and practices quite dissimilar to those of the Han peoples of north China. The peoples of southeast China cut their hair short, tattooed their bodies (both of which go against strong Han taboos) and practised forms of marriage in which the husband might move into the wife's parents' home or the wife might remain with her parents after the wedding. Refugees and emigrants from the north gradually spread Han Chinese culture in the area. From the fourteenth century the Chinese state conducted a series of military campaigns to gain control over the less acculturated peoples, and imposed on them a system of indirect rule through chiefs. The result of these successive rounds of immigration, acculturation and assimilation was that by the eighteenth century the peoples of Guangdong perceived themselves as members of several different categories: Cantonese, Hakka and Dan peoples who occupied the rich Pearl River delta and the less acculturated Yao, She and Zhuang who lived in the hills of north Guangdong. These groups shared many similar features, some of which were very different from those of the peoples of north China. Despite this, they themselves perceived a strict division between those who were Han and those who were not. The Cantonese and the Hakka created exclusive categories that defined them as Han, but the story of how they did so showed just how recent and fluid that identity was and how it could still sometimes be attained.

One of the most important ways in which families asserted their Han identity was to claim that their ancestors were immigrants from the north China plain. Genealogies were first written and then printed to substantiate those claims. These genealogies present elaborate stories of migration, often in several stages, from the north China plain to the family's current place of residence. The family is always traced back to a high official, often of the second or third century AD, despite the fact that the genealogies were mostly written more than a thousand years later. This is partly because of early laws relating to ancestral worship and the construction of lineage halls, which made some forms of these acceptable only to those of high status. However, the tracing of large families, not all of whose members were by any means wealthy, to an ancestor who was an official also expressed an allegiance to the values of the statewide elite culture. This respect for and involvement with elite culture was also shown in the reading aloud of classical texts at sacrifices and the widespread use of characters in boys' names from a predetermined sequence that marked which generation the boy came from, and thus signalled that relationship rather than age was the proper determinant of behaviour between people. The form of lineages had been a neo-Confucian invention and the compilation of genealogies and management of lineage affairs gave power to members of the scholarly elite.

Lineages claiming descent from official families of the north China plain could also be used by those whose claim to Han identity was dubious. One Guangdong lineage has a genealogy which claims that the family are Han Chinese whose ancestors had come from the north China plain but had somehow acquired non-Han Yao status. Many generations later they had switched back to their original Han status because it offered more protection in disputes with their neighbours. Apparently this family had once been registered as Yao aborigines but had subsequently assimilated and by the time the genealogy was written laid claim to Han Chinese status. Another example of the importance of genealogies in laying claim to Han Chinese identity is given by the Hakka, many of whose customs were similar to those of the less assimilated peoples of the province. Their women did not bind their feet and laboured in the fields performing the heavy work of agriculture. The Hakka also conducted some rituals similar to those common among the non-Han Yao and She. Finally the Hakka shared with the non-Han a structurally poor economic situation, with many Hakka villages being located on poorer and less profitable land, for example in the lower areas of the hilly lands to the north of the province. However, in the face of occasional slurs, the Hakka insisted that they were Han. Indeed they explained their different customs as being due to the fact that they were more like the original peoples of the north China plain. Lineages with detailed printed genealogies were an important part of the Hakka's self-identification as Han.

In such an environment the behavioural view of identity could also be manipulated. One of the most curious and yet most telling ways in which Han identity was constructed in the Pearl River delta area of Guangdong was the custom by which a woman on marriage did not immediately move to her husband's home. Instead she continued to live in her own parents' home and visited her husband only for the birthdays or death anniversaries of his parents or for other important festivals. Sometimes this might continue only till the birth of her first child, but many women postponed the move to their husband's home for many years. The woman might even use her dowry to buy a concubine for her husband. Such a practice would have been shocking to most people in north China, for whom the transfer of the bride to the groom's family's home was essential to the wedding. For them even for a wife to stay for a few weeks at her parents' home was regarded as improper and likely to give rise to gossip. To the modern observer the custom of delayed transfer marriage also looks remarkably similar to the marriage practices of the less assimilated Yao and She peoples. However, the practice of delayed-transfer marriage was common among wealthy Cantonese families and was used by them to distinguish themselves as Han from the lowly Dan who dwelt in boats, had no right to settle on land and practised forms of marriage in which the bride moved immediately to the groom's home. Thus a custom that inverted northern Chinese markers of identity was used by a very powerful group to distinguish themselves and came to be a form of social exclusion.

Conclusion

The common culture of eighteenth-century China had grown out of the structures of the state which promoted a single written language and education system through which it selected a bureaucracy who could be posted across the country. By the eighteenth century much of the content of this cultural system was accepted by ordinary people as well as the educated elite. Nevertheless, Chinese cultural identity continued to be a statement of power and status, a claim to affiliation with the ruling power. On the borders of the Chinese cultural area ethnic labels, including Han Chinese ethnicity, which implied membership of civilised society, were flexible but they could also be used as markers of social class. The ideas of culturalism meant that Han identity remained open, but it was also possible to manipulate them in such a way that Han Chinese identity was open only to those who could afford to adopt certain practices. Where this was done it was genealogies, lineages and other symbols that were particularly closely linked to the official state culture of the elite that were called into play. On the fringes of the empire as at its heart the ideals of culturalism permeated much of popular culture but were closely linked to elite values and practices.

Notes

1 *Chu Hsi and the Ta-hsueh: Neo-Confucian Reflection on the Confucian Canon*, trans. Daniel K. Gardner (Cambridge, MA: Council on East Asian Studies, Harvard University, 1986), p. 88.
2 Ibid.
3 Shang Yanliu, *Qingdai keju kaoshi shulu* (An account of official examinations in the Qing) (Beijing: Sanlian shudian, 1958), p. 255.
4 Quoted in Richard E. Strassberg, *The World of K'ung Shang-jen: A Man of Letters in Early Ch'ing China* (New York: Columbia University Press, 1983), p. 38.
5 Adapted from ibid., p. 145.
6 Cuthbert Collingwood, *Rambles of a Naturalist on the Shores and Waters of the China Sea* (London: John Murray, 1875), p. 115.
7 *The Book of Filial Duty*, trans. Ivan Chen (London: John Murray, 1920).

2

The Manchu empire

As the Son of Heaven in whom Confucian moral ideals were supposedly embodied, the emperor was at the heart of the culturalist view of the Chinese empire. Yet paradoxically during the eighteenth century, when that view was at its height, the emperor was not Han Chinese. Instead the imperial family were the descendants of nomadic tribal peoples of the open plains that lay to the north of the Great Wall, which ran along the traditional boundary of the Chinese empire. Moreover, although the emperors were sensitive to anything that might be construed as a criticism of themselves as barbarians, they were proud of their non-Han heritage. Eighteenth-century emperors made great efforts to preserve the distinctive Manchu customs of their people and in their rule over some of the non-Han peoples of their empire, especially the Tibetans and Mongolians, they portrayed themselves as the rulers of a Manchu empire that acted impartially towards its different subjects.

The Qing as a non-Han dynasty

At the beginning of the eighteenth century there were still many people alive who could remember the arrival of the Manchu armies some 50 years earlier as alien conquerors. By the time the armies moved down into the north China plain the rulers they fought for had already adopted many of the forms of the previous Chinese Ming dynasty government, taking a Chinese dynastic name 'Qing' and organising a civil service on the Ming model. However, their armies had been raised on the open plains that lay beyond the northern frontier of the Ming, from nomadic peoples such as the Jurchen and their more sedentary neighbours. The people who were the members of these armies had been given the new name Manchu by the founder of the dynasty, Nurgaci. As in south China, cultural identities on the peripheries of Han settlement were fluid; but in the north the growth of the Manchus as a military power encouraged many people to adopt

Manchu not Han customs. Some of the 'Manchus' who invaded the Ming empire were probably acculturated Han Chinese, but as a group the Manchus had very different customs from those of the Han. They spoke a language that was not related to Chinese and was written in a phonetic system adapted from Mongolian. Their military might was based on their cavalry and they prided themselves on their horsemanship and archery. Their clothes, even those of their leaders, were adapted to allow freedom of movement for riding and archery. Their women, like those of most non-Han peripheral peoples, had not adopted the practice of binding their feet.

Most of these customs continued to be restricted to the Manchus themselves and used by them as a means of self-definition, but the hairstyle was imposed on the Chinese. The men's hairstyle was one of the most distinctive features of the Manchu armies: the front of the head was shaved and the remaining hair plaited into a long queue that hung down the back. There was considerable resistance to the decree requiring all Chinese men except for monks to adopt this hairstyle. Before this time Chinese men had grown their hair long and worn it in a bun on the top of the head, usually covered with a piece of cloth, with the rest of the hair hanging down behind. Shaving the head was historically linked to shame and punishment. Moreover the Confucian classics stated that a man should hand on unharmed the body he received from his parents, which conformed to the popular taboo on cutting the hair. Thus the queue was initially regarded as immoral as well as simply being a foreign custom and a sign of defeat. A European living in China at the time described the Manchu capture of Shaoxing:

> They took this Town without any resistance, and so they might have done all the rest of the Southern Towns of this Povince of Chekiang. But when they commanded all by Proclamation to cut off their Hair, then both Souldier and Citizen took up Armes, and fought more desperately for their Hair of their Heads, than they did for King or Kingdom, and beat the Tartars not only out of their city, but repulst them to the river Cienthang: nay forced them to passe the River, killing very many of them.[1]

Although such resistance ultimately failed, it was an important feature of the conquest and shows that the imposition of the queue as a sign of submission was a major Manchu policy decision.

However, in the main the Manchus did not impose their customs on the Han Chinese but rather attempted to preserve them as the defining features of a privileged class. This proved to be difficult. After the conquest of the Ming empire the cultural demands on individual Manchus were quite different from those that had existed in the northeast. First, it became necessary to develop a corps of administrators who could supervise the Han Chinese bureaucracy. This required not only fluency in spoken Chinese but also a grasp of written documentary style and therefore the knowledge of the Chinese classics that underlay this. At first the emperors made considerable use of Han who had been incorporated into the Manchu state at an early stage as hereditary bondservants. Many of these men moved easily between Manchu and Chinese elite cultures. A contemporary description of one of the Kangxi emperor's favourite bondservants states:

> He thinks that the reading of books and the hunting of game are not things in natural opposition. Riding a swift horse and clutching the bow, the taut bowstring making a noise like a thunderclap – that is better than being hidden away in a carriage like most noblemen. And then to take the remaining arrows back home and entertain his friends, to get in heated arguments about ancient and modern, the different types of writers and the source and history of their merits, while the seated guests are silent since none can oppose him . . .[2]

Such fluency in both cultures was a product of the era of conquest. After the conquest the majority of the Manchu armies were sent to garrison major cities. Positions in these garrisons were hereditary and regulations forbade Manchu men from adopting other occupations, but a settled life within a Chinese urban environment naturally changed their customs. An eighteenth-century inspector reported of the Hangzhou garrison:

> Spoken Manchu has declined and the Manchus speak the same as the local Han Chinese. Local customs have corrupted their manners, and there are none among them to be emulated. Somehow it must be ordered that spoken Manchu not be forgotten.[3]

Traditional Western scholarship on China tended to understand these changes through the term 'sinicisation'. According to this argument, which is rooted in Chinese culturalist ideas, peripheral peoples who came into contact with Han Chinese civilisation adopted Chinese customs and were eventually absorbed into the Chinese people. Unlike eighteenth-century Chinese, who thought in culturalist terms of the peoples living on the periphery of the empire, Westerners applied the idea of sinicisation to the various non-Han dynasties and particularly the Qing. Statements that the Manchus had become sinicised were common in the nineteenth-century Western literature about China and were intended to disparage the Manchus for the loss of their martial culture and their conformity to what was seen as a weak and effeminate Chinese culture. Thus statements about sinicisation justified a story of greatness and decline based on past military success and present military weakness. In recent years the idea of sinicisation has been much criticised on the grounds that it obscures the processes and power relationships through which cultural change actually took place. New work on the Manchus has shown the extent to which Qing emperors tried to preserve Manchu culture, both by preserving the northeast as a Manchu homeland and by encouraging the continuation of northeastern cultural practices among Manchus resident in China.

Reports of language loss among Manchus garrisoned in China were a constant concern to the emperors, who wanted to preserve the Manchus as a separate group. Since Manchu identity was defined in terms of culture and lifestyle the emperors felt that preserving that identity required the preservation of their former culture. Manchu culture persisted much longer at court than in the provinces. (The bulk of the Manchu army had been settled in Beijing, which thus had a much larger community to support Manchu customs and religious practices.) The Qianlong emperor, who ruled from 1750 to 1793, enjoyed hunting as well as being a connoisseur of Chinese art, wrote easily in both Manchu and Chinese and was probably bilingual. He was concerned, however, to discover that some of his officials were beginning to write Manchu according to the rules of Chinese grammar so that genuine Manchu speakers could not understand it. He also complained that many Manchu officials could not conduct a court interview in good spoken Manchu.

The Qianlong emperor is famous for the flowering of Chinese culture, and especially the visual arts, that took place during his reign. Indeed today popular historical novels and plays often suggest that the emperor was not Manchu at all, but the son of Han Chinese who was smuggled into the palace. However, in reality Qianlong's patronage of Chinese art and literature was combined with the glorification of his Manchu heritage. He held campaigns to encourage Manchus resident in China to preserve their language and cultural practices, requiring, for example, that all Manchu degree-holders be examined in riding and archery. These campaigns were combined with sponsorship of the publication of many volumes on traditional Manchu history, culture and genealogy. In some ways the publication of this corpus of written literature actually worked to alter Manchu customs, which had previously been based very much on an oral heritage and on the lifestyles and customs of the northeast. The emphasis on genealogy as a defining feature of the Manchus, for example, was part of the gradual transformation of a Manchu identity defined by culture and lifestyle into an identity defined by descent. Nevertheless it is important to remember that the preservation of distinctive Manchu customs during this period was not just due to conservatism but was the result of conscious effort by the Manchu ruling elite.

Universal empire

The most obvious political reason for the preservation of a distinct Manchu culture was the role of a variety of other non-Han cultures in the Qing empire. The empire included Mongolia, Tibet, Manchuria and part of muslim Central Asia as well as China. These areas had very different customs, peoples and histories from those of former Ming China, and the Qing empire ruled them accordingly.

The Manchus had originally come to power in the area north of the

Great Wall bordering on Korea. Before their conquest of Ming China in 1644, they had been the dominant allies in a partnership with various Mongol tribes and these were absorbed piecemeal into the rising Manchu state. Shortly after the fall of the Ming the more distant Mongol groups north of the Gobi desert also began to pay tribute. The Mongols were governed by the Qing not through the system of counties and magistrates used for China, but through the Manchu system of communities, called banners, under hereditary command. The expansion of the Manchu empire to the north, both in the Manchus' own northeastern homeland and in Mongolia, had brought it into contact with the Russian empire, which was also expanding into Central Asia during this period. Previously fluid nomadic allegiances began to be replaced by borders between the two states negotiated by major treaties in 1689 and 1727 and marked on maps. Embassies were sent between the two states for major negotiations and a Russian mission resided in Beijing.

The westward expansion of the Manchu empire also brought it into conflict with the Jungars. The Jungar state was in many ways similar to that of the early Manchus. The Jungars were a Mongol group and they had created a highly mobile, completely militarised state. Operating among the nomadic peoples of Central Asia, the Jungar state did not consistently control one area of land, but rather moved from one place to the next depending on the military situation. Shortly after the northern part of Mongolia had begun to pay tribute to the Manchus it was invaded by the Jungars. A major Qing campaign led to the defeat of the Jungar forces there and the death of their leader Galdan. However the Jungar forces were not yet defeated and in 1717 they moved south to Tibet where they captured the city of Lhasa. Again Manchu forces were sent against them and drove them out, leaving a Qing garrison in control of Lhasa. The Jungars retreated west pursued by the Qing in a series of campaigns that ultimately brought a large part of muslim Central Asia into the Qing empire. In 1760 the newly conquered area was incorporated into the empire as Xinjiang, which means 'new territories'. This was to be the last major expansionist campaign of the Manchus, and by the time it was completed the Qing had come to control vast areas of northern and central Asia that were culturally quite distinct from the Chinese provinces that had formed the Ming empire.

ADMINISTRATION

In their rule over these peoples, the Qing emperors portrayed themselves as the monarchs of a Manchu empire that acted impartially towards its Tibetan, Mongolian and Han subjects. Manchu, Tibetan, Mongolian and Uyghur (one of the written languages of Central Asian Muslims) were all used for administrative purposes within the empire even though the central administration was, by the eighteenth century, conducted primarily in Chinese. One of the most visible forms in which the emperors expressed their commitment to a model of universal empire was the erection of stone steles inscribed in all five languages. This symbolic equality was reflected in the administrative arrangements of the empire. During the eighteenth and early nineteenth centuries the non-Han areas of the empire were not governed through the Chinese bureaucracy. Like other empires, the Qing manipulated existing power structures and ruled through native elites. The highest level of colonial government was the Lifanyuan, a special government bureau in Beijing. The Chinese term means 'ministry ruling the barbarians' but the Manchu title of the bureau meant 'ministry ruling the outer provinces'. The difference is instructive. Like the rest of the terminology of the central government the name 'Lifanyuan' had strong culturalist implications. However, in practice the bureau worked not towards culturalist assimilation but towards the preservation of the separate cultures and political structures of the different parts of the Manchu empire.

Mongolia had been ruled before the Manchu conquest by an aristocratic elite with independent princes who controlled separate territories. The Qing left this structure in place, allowing the Mongol princes to remain autonomous. The Manchus also sanctioned the continuation of much of the previous social order by giving titles to existing office-holders that confirmed them in power. Many of the Mongol princedoms were linked to the Manchu empire through dynastic marriages. The Qing also established a special legal code for the Mongols. This was recorded and administered in Mongolian and emphasised traditional Mongolian patterns of justice, such as fines paid in cattle and compensation for victims. However, over time this separate Mongol order was gradually diluted as the Mongol princes lost their independence, and as new posts were created diminishing their power. Capital cases could no longer be tried within Mongolia but had to be referred to the Lifanyuan in Beijing. Some elements of Chinese legal culture also began to be written into the Mongol legal code, for example, a concern with the relationship between the criminal and the victim, which was an important part of the Confucian moral order. However, the Qing continued to use a separate Mongol statute book throughout the nineteenth century.

The Manchus also took advantage of the rising power and institutional structures of Yellow Sect Buddhism in Tibet and Mongolia. Over the centuries Buddhism had adapted to the societies in which it was practised and doctrinal differences had played an important role in this adaptation. The dominant types of Buddhism in Tibet and China shared several features including an emphasis on bodhisattvas, souls who could have achieved nirvana but chose instead to remain on earth to help others. These bodhisattvas were worshipped as part of a pantheon that also included non-Buddhist deities. In other respects, Tibetan Buddhism was quite different from the Buddhism of the Han Chinese. This was partly because of the different religions and cultures that had existed before the arrival of Buddhism and partly because of the much greater involvement of Tibetan

Buddhism in the state. Buddhist sects with political patronage were a long-standing feature of the Tibetan state. The Yellow Sect, which was the most powerful organisation in eighteenth-century Tibet, developed as a reformist group in the fifteenth century. A key feature of the sect was the use of rein-carnation as a political institution. The first leader was succeeded by one of his disciples, as was common practice in most Buddhist religious orders, but when this man died his disciples looked for his reincarnation among children who had been born shortly after his death. Over the years an elaborate system was developed for finding the reincarnation, including dreams, omens and the young child's recognition of objects belonging to his predecessor. Because the new sect leader was chosen at a very young age, power until he was adult was in the hands of regents who also had complete control over his education and training. In other words, power was effectively gathered in the hands of an existing elite. This was especially true given the low life expectancy of children during this period. Reincarnation was, of course, a central part of Buddhist doctrine, but this was the first time the idea had been used to create a political structure in this way.

During the sixteenth and seventeenth centuries the Yellow Sect spread to Mongolia. Its head was invested with the title Dalai Lama by Altan Khan, one of the major Mongol princes before the rise of the Manchus. The system of office holding by reincarnations also spread: the Jebtsundamba Khutuktu, who was based at the great Mongol Buddhist shrine at Urga, was also appointed in this way. Then in 1642, just before the Manchu conquest of the Ming empire, the fifth Dalai Lama managed to become the dominant political power in Tibet, with the help of one of the Mongol armies that had moved south under Manchu pressure, and succeeded in controlling much of Tibet for most of the rest of the century.

The Manchus recognised both the Dalai Lama in Tibet and the Jebtsundamba Khutuktu in Mongolia as temporal powers. In doing so they strengthened and confirmed the Buddhist sects at the expense of other Tibetan and Mongol political elites. For their part, the Dalai Lama and the Jebtsundamba Khutuktu acted as rival lords as well as spiritual leaders. They gave titles to Mongol princes and even invested them in office, arbitrated disputes and received and sent embassies. However, the Qing exerted a certain degree of control, especially over the politically charged question of which child was to be chosen as the next incarnation. Not long after the Manchu conquest of China the Kangxi emperor ruled that henceforth the search for the new incarnation of the Jebtsundamba Khutuktu was to be conducted only in Tibet. This decree ended the previous practice of finding the new Khutuktu among the offspring of a Mongolian princely family, who then gained both prestige and power. When there was a dispute as to the identity of the sixth Dalai Lama (because the boy who was originally chosen refused to take holy orders), the emperor summoned the discredited incarnation to Beijing, although in the end he died on the way. Later the Qing decreed that if there were more than one contender for the position of Dalai

Lama the decision should be made by drawing lots from an urn they supplied for the purpose. From the start the system of politically powerful reincarnations had been successful precisely because of its openness to political manipulation by existing elites; the Manchus continued this practice.

Personal dealings with the greatest incarnations, the Dalai Lama and the Jebtsundamba Khutuktu, were also important to the Qing emperors of the eighteenth century and the existence of this Buddhist theocracy posed a problem of legitimacy to any form of imperial rule modelled purely on Chinese culturalism. The Tibetan Buddhist sects were widely revered not only in Central Asia, but also in much of China proper. The Qing emperors responded to this alternative view of the cosmos by presenting themselves as part of it, just as they presented themselves as part of the Chinese culturalist worldview. They invited the incarnations to Beijing, confirmed their positions, honoured them with high titles and treated them with respect. On these occasions the emperor might receive tantric initiation from the Tibetan lamas and generally presented himself as another incarnation, that of the bodhisattva Manjusri. Manjusri was the bodhisattva of wisdom who was associated with rulership. In this role the emperor formed a triad with the Dalai Lama, who was the incarnation of Avalokitesvara the bodhisattva of compassion, and the Jebtsundamba Khutuktu, or Vajrapani the bodhisattva of power. Fig. 2.1 shows the Qianlong emperor depicted as a bodhisattva on a Tibetan-style temple painting or tangka. Tangkas were painted to be hung in temples or on domestic altars where they functioned as icons and were intended to concentrate the mind on a certain manifestation of the Buddha. The design followed patterns that could easily be read by the believer. In this particular tangka the emperor is depicted in the centre wearing the monastic robes and distinctive hat of a Tibetan Buddhist incarnation. In front of him offerings are laid out on an altar. Around and above him are displayed images of many other bodhisattvas and incarnations reaching up to the heavens which are depicted at the top of the picture. The emperor is depicted as an intrinsic part of the whole Tibetan Buddhist system and an appropriate object for worship.

The cult of Manjusri developed in the Wutai Mountains in the north of Shanxi province. The Kangxi and Qianlong emperors repeatedly visited the site and paid for the construction of dozens of temples. Wutai was only one of the Yellow-sect shrines that grew up in China. The emperors' interest meant that Beijing became a centre of Tibetan Buddhism. Indeed, after the ascension of the Yongzheng emperor to the throne in 1732 his former palace in Beijing, the Yonghegong, was converted into a major Tibetan Buddhist temple. Outside China proper at Rehe, their summer retreat on the Manchurian plains, the emperors not only built Lamaist temples but also constructed a miniature version of the Potala Palace, the official residence of the Dalai Lama. The Qianlong emperor even used one lama with whom he had a particularly close personal relationship as a mediator between the Tibetans and Mongols. In other words, the emperor's presentation of

Figure 2.1 The Qianlong emperor as a Tibetan bodhisattva
Source: *Orientations* 26.7, 1995

himself as a Buddhist ruler was an important part of the relationship
between the Qing and the non-Han areas.

ASSIMILATION

Culturalist arguments tend to assume that the Qing state used education
and Han immigration to promote assimilation to Chinese cultural models. Although this was true of the state's attitude to most of the non-Han
peoples of the south, it was not true of policies towards the north. In fact
the Qing invested a great deal of effort in trying to stop the acculturation
of the peoples of north and central Asia. Understanding that Han
Chinese immigrants were the front line of acculturation, the state
attempted to prevent them from residing in the non-Han areas of the
Manchu empire.

The political systems of Muslim Central Asia before the Qing conquest
were quite different from those of Manchuria, Mongolia or Tibet and the
Qing administration of the new province of Xinjiang reflected this. There
had originally been considerable Han Chinese opposition to Qing expansion into this area. Influential members of the Han Chinese elite felt that
such vast military campaigns conducted well beyond the Chinese cultural
area were wasteful of lives and resources. One of the results of this opposition was that after Xinjiang was established as Qing territory considerable
efforts were made to make it self-financing. In order to achieve this the Qing
took over the tax structure and much of the bureaucracy. The continuation
of the bureaucratic framework can also be seen in the way the legal system
functioned. The colony had two separate legal systems: Qing law, which
was applied by officials of the central state, and Muslim sharia law, which
was applied by the secular and religious leaders of local communities. In
general, these two different systems were applied to cases along ethnic lines.
The existence of a legal system for Han Chinese marks the importance of
Han Chinese immigration into Xinjiang both before and after the conquest.
Initially, the Qing planned to segregate Han Chinese in Xinjiang as they had
done in their other dominions: travel was restricted by a requirement for
road passes and Han were not allowed to settle in the more strictly Muslim
south of the region. There were also efforts to prevent Han Chinese from
marrying local women, for fear that rumours of sexual exploitation would
anger the locals. These policies were never successfully implemented, but
even at the end of the eighteenth century they still existed and marked the
Qing government's intention to rule its dominions according to practices
and standards different from those applied in China.

In Mongolia, trade between the Mongols and the Han Chinese had long
been essential. The Mongols exported livestock, primarily horses and sheep,
and imported silk and tea. Silk, tea and other Chinese exports were also
traded through Mongolia to the Russian empire beyond. The Manchus did
not ban the trade, which was essential to the Mongols' livelihood, but they

did try to restrict the activities of the Han Chinese merchants. Trading houses were supposed to be licensed and were required to have their licences renewed each year in Beijing. Moreover, regulations forbade any intermarriage between Han Chinese and Mongols and banned Chinese merchants from living in buildings or even in the felt tents used by Mongols in winter. This was intended to restrict the trade to the summer season, when the merchants could live in tents, and thus prevent Han immigration into Mongolia.

However, government attempts to prevent acculturation in Mongolia were not successful. Both Mongol princes and Manchu officials had invested in the businesses run by the Chinese merchants in Mongolia, and were profiting from the trade. By the end of the eighteenth century Chinese merchants were building shops, and trading towns began to grow up with largely Chinese inhabitants and buildings. The extent of Chinese immigration is revealed in an 1808 petition stating the grievances of one group of Mongols against their hereditary prince:

> The Prince has allowed the Chinese people, who were permitted to stay here for a limited time, to build up houses and enclosures and allowed them to settle down in the neighbourhood or in some other nearby villages. The Chinese carpenters Luusan, Dalai, Zayaat, Das, Senge, Dalai, Nomt and Kharsuvuu are settled close to the Prince's residence; in Zargalant, a neighbouring place, there are two Chinese named Bayandai and Luusan, they also have houses and enclosures. Some of the Chinese who had separated from the above mentioned are all settling in various scattered places in our banner and running a business there.[4]

The petition goes on with a long list of villages and the names of the Chinese resident there. Dislike of Han Chinese immigration led to occasional rioting against Chinese shops and businesses throughout the eighteenth and nineteenth centuries. Fear of the instability such friction generated in a sensitive border area was doubtless one of the reasons behind the Qing attempts to ban Han immigration.

The combination of twentieth-century politics and nationalist historiography means that while there are excellent studies of relations between Mongolians, Muslim Central Asians and Han Chinese during the eighteenth century, histories of Tibet have been absorbed with questions of political sovereignty during this period and cultural relations have been largely ignored. What sources there are suggest that Han Chinese traders from the neighbouring province of Sichuan entered Tibet in quite large numbers. Many names of vegetables and other foods were adopted from the Sichuan dialect into Tibetan during this period and Chinese cooking styles became fashionable in upper-class Tibetan homes. The dress of Manchu and Chinese officials also became the state dress for the ruling classes. Despite the emperor's proclaimed engagement with Tibetan culture, acculturation to elements of Han Chinese life was also undoubtedly part of the Tibetan experience during the eighteenth century.

The Manchu policy of separation was limited, and to some extent contradictory, as Han Chinese officials increasingly came to dominate the highest positions in the empire. Nevertheless, during the eighteenth century the non-Han areas of north and Central Asia were ruled by the Manchus and not by the Han Chinese. Han officials were seldom posted to these areas and the highest appointments were almost always reserved for Manchus. The term 'Amban', used for the Qing imperial residents in Tibet, Mongolia and Xinjiang and reported as their title by nineteenth-century Western travellers, is a Manchu, not Chinese, word. Similarly, the treaties concluded with the Russians that fixed the northern borders of the empire show that with respect to the powers of Central Asia that lay beyond their empire the Manchus conducted a pragmatic diplomacy that largely ignored the tradition of culturalism.

The Han and the universal empire

The fact that the dynasty promoted a closed hereditary ruling group and used the non-Han cultural features of that group as a means of ruling a vast empire affected Han Chinese attitudes towards the state. On the one hand, as we might expect, the policy created a sense of grievance among Han Chinese, who felt that they were excluded from political power by an alien group. However, paradoxically, the Manchu ideology of the universal empire also worked to strengthen Chinese culturalism. This came about because the Manchu emperors, unable to justify their rule by descent, turned to the promotion of the moral system of orthodox Confucianism as a source of legitimacy.

Strengthening of culturalism

The Qing dynasty, because of its self-proclaimed non-Han origins, was unable to claim legitimacy through descent. Groups rebelling against the Qing often claimed descent from the Ming, or even the earlier Song, royal family, showing that descent lines were a popular way of understanding legitimacy. However the Confucian classics also provided a model of legitimacy based on virtuous rule. The Qing laid claim to Confucian virtue both in the structures of the state and through the actions of individual emperors. The dynasty continued the Ming system of examinations in the Confucian classics as a way of selecting office-holders, ensuring that the officers of the government would have the means to display an aura of moral legitimacy. Moreover, exam candidates were required to emphasise the moralistic commentaries of Zhu Xi even when, especially by the nineteenth century, scholarly trends were leading them in other directions, such as evidential research. Meanwhile Qing patronage of scholarly research resulted in the codifying and reprinting of the Confucian canon, the Kangxi emperor's summary of Confucian morality was required learning for exam candidates, and the Qianlong emperor provided a much-reported model of filial piety in his treatment of his mother and the elaborate funeral he provided for her. Thus the Qing used both state structures and imperial behaviour to demonstrate virtue and Confucian legitimacy and this emphasis on the dynasty as the embodiment and central point of moral values worked to increase the importance and orthodoxy of culturalist views that saw China as the centre of civilisation.

Han Chinese officials, along with all the multitude of examination candidates who aspired to be officials, used this emphasis on the Qing state as a centre of moral virtue to justify their position as collaborators with an alien dynasty. They needed to do so because there was, in fact, a long tradition of opposition to non-Han dynasties. From the tenth to the thirteenth centuries much of north China had been ruled by the Liao and then the Jin dynasties, whose ruling classes were drawn from the Khitan people of Inner Mongolia and the Jurchens of Manchuria respectively. Much of the history of the culturally Chinese Song dynasty, which was ultimately forced to retreat to the south, was written in terms of its resistance to these northern peoples and their dynasties. Historians of this period have argued that loyalty directed not to the dynastic house but to the Chinese state existed from the time of these Song-dynasty battles against the Jin, and that this ideology was used by rebels to legitimate their cause. Stories of the generals and battles of those days were to become part of the common currency of late nineteenth- and early twentieth-century Chinese nationalism. Although the Chinese loyalist heroes of this period were occasionally also admired by Manchu writers, it is clear that an ideology of opposition to alien rule was available to Han Chinese officials and scholars.

Eventually both the Song and the Jin fell to the heirs of Genghis Khan, who ruled China for a hundred years as the Yuan dynasty. During the late thirteenth and early fourteenth centuries China was part of a Mongol empire that spread right across central Asia. This vast empire facilitated trade, the movement of officials from places as far away as Persia to serve in China, and even the introduction of Arabic astronomy to the court. Qing scholars were particularly interested in the situation of the Chinese under the Yuan. Some had taken up the strands of racial difference, emphasising the ultimately alien quality of the barbarians; for others culturalism enabled them to rationalise taking office. The two ideas are illustrated in a story well known in the Qing about two Yuan-dynasty scholars. One of them was said to have explained that if he did not hold office under the Yuan he would not be able to implement Confucian ideals. To this the other replied that only by refusing to hold office could he honour those same ideals. Under the Qing, as under the Mongols, the task of justifying service to an alien dynasty meant that officials tended to emphasise moral values and hence culturalism as the rationale behind the state.

Anti-Manchu feeling

But was the fact that the Qing dynasty preserved a sense of ethnic difference important to the majority of the population? It has often been claimed that widespread and persistent ethnic antagonism underlay the eventual fall of the Qing dynasty. This was an important argument of the revolutionaries of the 1900s who were under constant attack for their own alien and un-Chinese ways. In answer to this they attempted to tar the dynasty and much of the social order with similar charges of being un-Chinese. Later historians were greatly influenced by these views in their understanding of the eighteenth and nineteenth centuries and it is only in recent years that such ideas have begun to be questioned. I will discuss three examples of these tensions: the suppression of scholarly anti-Manchu writings during the compilation of an imperial library, popular secret-society uprisings and finally the huge Taiping rebellion. All of these have in the past been used as evidence of widespread, but suppressed, anti-Manchu feeling. While it is undeniable that such feelings existed by the late nineteenth century, I want to look here at the way in which they were expressed and what that tells us about the relationship between opposition to the Manchus and culturalism.

LITERATURE

The eighteenth century was a period in which many encyclopaedias and great compilations were put together under imperial patronage. The greatest of all of these was the Complete Books of the Four Treasuries, a project to assemble copies of all known books and to publish a library. The library consisted of newly edited texts of all major works and summaries of less important works. At the same time that the books were collected and edited, unacceptable works were to be found and destroyed. In practice the project only dealt with books considered to be of some literary value; this was not a survey of popular culture. The editors concluded that some of these works were unacceptable to the dynasty and this led to commands by the emperor to ferret out more such works. Some works were censored with, for example, the character for rabbit being removed from transliterations of Manchu historical and geographical names. Other cases were considered to be subversive and ended with the execution of the individuals involved and even their families. The most famous case was that of a man called Wang Xihou, who had written a dictionary. The standard dictionary of the period was, and indeed still is, the great work compiled under the patronage of the Kangxi emperor. Unfortunately Wang Xihou used the tabooed personal names of several Qing emperors as examples in his dictionary. This was interpreted by the editors as implying that he did not consider the Qing to be legitimate and ended with the execution of the author and the demotion of several officials. The cases that arose from this and other similar charges were both frightening and well known. The legal persecution has often been cited as an example of Manchu sensitivity to ethnic slurs. By emphasising the violence of the punishments, later authors have implied that it was only by such severe means that the Manchus were able to suppress the natural Han antagonism to alien rule.

However the censorship that followed the Four Treasuries project was by no means only related to either Ming loyalism or slurs on the Manchus as such. Since the texts concerned were destroyed, the exact nature of some of the material that was censored is unclear. But, as the case of the unfortunate lexicographer, Wang Xihou, shows, some of the texts considered most offensive were not intended to criticise the dynasty. It is also important to note that as well as disparagement of the Manchus, criticisms of the current Confucian orthodoxy were considered subversive. Moreover, the way in which the search for subversive material was set up, with rewards for men who were qualified for official posts but had not yet received appointments, meant that these men, almost all of them Han, generated many of the cases. The campaign was eventually called off when it became clear that the censorship was being used by such men and others to bring false accusations against personal enemies. Thus recent scholars have seen the events as reflecting problems within the predominantly Han bureaucracy as much as Manchu–Han tensions. For most of these Han officials the Manchus were now firmly on the side of Confucian orthodoxy.

SECRET SOCIETIES

Twentieth-century revolutionaries also saw early anti-Manchu feeling in the history of the secret societies that held occasional rebellions throughout the eighteenth and nineteenth centuries. One of the most important of these societies was the Tiandihui, whose members fought under the slogan 'Overthrow the Qing! Restore the Ming!' and claimed that the society had been founded by the remnant of the monks of Shaolin monastery. According to the legend the society later told, the monks of Shaolin monastery helped the Kangxi emperor to fight a barbarian people and returned to their monastery in triumph, but the emperor then treacherously burned their monastery to the ground. Five of the monks escaped to Guangdong where they met a man who introduced them to a descendant of the Ming royal family. The monks and the Ming loyalists then joined together in a society dedicated to overthrowing the Qing. They were also said to have fished out of the sea a cauldron inscribed with the slogan 'Overthrow the Qing! Restore the Ming!' This legend places the society squarely in a tradition of anti-Manchu activity, which it traces back to the beginning of the dynasty. It was important to the early twentieth-century revolutionaries who wished to recast their secret-society collaborators, often seen at the time as criminals and bandits, as nationalistic anti-Manchu rebels. However, the legend itself is not recorded before the mid-nineteenth century and recent studies of the origins and ideology of the Tiandihui suggest a rather different view.

The Tiandihui seems to have begun among the floating population of Fujian province. Anyone who learnt the secret passwords and initiation rituals of a Tiandihui society could create his own group. This was often a moneymaking venture since new members would expect to pay to be initiated into the society. They would then go through the rituals, learn the passwords and swear brotherhood with the other members of the society. Members might provide each other with mutual aid, such as loans for weddings or funerals, and also with support if they got into trouble either with other gangs or bandits or with local officials. Although the different groups thus founded might refer to themselves as branches of a larger society, since to do so enhanced their prestige, in practice there was seldom any link between different Tiandihui groups. This structure, which implied larger support while leaving organisers free to pursue their own goals, also made it very easy for the society to spread rapidly across the country. Provinces like Guangxi and Taiwan were undergoing massive immigration. The new immigrants needed help and support and often found this in the bonds that linked people from the same native place. In addition, both provinces had large populations of unassimilated non-Han peoples also competing for resources. There was intense rivalry between all these different groups in what was already a violent frontier society. At the same time there was considerable resentment at the government corruption and abuses of power by local officials that went with this uncontrolled frontier situation. In these circumstances both recent migrants and existing villagers needed the support of larger structures for protection. Secret societies were one of the kinds of organisation that filled that need and they flourished in these areas.

Secret-society uprisings grew out of resistance to the government in societies where violence was a part of life, and most concentrated on immediate goals such as looting or resisting arrest. However from the early nineteenth century the societies began to make use of anti-Qing slogans and ideas to legitimise their leaders. A tradition of Chinese resistance to alien rulers was certainly one of the forms of rhetoric available to their leaders. A proclamation issued by another secret society, the Small Sword Society, which organised an uprising in Shanghai in 1853, reads in part:

> It can be found in historical records that enlightened emperors of old defeated the peoples of the north and west to protect the territories of the Xia, and drove out the barbarians to bring peace to China. ...
> Since the Manchurian bandits captured the throne, rituals and propriety have ceased to exist, and all sense of shame has been lost. All

over the county, there are officials with the hearts of wolves and the practice of dogs, who are oppressive, and whose demands are arbitrary. They sell official posts and titles, and the Imperial Court is thus staffed with people with rabbit heads and deer breasts. The government offices are like a market: those who have money may live, and those who do not die. Officialdom behaves like bandits, creaming the people's fat, stripping them of their oil. Nomination to official titles is unjust, employment is wasted. [Manchu] bannermen fill the Imperial Court, and brilliant people from all quarters fall to the wayside.[5]

This proclamation attacks the Manchus as aliens whom the people of China should drive out and refers to historical examples. However the references to officials as animals do not attack the Manchus so much as criticise the corruption of the court, and in particular the failure of the court to give appointments to the men who have succeeded in the examination system. The Manchus in this context are objectionable primarily as a hereditary group filling posts that should be held by those who have passed the exams. Clearly the writer of this proclamation feels great resentment on this point; many of the people who ended up leading uprisings had in fact attempted to operate through the Qing system and had turned against the Qing only after they failed to gain official appointments. Opposition to the Qing as Manchus was then merely one of the available lines of rhetoric that could be used to attack the government.

THE TAIPING REBELLION

The Taiping Rebellion, by far the greatest of the rebellions of the eighteenth and nineteenth centuries, also made use of this rhetoric, though again it is not clear that ethnic antagonism was central to the uprising. The rebellion began with a failed examination candidate, Hong Xiuquan, who came from a relatively prosperous family in a village in central Guangdong. After his third failure in the exams he came home to his family and collapsed, ill. While he was ill he had a curious vision in which he was taken up to heaven. There he was admitted into the presence of the Old Father who told him that demons had invaded the earth. Hong was then ordered to do battle with the demons, given a golden seal and sword, and sent back to earth. After his fourth failure in the exams several years later Hong made angry accusations against the government and Manchu officials. It was around this time that a visitor picked up a Christian pamphlet that had been lying in Hong's cupboard and suggested Hong read it. When he did so he found that it enabled him to interpret the strange vision he had had when he was ill. Clearly the Old Father was the Christian God and Hong was the younger brother of Jesus and had been sent down to earth to do battle with the demons. Hong identified the demons with the deities worshipped in his villages, destroyed their statues and left home to preach the Christian religion. At this stage Hong's thinking was primarily concerned with opposition to idolatry, rather than with political rebellion.

Hong's travels took him to the neighbouring province of Guangxi and there among the immigrants and frontier communities he and his followers built up a new religious group, the Society of God Worshippers. Members of the society followed a strict version of the Ten Commandments and destroyed statues of local deities. A military campaign against bandits in the area led refugees and some of the groups of bandits to join forces with the society. Heterodox religious sects, whether Buddhist or Christian, were illegal and in the violent conditions of the Guangxi frontier were almost bound to come into conflict with the authorities. In 1850 members of the Society of God Worshippers were arrested and attempts to release them brought the society into direct conflict with the state. Hong Xiuquan declared a new state, the Taiping or Heavenly Kingdom of Great Peace. The group was encircled by government troops but broke out and began to move towards the northeast. As they went the Taiping captured towns and cities but broke out when the government troops began to besiege them and moved onwards. They plundered the cities to gain money and supplies. Although many people fled before their advance, some had little alternative but to stay, and, since the pursuing Qing troops killed collaborators with an almost equal ferocity, many were driven to join the Taiping forces. In 1852 the Taiping captured the great cities of Wuchang and Hankou on either side of the Yangzi River and sailed down the river to Nanjing, which they took and established as their capital.

By the time the Taiping reached Nanjing the leaders had shifted their attention away from idolatry and, as their political goals developed, had begun to identify the Manchu forces as the demons to be opposed and to take up the rhetoric of opposition to the dynasty. An excerpt from a Taiping proclamation issued in 1852 gives a sense of the new rhetoric:

> The Chinese have Chinese characteristics; but now the Manchus have ordered us to shave the hair around the head, leaving a long tail behind, thus making the Chinese appear to be brute animals. The Chinese have Chinese dress; but now the Manchus have adopted buttons on the hat, introduced barbarian clothes and monkey caps, and discarded the robes and headdresses of former dynasties, in order to make the Chinese forget their origins. The Chinese have Chinese family relationships; but the former false demon, Kangxi, secretly ordered the Tartars each to control ten families and to defile the Chinese women, hoping thereby that the Chinese would all become barbarians. The Chinese have Chinese spouses; but now the Manchu demons have taken all of China's beautiful girls to be their slaves and concubines. Thus three thousand beautiful women have been ravished by the barbarian dogs, one million pretty girls have slept with the odorous foxes; to speak of it distresses the heart, to talk of it pollutes the tongue.[6]

In line with their opposition to the Manchus, Taiping soldiers abandoned their queues and grew their hair long. Later, when they took Nanjing, they systematically killed the Manchu garrison of 30,000 men and their wives and families.

The anti-Manchu beliefs of the Taiping were combined with extreme heterodoxy: Hong Xiuquan's original vision had included the beating of Confucius as well as the command to expel the demons. Thus the Taiping vision of society was opposed not only to the Manchus but also to most of the forms and structures of the Chinese state. Zeng Guofan, the general who eventually defeated the Taiping, was known both to his contemporaries and to later generations as an exemplar of Confucian orthodoxy. Although the anti-Manchu nature of the rebellion frightened the Manchu court and probably exacerbated their sense of Manchu–Han difference, the vast majority of Han Chinese were also opposed to the rebellion. They accepted the link between the Qing dynasty and orthodox Chinese culture, while suffering from the devastation and violence of the rebellion.

Ordinary people's attitudes are illustrated in the story of the Cheng family in Anhui, north of Nanjing, who fled from the approaching Taiping armies in 1856. In the chaos the mother and her two daughters aged 15 and 16 became separated from the father and son. The girls were each carrying the bundles of embroidered clothes they had made and that would form their dowries. On the road the mother and daughters met a group of Taiping soldiers, terrifying with their long hair hanging down to their shoulders and swords in their hands. Hoping for loot the soldiers ripped open the girls' packages and amused themselves cutting the careful embroideries into pieces. One of the girls, furious, cursed the soldiers as 'long hairs', and the soldiers in response killed both girls and then their mother. Father and son, reaching the place, saw a crowd standing round, recognised the corpses, but, too frightened to take them for burial, simply fled. For these people, as for so many, the Taiping were terrifying outsiders, their long hair a sign of difference from, not of unity with the Han people.

Conclusion

This chapter has argued that although there was a tradition of antagonism to alien rule in China, culturalist thinking could also be used to justify and legitimise non-Han dynasties. Thus, the Qing were able to preserve a non-Han identity and retain their position as a politically privileged minority. This also allowed them to manipulate the symbols of power that existed in inner Asia and thus provided legitimacy for their rule there as well as in China. During the eighteenth and early nineteenth centuries they were thus successful in maintaining both their universal empire and Chinese culturalism and, indeed, each reinforced the other. However, the political pressures of the nineteenth century were to destroy this close relationship between culturalism and empire.

Notes

1 Martin Martinius, *Bellum Tartaricum or the Conquest of the Great and Most Renowned Empire of China* (London: John Crook, 1655).
2 Quoted in Jonathan D. Spence, *Ts'ao Yin and the K'ang-hsi Emperor, Bondservant and Master* (New Haven: Yale University Press, 1966), p. 66.
3 Quoted in Pamela Kyle Crossley, *Orphan Warriors: Three Manchu Generations and the End of the Qing World* (Princeton: Princeton University Press, 1990), p. 71.
4 *Petitions of Grievances Submitted by the People (From the 18th to the Beginning of the 20th century)*, trans. S. Rasidondug (Wiesbaden: Otto Harrassowitz, 1975), pp. 27–8.
5 Trans. in David Faure, 'Secret societies, heretic sects, and peasant rebellions in nineteenth-century China', *Journal of the Chinese University of Hong Kong* 5.1 (1979), p. 192.
6 Trans. in Franz Michael, *The Taiping Rebellion: History and Documents* (Seattle: University of Washington Press, 1971), vol. 2, pp. 145–6.

PART
II

CONSTRUCTING A MODERN
NATION

3

The world of nation states

The ways in which the Qing empire dealt with foreign affairs grew out of the ways in which its internal structure and identity were perceived. There were thus two possible models for foreign affairs, one based on the theory of culturalism and the other on the idea of an international empire. During the eighteenth century there was little conflict between these two models. However, when the state came into conflict with the Western powers the differences between the models became acute and began to play an important part in court politics, creating ethnically based Han and Manchu political constituencies within the bureaucracy.

Changing models of foreign affairs

The model of foreign affairs based on the theory of culturalism is known as the tribute system. In this system, as famously described by John K. Fairbank, the representatives of foreign countries visiting China were treated as bearers of tribute from their country to the emperor of China. They travelled from the borders of the country to its heart in Beijing and there presented their tribute of gifts and local products to the emperor, received gifts in return and then returned to their homelands. The system preserved the ideal of a single moral universe whose values were embodied in the Confucian texts and the Chinese system of government. China was seen as the centre of the world and also the centre of morality; other nations, by definition less civilised, paid tribute that showed the subservient status of their kings to the Chinese emperor. This system worked best for some of those neighbouring countries that had long been part of a Chinese cultural area, in particular Korea, Vietnam and the Ryukyu Islands. Korea sent annual embassies and others to thank or congratulate the emperor or to offer condolences on his death. These embassies expressed the ritual subservience of the Korean king, by requesting, for example, a copy of the imperial calendar every year, but they also dealt with such matters as fixing the border between the two states and setting up military posts and colonies in the border areas. In the tributary countries elites accepted the value of elements of Chinese culture and thought, while their rulers used the legitimacy conveyed by their relationship with the Chinese state to strengthen their own power. However the model of the tribute mission was also plausible for complete outsiders: a Dutch embassy of 1794 presented itself in accordance with the tribute model. This was possible since there were relatively few demands made on the mission beyond the humble language and posture expected of its members. Moreover, both the gifts offered by the court in return for the tribute and the private trade done by members of the mission meant that a tribute mission could be extremely profitable. When the Netherlands sent a tribute mission Dutch merchants were merely accommodating to the outward forms for national or personal advantage. However, for the Chinese the idea of China as 'all under Heaven' and the emperor as the 'Son of Heaven', whose moral influence spread beyond the boundaries of the state, appeared as proof of the universality of Confucian moral structures and worked to legitimate the scholarly class and its position within a culturalist world order.

The other model of foreign affairs was that provided by the Manchu dynasty's model of itself at the head of a multi-national empire. Within this empire it dealt with the different peoples according to their own customs and needs. The model of foreign affairs that corresponds to this view of the empire can be seen in the dynasty's relations with Russia. Embassies were sent between the two states for major negotiations and there was a permanent Russian mission in Beijing. However, this pragmatic model of foreign affairs was used almost exclusively with relation to the powers of north and Central Asia, which the Qing regarded as strategically threatening, a situation that created problems when in the nineteenth century Western traders on the south coast began to cause trouble.

The British threat to the tribute system

During the eighteenth century the European states that had any contact with China had accepted the general outlines of the tribute mission. Indeed, between 1655 and 1795 there had been 17 European missions to China, all of which had been largely compatible with the tribute system. Even the British embassy led by Lord Macartney in 1793, in which Lord Macartney famously (to us) refused to kowtow to the emperor, carried gifts labelled as tribute from the kingdom of England, and whatever Lord Macartney's actual actions the Chinese records stated that he had kowtowed. An eighteenth-century illustrated volume describing the customs of tribute-bearing peoples shows how the Europeans were assimilated into conventional Chinese models of non-Han peoples. The illustration of the English shows a man and a woman in eighteenth-century dress (Fig. 3.1). The man wears a

Figure 3.1 The English as seen by the eighteenth-century Chinese
Source: *Huang Qing zhigong tu* (Tribute-bearers of the Qing Dynasty).
Taibei: Shangwu yinshuguan, 1986, vol. 1, p. 46

sword while the woman's chest and lower arms are bare, features which are reminiscent of the illustrations of Taiwan native peoples in the same book (Figs 1.4 and 1.5) and suggestive of barbarian status. The written description that accompanies the picture reads:

> This barbarian people's clothing and adornment resemble that of a country that is very wealthy. The males mostly wear wool and love to drink wine. The females, when they have not yet married, bind their waists, desiring that they be slender. They wear dishevelled hair which hangs over their eyebrows, short clothing and layers of skirts. When they go out for a walk, then they add a big coat.[1]

Like other non-Han peoples the English are understood primarily in terms of their clothing and customs, and the structure of the brief paragraph implies the power relations that were expected between peripheral peoples and Chinese civilisation. In fact, much more information about Europe had come from the Jesuit missionaries of the seventeenth and eighteenth centuries who had been useful to the court and were acknowledged to be experts in such specialist fields as astronomy and mathematics. It was understood that their religion was not entirely compatible with the Confucian system, but they argued from Confucian texts and had been treated much like other heterodox sects. The threat to the Confucian system was not from Jesuit Christianity but from the European and American traders who began to arrive in the southern city of Guangzhou.

At first the Chinese state dealt with the small community of foreign traders in Guangzhou according to a model used for non-Han merchant communities in peripheral regions: the foreigners were to live in their own part of the town with a headman who would administer their affairs and be responsible for their behaviour to the Chinese authorities. The role of headman was played by the representatives of the British East India Company. In addition, the foreign traders were controlled through an arrangement where they were compelled to deal only with a monopoly of Chinese merchants (the Cohong) and the trade was taxed through a Superintendent of Maritime Customs for Guangdong appointed by the court. From the late eighteenth century all European trade was supposed to be confined to Guangzhou and the major tea and silk trades were confined to the Cohong monopoly. Under these conditions the trade was extremely profitable for all concerned and the Chinese merchants of the Cohong grew fabulously rich.

However, by the 1830s the very size of the trade was beginning to put pressure on the system. This pressure was increased when the East India Company's monopoly ended in 1834. Private trade had been growing fast in the preceding years, as had imports of opium, which foreign traders hoped would balance their huge exports of tea and silk. After 1834 competition between the East India Company's opium and opium from other Indian sources caused a drop in prices and a consequent boom in the quantity that was being sold. The expansion of the trade combined with the fact that opium was illegal in China meant that more and more trade was taking place outside the monopoly and causing disorder in the areas around the city. Pressures of this sort led to calls by the foreign traders for a new system. In England ideas of free trade were increasingly popular and the British merchants became more and more resentful of having to deal in China through the monopoly Cohong. They began to demand new rights that would break the Cohong's power, specifically the opening of other ports to European trade and the establishment of a fixed rate of tax.

The British merchants also resented being thought of as savages or barbarians. The British interpreter Thomas Meadows reported some years later in 1852 that:

The Chinese do habitually call and consider Europeans 'barbarians'; meaning by that term 'people in a rude, uncivilised state, morally and intellectually uncultivated' ... Those Chinese who have had direct opportunities of learning something of our customs and culture – they may amount, taking all Five Ports, to some five or six thousand out of three hundred and sixty millions – mostly consider us as beneath their nation in moral and intellectual cultivation. As to those who have had no such opportunities, I do not recollect conversing with one, and I have conversed with many, whose previous notions of us were not analogous to those we entertain of savages. They are always surprised, not to say astonished, to learn that we have surnames, and understand the family distinctions of father, brother, wife, sister, etc.; in short, that we live otherwise than as a herd of cattle.[2]

The emphasis on family relationships (institutionalised in surnames) points to the importance of Confucian values in defining civilised, and hence Chinese, behaviour. We have already noticed that Guangdong was an area where Han ethnicity was relatively recent and an important marker of status and power. The Han Chinese families of the Pearl River delta around Guangzhou bolstered their position both through their customs and practices and by their assertions of the links between those customs and practices and the values of the Confucian classics. However, it was clearly irritating for Europeans and Americans, whose expansive new culture was built on the image of themselves as the bearers of civilisation to the non-Western world, to be treated as uncivilised barbarians. Meadows states the conflict quite explicitly when he comments that Chinese notions of Westerners are 'analogous to those we entertain of savages'. The Europeans' response was to emphasise their own civilisation and the savagery of the Chinese. This they found exemplified in the methods of the Chinese legal system, which led to the concept of extra-territoriality, one of the pillars of the later semi-colonial treaty settlement. Western resentment of Chinese attitudes also led to a fanatical emphasis on prestige in official contacts, which eventually made the formalities of the tribute system impossible.

Into this increasingly difficult situation in Guangzhou stepped Lin Zexu, a new official sent directly by Beijing. Lin Zexu was not particularly interested in the concerns of the Western traders, so to understand his actions we need to turn to the attitudes of the court in Beijing towards the Guangzhou trade. The court was aware that the balance of trade in Guangzhou had shifted from the export of tea and silk, paid for largely in silver, to the import of opium. Ministers viewed opium smoking as morally objectionable, but this was not their major concern with the trade. Instead they saw the trade as a possible explanation for recent rises in the price of silver in relation to copper, which were disturbing the economy and especially tax collection. The outflow of silver to pay for opium imports was not the only explanation for rising silver prices given by Qing officials at the time and the view of economic historians today is that, though there may have been an outflow of silver from time to time, in general imports of opium were in fact balanced by exports of tea and silk. However that may be, when Lin Zexu proposed ending the opium trade to solve the currency problems, the court accepted his proposal and sent him to Guangzhou to carry it out.

The 'Opium War' that followed this decision has long been viewed as marking the beginning of a new period in Chinese history, which means that there is an unfortunate tendency to imagine that everyone knew at the time how important the issues relating to Western traders in Guangzhou were. This is not the case. As many historians, most recently James Polachek, have argued, Guangzhou and its affairs were regarded by the court as peripheral and not of strategic importance. A glance at a map shows the immense distance between Beijing and Guangzhou, especially at a time when travel was almost entirely by land. Guangzhou was at the outermost reaches of the empire and its people, despite their endless efforts to defend their customs in Confucian terms, were not considered by the northerners to be fully Chinese. Meanwhile strategic thinking was concentrated on the northern and northwestern borders, which had produced China's earlier conquerors. Lin Zexu and his supporters in court viewed the Westerners as traders and pirates, tied to the sea and with no serious political ambitions. For this they had a well-known model in the Japan-based coastal raiders of the sixteenth and seventeenth centuries. Seeing the matter in this light, Lin Zexu took up his post in Guangzhou intending to stop the opium trade quickly and effectively, and thus solve the currency crisis. With this in hand he would then be in a good position to get himself appointed to the governor-generalship of Guangdong and Guangxi. His ultimate political aim seems to have been quite different, namely the reduction of the power and expenditure of the Yellow River Conservancy through changes in the way in which tribute grain was shipped from the Yangzi delta to Beijing. He arrived in Guangzhou in 1839 and immediately took action, dramatically destroying 20,000 chests of opium and imprisoning the foreigners in their quarter until their headman agreed that they would not trade opium in future. In this dramatic style Lin Zexu precipitated the tensions among the foreign traders in Guangzhou into a full-blown crisis.

The British consul summoned help and a fleet sailed from India to take reprisals on the Chinese government. Given the earlier objections of the British traders to the mechanisms of trade in Guangzhou, it is not surprising that the British expedition soon acquired the additional aim of forcing the Chinese to agree to alter the trading system. The Opium War, as it became known, fell into two stages. First British troops besieged Guangzhou but then agreed to accept a ransom and withdraw. During the siege the troops looted and raided villages and stories circulated of rape and of their having opened the tombs of the villagers' ancestors to see how the corpses were embalmed. In the atmosphere of panic that naturally resulted, the local gentry began to raise militia forces. This was in any case very much in line with the ideas of the new imperial commissioner, Lin Zexu, and his supporters at court, who believed that the solution to many of the state's problems lay in the moral regeneration of the local gentry and their active involvement in the management of their communities. It was also a natural response in an area that had a history of feuding between powerful lineages that often led to serious fighting between villages.

What was to become the most famous incident of the war occurred near the village of Sanyuanli, a few kilometres from Guangzhou, when a small group of British troops got lost in a violent rainstorm. Because of the rain their muskets would not fire and they were then met by a crowd of more than 7,000 villagers with all the arms they could muster. One of the British soldiers was pulled out of line and killed by the villagers and 14 more were wounded before another party of troops came back to rescue them. Exaggeration of these events resulted in the news of a great victory by the villagers and the next day 12,000 more gathered, but were dispersed by Qing officials who had already agreed to ransom the city from the British and did not want more trouble. The battle of Sanyuanli has subsequently been considered by Chinese nationalists to be the first major illustration of patriotic resistance to foreign imperialism. Other writers have argued that the villagers who took part were merely xenophobic. Neither assertion can easily be proved. The huge crowds of villagers who gathered round Sanyuanli were quite probably motivated neither by love of the Qing empire, which did not appear at the time to be significantly threatened, nor by an irrational fear of foreigners, but by a quite rational desire to protect their lives and property from an invading army.

During the second stage of the war the British fleet sailed north to the mouth of the Yangzi and then up to Dagu just outside Tianjin, threatening the court in Beijing. Lin Zexu was held responsible for the war, dismissed and sent into exile while the British were persuaded to return to Guangzhou. There negotiations were held about British demands to change the trading system, but these failed and the next year the British fleet sailed north again. They captured the county town of Shanghai and the major internal port of Zhenjiang and threatened Nanjing. Negotiators were sent by the court to deal with them and the two sides made an agreement, the Treaty of Nanjing, which laid down new rules about trade and the management of the British community in China. The treaty achieved the British expedition's primary aim of ending the Guangzhou Cohong's monopoly over the Western trade by opening five more ports to foreign trade and replacing the flexible system of taxation with fixed tariffs on imports and exports. In addition to this, the British were allowed to keep the small rocky island of Hong Kong, which they had occupied during the war, and were paid off by the Qing government. However, negotiations were hampered by the fact that the British negotiators were demanding to be treated as the victors in a war between states as the recent events would have been understood in Europe, while the Qing emperor was receiving reports that described the British as rebels and assumed that the aim was to pacify them. It was thus inevitable that the terms of the treaty would be understood differently by the two sides, a situation that was exacerbated by difficulties in translation and hence in the terminology of the Chinese and English versions.

The chief Qing negotiator of the Treaty of Nanjing was a Manchu named Qiying and British negotiators noticed both the presence of the 'Tartars' and their greater flexibility when compared to the Han Chinese officials. This reflected the growing power over foreign relations of a Manchu faction at court that was to dominate official foreign policy for most of the next 10 years. The Manchu tradition of pragmatic and flexible relationships with the various peoples on the borders of their empire, as well as the Manchus' own differences from the Han population, enabled them to be relatively flexible, especially about the outer forms of foreign relations with which the British were so concerned. They were aware of the military strength the British fleet had displayed and in the years following the treaty their primary policy aim was to avoid trouble. However, such an approach was contingent on the continued dominance of the Manchu faction at court.

Chinese objections to the treaties

It was probably inevitable that the Treaty of Nanjing would not be fully implemented. Firstly, by this time Qing emperors had relatively little control over their officials in the provinces and had considerable difficulty getting any policy changes implemented. In addition to these general problems, it was immediately obvious that powerful vested interests in Guangzhou were going to suffer as a result of the treaty settlement. The fortunes of the Guangzhou monopolists and tax collectors had been of little interest to the Manchu negotiators in Nanjing, but the implementation of the treaty affected them greatly. Both the opening of five more ports to foreign trade and the replacement of the previous taxation system with a fixed tariff shifted trade away from the Guangzhou merchants. In Guangzhou relations between the British and Chinese deteriorated; foreigners out walking were stoned and fights broke out. This would not have been important if the people of Guangzhou had not been supported by powerful interests at court.

At court in Beijing many officials had been raised in a strongly moralistic school of politics. This was a product of the examination system, success in which demanded both the expression of morality and the cultivation of relationships within the bureaucracy. The simple fact that most Han officials had risen through the strictest form of the examination system, while most Manchu members of the court had not, tended to bring about divisions at court, where the moralistic style of such officials as Lin Zexu and later Zeng Guofan was the preserve of Han Chinese. The result was a Han Chinese faction whose members were aware of their weakness with relation to the Manchu aristocrats dominating the court and were searching for ways to increase their own power. They knew that the legitimacy of their power rested on the examination system and thus on the preservation of the ideas and morality it embodied. This gave them a much greater investment than the Manchus in the ideals that lay behind culturalism, and they quickly perceived that that ideal was threatened by the treaty settlement. In addition an influential group of Han Chinese literati shared Lin Zexu's ideals about the moral renewal of local society and were connected with him through factional alignments. Their desire to defend Lin Zexu and to attack the Manchu negotiators meant that they had to take a certain line about the war that had just taken place. They depicted the first stage of the war, in which the British besieged Guangzhou and then left to sail up the coast, as a victory by Lin Zexu and the local militia forces. The incident at Sanyuanli village was described as a major victory for the militia, by dint of considerable exaggeration of the numbers of British dead. To make this victory important Lin Zexu and his defenders claimed that Guangzhou was the pirates' real aim and only when they were driven off by the successful defence did they move north looking for a weak point in China's coastal defences. This then showed that the war could have been won and that the later failures were due to poor management rather than inherent weaknesses. The British were by no means the only rebel band to capture county towns and even major cities during this period, and the war was to be dismissed as pirate raiding in a peripheral region.

The Han Chinese literati faction's refusal to accept either the Qing defeat or the subsequent treaty meant that it was impossible to implement the Treaty of Nanjing fully. Failure to do so led to tension between the factions at court in Beijing and on the ground in Guangzhou. Frustrations on both sides led to another war, the Second Opium War (or Arrow War) of 1857, fought over a petty and dubious incident in which the British consul demanded an apology from the Guangdong governor general for the boarding, by Qing officers searching for pirates, of a ship named the *Arrow* and the arrest of some of her crew. The *Arrow* was a new mixed design of ship with Chinese sails and a Western hull, and was owned by a Chinese resident in Hong Kong. The British stood on very weak ground and the Guangdong governor general, who was a supporter of Lin Zexu and his strong policies, refused to provide the required apology. After issuing an ultimatum, the British, acting together with the French, took the city of Guangzhou and governed it for the next three years, shipping the governor general off to Calcutta. In a repeat of events 15 years earlier, a British fleet moved north round the Chinese coast. This time, however, they captured the city of Tianjin, Beijing's main port. There they negotiated the Treaty of Tianjin, the provisions of which went well beyond those of the earlier Treaty of Nanjing. The Qing were forced to agree to the opening of 10 more Treaty ports where foreigners would be allowed to live and trade, and foreign travel was to be permitted throughout the country. The expectation that much trade with foreigners would now take place in China's interior provinces was provided for with a requirement that internal Chinese customs should not amount to more than 2.5 per cent of the value of the goods traded. The British also, as before, demanded a financial indemnity. The most problematic item in the treaty was the requirement that foreign diplomats should be allowed to reside in the capital. This did not take place until 1860, when a foreign expedition of some 17,000 British and French troops entered the capital and sacked the emperor's Summer Palace.

The Treaty of Tianjin formed the basis for the so-called treaty system in which Westerners and their communities, known as 'concessions', held a privileged place within Chinese society. The requirement that foreigners live in their own communities administered by their own headman had originally been imposed by the Qing state. However, these communities grew into areas of legal privilege available to all foreigners but to Chinese only at a price. The privileges of the foreign concessions were of two kinds: preferential taxation and the application of British commercial law. The preferential taxation of businesses based in the concessions was due to the fact that although the Qing state had been forced to agree to taxation through a single tariff for foreigners it had not changed the taxation arrangements for its own merchants. Thus foreign merchants paid a low and predictable rate of tax on their businesses while Chinese merchants outside the concessions continued to pay higher and, more importantly, unpredictable amounts of tax, with the sums dependent largely on personal relationships with government officials. The natural result of this was that the foreign merchants made these privileges available to the Chinese, but at a price: by the time of the Treaty of Tianjin British merchants were already operating a black market in transit passes for goods. The application of British commercial law made legal action possible in business disputes and made the outcome relatively predictable. This was in contrast to the Chinese legal system in which business disputes tended to be shrouded in criminal accusations. The privileges for foreign businesses within the concessions gave huge advantages to foreign merchants and consequently Chinese domestic trade too began to operate through the concessions. This was done at a price and the rewards accrued to the foreign firms of the concessions. Perhaps the most outstanding example is the almost total takeover of the coastal trade by foreign shipping in the years immediately following the Treaty of Nanjing.

The Qing government was tied to the treaty system by the revenue provided to it by the new foreign-run Imperial Maritime Customs. This was an innovation established as a result of local negotiations in Shanghai in 1853, during the secret society Small Sword uprising mentioned in Chapter 2. When the Small Sword society captured Shanghai county town, the British consul decided to take over the collection of the tariff on foreign trade. The Shanghai local government was soon restored to office, but the British consul refused to hand over the back payments unless foreign inspectors were employed to run a Western-style customs service to collect the tariff. An agreement was made whereby Westerners were employed by the Chinese government as officials to collect the customs tax, which was then handed over to the central government. The significance of this arrangement lay in the fact that because of the aftermath of the Taiping Rebellion and resulting military reforms the Chinese provinces were significantly reducing the amounts of money they were handing over to the central government. The large and reliable revenue provided by the foreign-run Imperial

Maritime Customs thus became a major financial pillar of the central government, and was later used as security for the foreign loans that provided yet more income for the otherwise cash-strapped central government. Under these circumstances the central government gradually became dependent on the treaty system. This naturally affected the balance of power at court.

Growing political power of the Han Chinese

From the 1840s diplomatic engagement with the foreigners had been largely a Manchu preserve. The remnants of this can be seen in the institutions set up by the court after the Treaty of Tianjin in 1860 to deal with foreign affairs. Diplomacy was to be controlled by the emperor's brother Prince Gong through a special bureau known as the Zongli Yamen, or General Affairs Bureau, which took charge of all matters related to the Westerners. The Zongli Yamen was initially an entirely Manchu organisation, though it soon employed large numbers of Han Chinese. Shortly after it was founded it established an interpreters' college in Beijing to train Manchu bannermen in foreign languages and thus continue the Manchu dominance of diplomacy. The organisation of the Zongli Yamen was intended to maintain the separation between Han culturalism and Manchu diplomacy. Through it the court would combine the reality of new treaty concessions with the appearance of respect for those members of the scholarly elite who had opposed them. But changes in the balance of power at court had by now made such a separation impossible to achieve. The different reactions to the Treaty of Nanjing in 1842 and the Treaty of Tianjin in 1858 illustrate a significant change in foreign policy that had already occurred by the time the Zongli Yamen was set up. The clearest example of this shift is the extreme resistance to the idea of foreign diplomatic representation in Beijing when this was demanded by the foreign negotiators in 1858. Foreign diplomats were only allowed to reside in Beijing after British and French troops had entered the capital and stormed the emperor's summer palace. Foreign missions permanently in residence in the capital did, of course, undermine the symbolism of the tribute system. However, a Russian mission had existed in Beijing for nearly 200 years. The acceptability of this Russian mission was premised on Manchu models of international empire and the pragmatic conduct of foreign affairs. By 1860 this model of foreign affairs had been abandoned in place of a passionate, but by now totally implausible, belief in the tribute system.

This new emphasis on the tribute system grew out of the military reforms that followed the Taiping Rebellion. Throughout the period of the Opium Wars the Qing dynasty was primarily concerned with the Taiping, who were eventually defeated under the command of Zeng Guofan, a committed Confucian and a leading member of the Han scholarly elite. Zeng Guofan's ideas arose from much the same background as those of the ill-fated Lin Zexu. Like Lin Zexu he believed that what was needed to solve the state's problems was the moral renovation of local society, starting with the local gentry and involving the mobilisation of peasant militias in times of trouble. He had raised an army based on these principles to fight the Taiping, selecting members of local elites, many of whom had examination degrees, as officers. They then recruited soldiers from their home districts who were paid by levies also raised in the area. The resulting army had a strong local base and tight lines of loyalty between commander and men. The structure of the army also circumvented the Manchu banner forces with their strong ties to the dynasty.

After the death of the Xianfeng emperor in 1859, the rise of the Han Chinese literati continued because of the weakness of the central government. The empresses dowager Cian and Cixi, the mother of the new Tongzhi emperor, succeeded in becoming regents. Cian died a few years later, but Cixi ruled for more than 40 years. Initially the new regents were weak because of their lack of experience of government. However, even in later years, Cixi was hampered by the fact that a female regency was not a legitimate form of government. This meant that the regents were dependent on the general support of the court. In fact the whole period has been described by Luke Kwong as one of coalition government where power was dispersed rather than concentrated in the person of the emperor. One of the most obvious results of the dispersal of power within the court was the rise of the provincial governors general. These men headed the provincial bureaucracies and were the highest officials stationed outside Beijing. With a weak central government they began to abrogate more and more powers to themselves. Zeng Guofan and others had raised armies to fight the Taiping that were financed from locally raised revenue. At the same time, the devastation caused by the Taiping and other rebellions meant that in these areas the land tax, which went to the central government, often had to be remitted. In effect what this meant was that more of what was being extracted from the provinces through taxation was going to the provincial governments and less to the central government. The trend continued as the central government allowed regional governors general to continue to raise taxes for local purposes after the end of the rebellion. Gradually the central government began to lose control over provincial revenue. The impact of this process was initially concealed, however, by the rapidly increasing revenues from the new foreign-run maritime customs which were being received by the central government. Meanwhile the governors general in the provinces began to use their new resources to build up the power of their positions and bureaucracies.

Like the central government, the regional governors general were primarily concerned during this period with the necessity for military reforms that would enable the state to resist rebellion or invasion. During the 1860s they were the leading force in a series of reforms, known as the 'self-strengthening' movement, that were driven by the recognition of the superiority of Western weapons, which had been demonstrated both in the British and French march on Beijing and in the campaigns against the Taiping, where Qing soldiers had used imported arms. In the 1860s plans were put forward and accepted to manufacture these weapons. The Jiangnan Arsenal was established in 1865 with its own language school and translation bureau so that the staff could understand the foreign technical manuals involved. A couple of years later a naval dockyard was set up in Fuzhou with a school that taught courses in either engineering and French or navigation and English. The dockyard employed as many as 70 foreign members of staff as well as the local degree-holders, who acted as managers, and the students. Officials in charge of these enterprises were quick to realise that military modernisation required more than armaments. It was also necessary for staff study to first foreign languages and then the technical skills without which the arms could not be effectively used. Railways and telegraph lines were needed for military communications. Building railway lines required steel, and steel mills created a demand for high-grade coal. Thus officials began to set up the forerunners of a whole variety of modern industries. They saw that success in these ventures, given the official context, would require changes in the system of education and thus in the examination system that drove it. The director of the Fuzhou Naval Dockyard, for example, proposed that mathematics should be included in the examination system for appointing government officials. The near bankruptcy of the central government and the importance of regionally based and funded armies in defeating the Taiping meant that the majority of these projects were funded and controlled by the increasingly powerful group of Han Chinese regional officials.

The degree of the involvement of the powerful governors general in self-strengthening projects can be illustrated by the interests of Li Hongzhang, Governor General of Zhili and Commissioner of the Northern Ports. Li Hongzhang had begun his high official career as a protégé of Zeng Guofan in the battle against the Taiping and then the Nian rebels who rose up in the power vacuum created by the Taiping chaos. Later he invested the training funds for his army in a modern shipping operation, the China Merchants' Steam Navigation Company, for which he also acted as official patron. Li Hongzhang's close involvement with the company meant that in later years he was able to use its ships for transporting his troops and to develop his own naval forces. Further funding for these activities was acquired from his control over customs revenues from Tianjin, north China's major port. The men like Li Hongzhang who came to power in the provinces during and after the suppression of the Taiping were Han Chinese and they gradually also came to control the foreign-affairs issues of their regions. *Modern Times*, a novel published in 1905, describes a visit by a foreign missionary to a high provincial official (probably based on Zhang Zhidong, another well-known governor general). When the missionary arrives in the city he goes to a special foreign affairs office to inform them of his desire to visit the governor general.

Now the Foreign Affairs Office had long since received the Viceroy's instructions concerning foreigners. One of the Viceroy's strengths was his capacity to deal with different situations and to adapt to changing circumstances. Aware that over the years China had steadily declined, and that she was no longer as powerful or prosperous as other nations – that there were areas, even, in which she had to depend on foreigners – the Viceroy had completely discarded the arrogance of his youth, and had become very accommodating. He constantly instructed his subordinates in the following manner: 'In all your dealings with others, be guided by the principle of courtesy. Praising people will never lead to trouble. Since in our present circumstances we cannot win a fight, it is essential to enter into negotiations with them. Can we afford to adopt an attitude of superiority when our country's fortunes have reached such a low ebb?'[3]

Individuals like Li Hongzhang and Zhang Zhidong became increasingly pragmatic and realistic in their appreciation of the military capabilities and hence the options of the Qing state. However, the factional affiliations of court politics meant that the very prestige of these men provided backing for culturalist dealings with foreigners. Most of the regional power-holders of the late nineteenth century began as protégés of Zeng Guofan, who was famous for the strictness of his personal morality and his moralistic style of government. He insisted, for example, on going home to mourn the death of his mother for three years at a crucial stage in his military career. Filial piety lay at the heart of the Confucian morality and mourning the death of a parent was central to its expression. All officials were supposed to resign their posts on the death of a parent, but few as powerful as Zeng Guofan actually did so. Zeng Guofan's action was a public display of extreme morality, a statement to all that, for him, moral values were at the heart of government. Zeng Guofan's rise to power and the rise of the Han scholarly elite at court brought an end to the pragmatic Manchu control of foreign policy. The new power of the Han scholarly elite meant that until the end of the century the dynasty would derive its legitimacy from anti-Western conservatism. An emphasis on Confucian morality at the heart of government led naturally to a commitment to the values of culturalism in dealing with foreign affairs. Ultimately, therefore, the rhetoric of the tribute system was to be combined with the reality of the treaty system.

Local elite support for culturalism

Culturalist ideas tended to be concentrated among officials, degree-holders and educated men who aspired to the status of scholars, and were often expressed in attacks on Christianity, which was also unpopular with many ordinary people. Whereas for the central government the crucial issues of Western interference were essentially those of armed intervention, for local officials and degree-holders Christianity could be seen as the most serious threat to the imperial order. For if the social order was based, as these men's power was, on the premises of Confucian morality, then Christianity as a heterodox religious sect undermined that social order. Serious incidents tended to blow up with respect to the large Catholic communities, many of which had existed since the eighteenth century and were deeply embedded in local society, rather than the more recent and much smaller Protestant missions concentrated round the treaty ports.

The role of official and scholarly elite support for anti-Catholic rioting is illustrated by the stories of two otherwise quite different incidents that occurred in 1862 in Nanchang, the capital of Jiangxi province, and in 1870 in Tianjin. Nanchang had long had a large Catholic community and the community's position was strengthened by the commitment not to persecute Catholics laid down in the Treaty of Tianjin. When, in 1862, a new Vatican official was appointed to take charge of the Jiangxi Catholic community, he demanded to be treated as of equivalent rank to a governor general and that the new treaty provisions should be widely advertised. The demand for high status for the foreign representative of a heterodox religion was in direct conflict with culturalist Confucian views. In response a couple of senior members of the gentry, one a member of the prestigious Hanlin academy in Beijing and the other a local lecturer, wrote and circulated two strongly anti-Christian manifestos. A new provincial governor took office, Shen Baozhen, the son-in-law of Lin Zexu, and not only did not treat the Vatican official with the rank he demanded but refused to see him at all. While all this was going on candidates began to gather for the provincial exams in the city. Given the degree of support from the political elite, it was hardly surprising when a riot broke out and much Catholic property was destroyed. The affair was not calmed by the new governor's announcement at the end of the first day of rioting that no arrests would be made. Acting in the same spirit he later refused to implement the compromise worked out between the Beijing government and French diplomats and was said to have claimed that the affair was 'a gratifying result of two hundred years of nurturing the scholar gentry'.[4]

In Nanchang the victims of anti-Christian rioting were Chinese Catholic families and businesses, and the governor succeeded in keeping Vatican officials out of the province. However victories like this exacerbated tensions elsewhere. A much more diplomatically serious incident occurred in 1870 in Tianjin, where French nuns had been offering money for orphans. In a society where daughters were regularly sold by their families it was not surprising that this was seen as a purchase and, eventually, that a man was arrested and confessed to kidnapping children for sale to the orphanage. The scandal was worse because the orphanage was eager to take dying children and consequently had a very high death rate exacerbated by epidemics, one of which had recently broken out. Negotiations with the French authorities, who resided in the same compound as the orphanage and cathedral, brought an agreement that Chinese officials would be allowed to inspect the orphanage. However, when the city's three leading officials turned up with a large crowd of local dignitaries, the French consul panicked, shot at the magistrate and killed one of his attendants. In the ensuing rioting the consulate, cathedral and orphanage were all burned down and nineteen foreigners were killed as well as many Chinese Catholics. A major crisis was only averted by the fact that the Franco-Prussian War had just broken out when the news reached Paris.

Although the Tianjin riot was the most serious incident in terms of the loss of foreign lives, intermittent outbreaks of anti-Catholic violence were a feature of the period. Such outbreaks and especially the government's obvious unwillingness to punish the perpetrators of the violence fed the long-standing resentments of the foreign community in China at their unequal status, but above all strengthened the culturalist ideologies from which they arose.

The new modernisers and the origins of nationalism

However, culturalism was no longer the only possible attitude towards foreigners. During this period we also see the growth of a quite new community of Han Chinese who had personal, and often financial, interests in the legitimation of new ways of looking at the international order. Initially many of the opportunities connected with Western trade came through emigration. The great sea-trading routes transported not only goods but people; indeed the so-called 'coolie trade' in which Chinese workers were shipped as bonded labourers from Guangdong to Southeast Asia was one of the scandals of the age, rivalling even the opium trade. Many bonded labourers lived poor and died young in the countries to which they went, but other Chinese from the same places grew wealthy in their adopted homelands. For much of the eighteenth and nineteenth centuries Chinese merchants held immensely profitable concessions to sell opium in Southeast Asia. Many emigrants, and especially those who did well, maintained close links with their families, home villages and counties in China, using them as a source of reliable labour, sometimes sending their children home for their education, and even shifting their place of residence back and forth as the need arose.

The family of Sun Yatsen, the revolutionary who eventually became China's first president, provides a case in point. Sun's father was a small farmer and trader in Xiangshan county just across the mouth of the Pearl River from Hong Kong, and an elder brother emigrated to Hawaii. Sun Yatsen was sent to Hawaii as a child to live with his brother and was educated at a British-run school there. He then came back home to study at the Western-style medical school in Hong Kong and to marry a local woman. In these situations a new kind of Chinese identity developed that grew out of personal discontent with earlier culturalist ideas, but was also heavily influenced by contact with Western ideas in a variety of forms. The huge number of Chinese who emigrated to Southeast Asia had come into contact with the European colonies that were being formed there. In these new states the culturalist ideas of the immigrants interacted with the racist attitudes of the colonisers, which were gradually being institutionalised during this period. At the same time citizenship of these colonial states allowed the emigrants and their children to return to their home villages under the often convenient protection of foreign extra-territoriality. In this situation they became aware of their Chineseness in a new context of nation and race.

As the Western presence in China expanded, foreign trade also provided employment in China itself. The early years of Tang Jingxing and Wu Tingfang give an idea of the kinds of opportunities that were becoming available. Tang Jingxing, who was born in Xiangshan county in 1832, was educated at Hong Kong mission schools and, on graduation, became an interpreter for the Hong Kong government. Some years later he moved to Shanghai to be an interpreter and clerk in the new Western-run Imperial Maritime Customs. Wu Tingfang was born in Singapore, but his family returned to Guangdong when he was still an infant and his early education took place in the suburbs of Guangzhou in the traditional Chinese style. However at the age of 13, when parents began to make choices about their sons' future careers, he was sent to a missionary school in Hong Kong, and after his graduation became a translator for the Hong Kong police court. Tang Jingxing and Wu Tingfang are famous because of their later achievements: Tang Jingxing became the manager of several of Li Hongzhang's modern-style business enterprises, while Wu Tingfang qualified as a barrister in London and led a distinguished career that included a spell as Chinese ambassador to America. The story of their early lives suggests the kind of new career opportunities that parents in areas close to the treaty ports were seeing and investing in. Employees of Western organisations, emigrants and those who worked within the foreign affairs side of the Qing empire began to understand the attitudes that underpinned Western power. Moreover, the acceptance of at least parts of that ideology was necessary for success in their careers. Western business practices rested on an elaborate ideological foundation that was closely linked to the political structure of the European states and very different from that employed by contemporary Chinese businesses. The compradors who made fortunes acting as the middlemen between Western companies and Chinese society had to understand the ideas of Western company structures and banking. Such understanding was not, however, limited to business practices, but inevitably brought with it new ideas of the role of the state in society.

The new career opportunities related to foreign trade and influence caused parents like those of Tang Jingxing and Wu Tingfang to choose to send their sons to missionary schools. In doing so they accepted that their children would not rise to the highest power in the state through the examination system, and made choices that were intended to enable them to do well financially after a relatively cheap education. The primary aim of this education in the parents' minds was the acquisition of foreign languages for future financial benefit, but for the teachers and school governors the aim was the conversion of the children to Christian belief. Given the children's daily contact with the missionaries it is hardly surprising that some of those who studied in missionary schools did indeed become Christian. The Protestant Christianity many of them accepted, often closely linked in educational institutions to Western science and medicine, put a further barrier between themselves and the culturalist worldview of many of their peers.

The emigrants and men who staffed the Western trading houses and administrations of the treaty ports were joined in their increasing discomfort with culturalist worldviews by men who had built up careers as specialists in foreign affairs for the Qing government. These men were far fewer in number than those who grew wealthy and powerful through the treaty ports, but they tended to have better traditional education and therefore easier contacts with the bureaucracy and with the mainstream of contemporary elite culture. They played a crucial role in spreading new ideas of identity to a wider audience. Yan Fu, who later became famous as a translator, provides a good example of the kind of people who became involved in the government's early modernisation enterprises. Yan Fu had received a good early education, but when he was 14 his father died and the family could no longer afford his schooling so he was sent to take the exams for the new naval school, which charged no fees and gave students a monthly wage. He graduated after five years and in 1877 the government sent him to England to continue his education in naval science at Portsmouth and Greenwich. On his return from England Yan Fu became a teacher at the Jiangnan Arsenal school and then dean of Li Hongzhang's new Beiyang Naval Academy. Yan Fu's original entry into the naval school was by no means an optimal career choice, merely the lesser of several evils in a situation in which his family could not afford to continue his regular education and the new dockyard had been founded nearby. However, by the time Yan Fu was an adult, his heavy investment over many years in the learning of the ocean barbarians meant that the legitimacy and value of that learning had become essential to his own sense of self-worth. For Yan Fu, and an increasingly large number of others like him, culturalism was becoming psychologically unacceptable and a new way of looking at the world had to be found. In their search for this they were to develop that new sense of identity that we know as modern nationalism.

At the same time as the modernisers sought a new sense of identity, they began to look beyond the Western technical skills so important to the self-strengthening movement to the underlying differences between Chinese and Western culture. The foreign-language element of their education made analyses of the underlying structures of Western ideas possible. To Yan Fu, reading books on political economy in London, it began to seem obvious that the power of the Western nations lay not merely in their weapons but also in the ideologies that underpinned their states. Later, after his return to China, he began to translate some of the works he felt were most important into elaborately beautiful classical Chinese, interspersed, as was the practice in classical Chinese texts, with his own commentaries and explanations. Among the ideas that he felt were most important were those that we now think of under the heading of Social Darwinism. In total contrast to the culturalist view of an eternally expanding moral centre through which barbarians were inevitably drawn towards civilisation, Yan Fu described a world that was at once savage and ruled by the laws of nature, a world in which nation states competed for power and those that failed were wiped out. This was the new world of nation states in its harshest form and in its very violence it appeared to provide an accurate analysis of the expansion of the European empires into the rest of the world. Of all the ideas that Yan Fu translated this was the most influential because it fitted so well with what his readers saw around them.

For men like Yan Fu the increase in the use of Western ideas and the adoption of further Western technologies was in their interest, for with the advance of these ideas they became not merely experts on the foreigners, but experts on government. This was particularly important for them because they were usually under attack for being un-Chinese. Some of the men who had studied abroad longest had adopted Christianity and married Western women. Many returned to their homes wearing strange clothes and hair-styles. Many years later Wu Tingfang explained why he had gone back to wearing Chinese-style clothes after returning from his long period abroad:

> That was the Qing dynasty! When students returned from studying abroad, we needn't talk about those who became officials; but even those who did not become officials also grew queues. Otherwise ordinary people would look askance at them, and if they did not call them revolutionaries, then they laughed at them as slaves of the foreigners. Everyone wants respect, so who is willing to be a slave of the foreigners? Everyone wants to live, so who is willing to be a revolutionary when revolutionaries are being strictly suppressed'?[5]

There has been considerable discussion over whether men like Wu Tingfang and Yan Fu can be considered nationalist. In his study of Yan Fu, Benjamin Schwartz suggested that nationalism should be defined as a state of mind 'where the commitment to the preservation and advancement of the social entity known as the nation takes priority over the commitment to all other values and beliefs'.[6] Few faced such stark choices, but it is clear that a

new type of Chinese identity, heavily influenced by Western ideas and practices, was beginning to develop among a small but growing group of the
population who had close contact with European, American and colonial
lifestyles. It is also clear that this group had begun to have a strong interest,
both psychologically and financially, in the expansion and legitimation of
these new forms of identity.

Loss of the tributary states

It was not, however, until the huge psychological blow of the loss of China's
traditional tributary states that new ideas about identity began to spread
beyond the small group of men closely involved in the government and in
Western trade. The loss of Vietnam and Korea made it immediately obvious
that the ideas of culturalism simply did not any longer provide an accurate
depiction of the world. Although it was still possible to argue that culturalism described how the world should be, it clearly did not describe how the
world actually was.

In 1862 the Vietnamese government signed a treaty ceding part of the
country to France and giving France control over its foreign affairs. A
further treaty in 1874 effectively made the country a French protectorate,
though still independent in name. The Vietnamese government responded to
the increase in French power by seeking to strengthen its long-standing ties
with China. Vietnam had fought both the Ming and Qing dynasties to
prevent excessive Chinese interference, but had usually continued to recognise some role for China in its politics. Now the Vietnamese government
continued to send tribute missions to Beijing in an attempt to use China to
balance the French. In 1884 the French therefore entered into negotiations
with the Qing over Vietnam. This provoked violent dispute within the Qing
court between those, led by Li Hongzhang, who was conducting the negotiations, who realised that the Qing armed forces could not resist a French
attack, and those purists who emphasised, in true Confucian fashion, the
importance of men's spirit rather than weapons. In this situation an agreement was reached by Li Hongzhang and the French ambassador, but
Chinese troops on the ground in Vietnam continued to resist and the French
took matters into their own hands, moving north from Vietnam up to
Fuzhou where they sank the new Chinese fleet and destroyed the newly built
Fuzhou Naval Dockyard. After this defeat Li Hongzhang's agreement was
accepted and Vietnam was no longer part of the Qing empire.

Ten years later came the loss of Korea. Korea had been among the
earliest Manchu conquests and had continued to conduct elaborate tributary relations with the Qing. From the early 1880s there had been
considerable dispute in Korea over whether or not to try and modernise the
government and if reforms were to be undertaken how much influence
either China or Japan should have over them. After court power struggles

with considerable involvement by Chinese and Japanese forces, the Qing had negotiated with the Japanese and both sides had agreed to withdraw their troops. Li Hongzhang, who was based in north China facing the Korean peninsula, then sent the head of his military operations, a young man named Yuan Shikai, to Korea where he dominated court politics for almost 10 years from 1885. It was already becoming clear to those actually involved in the three countries' relations that the formalities of the tribute system were no longer a possibility. Into this tense situation erupted the religiously motivated Tonghak Uprising. Chinese troops were sent to crush the uprising, and Japan took this as a breach of the previous agreement. In the war that followed the Japanese decisively defeated Li Hongzhang's army and navy in 1895. The Qing were forced to agree to Korean independence from China, cede the island of Taiwan to Japan and give Japanese the same kind of treaty rights in China that Westerners had.

The impact of the loss of first Vietnam and then Korea on Chinese ideas about the state was much greater than the previous minimal connection of these territories with the Qing might appear to warrant. This makes sense only if we see that the loss of Vietnam and Korea was the moment at which the culturalist world order was destroyed. For those whose beliefs in culturalism had already been shaken by extensive contact with Western ideas and institutions the result was complete disillusionment with the Qing state. Sun Yatsen, studying in a British medical college in Hong Kong, later dated the start of his revolutionary thought to the Sino-French war and claimed that he organised his first revolutionary uprising in Guangzhou in 1895 shortly after the defeat by the Japanese. But the defeats also began the process of the destruction of the culturalist world order from within. The scholar Kang Youwei, also from the area just around Hong Kong, tried to organise a petition of 1,200 candidates for the highest degree in Beijing to oppose the signing of the 1895 treaty with Japan. Kang Youwei was later to play a crucial role in transforming the nature of Confucian belief from an all-embracing culturalist world order to a much more relativist belief. Indeed he even tried, not very successfully, to make Confucianism into a national religion. While Kang Youwei's own ideas were always considered eccentric, many other scholars at this time began to cast their understanding of Confucianism in relative terms, a process described by Joseph Levenson as the moment of transition from culturalism to nationalism.

Exclusion and opposition

With the destabilising of Confucian ideology and the increasing disillusionment of the treaty-port intellectuals came the beginnings of elite opposition to the dynasty. Both the Confucian scholars and the men of the treaty ports were unhappy at their exclusion from power. The causes of the scholars' dissatisfaction with the exam system have already been discussed, but the widespread sale of government office to fund the suppression of the Taiping rebellion had exacerbated their feelings of being unfairly treated. The experts on Western affairs, with their knowledge of the sources of Western power, felt that they too were being unfairly excluded from the government. Moreover, their training made it next to impossible for them to succeed in the highly competitive examination system. Yan Fu tried and failed three times to pass even the lowest level of the exams. Men like Yan Fu and Tang Jingxing were sometimes invited into the service of high officials, but were restricted by their lack of examination qualifications to positions as foreign-affairs experts, when they felt that their knowledge should be at the centre of government reforms. Even scholars and regular officials who took up positions relating to foreign affairs tended to find themselves sidelined: one of the problems of the Fuzhou Naval Dockyard was the attempts of its staff to succeed through the regular examination system which distracted them from their jobs.

The events of 1898, known as the Hundred Days' Reforms, pointed up the lack of access of the reformers to the centres of power. In 1898 the young Guangxu emperor should have taken power after the regency of his aunt the Empress Dowager Cixi. The Guangxu emperor was interested in reform and gave audiences to several individuals closely associated with ideas of reform, including Yan Fu and Kang Youwei. In addition he agreed to a variety of proposals for change that went considerably further than the court had yet thought tolerable: the abolition of the formal stylistic criteria hitherto demanded of exam essays, the establishment of schools teaching modern subjects in the provinces, measures designed to stimulate agriculture, industry and commerce, and the use of Western-style drills by the army. He also called for the abolition of many government sinecures, though this seems to have been more of a personal crusade for frugality in government. These proposals were not radical: complaints about the essay style required in the exams had been made since at least the eighteenth century. However, for reasons that are not fully understood but may have related to fears of a Western-backed coup, the regent Cixi lost her nerve over the process and resumed personal power, banishing the emperor to part of the Summer Palace and executing several supporters of Kang Youwei. Kang and his disciple Liang Qichao fled to Japan.

In the events of 1898 we see the beginnings of the alliance between the scholarly elite and the experts on Western affairs that was eventually to overthrow the Qing. In large part their hostility towards the government must be put down to resentment at their exclusion from power. However the loss of Korea and Vietnam, which shattered the culturalism of many of the scholarly elite, also opened the way for extending new ideas about identity and the nature of the state to a much wider audience.

The Boxer Uprising

So far we have looked at the response of China's political elite and the population of the treaty ports to the Western presence in China, but in order to understand the development of Chinese nationalism it is also necessary to consider popular attitudes. This is difficult because most people did not leave written records, let alone accounts of their opinions on international relations. However, the Boxer Uprising of 1900, when all over the north China countryside groups of villagers burned down churches and murdered their Catholic neighbours, was a moment when many people acted out their attitudes and sense of identity. The feelings that gave rise to such tragedies were greatly exaggerated by a severe drought and the political tensions at court, but it is possible to use the uprising to try and understand how popular views about Chinese identity were changing as a result of the Western presence.

Across rural north China Boxer groups began with young men assembling, usually in temples, and taking part in a strange new form of martial art in which they were possessed by spirits. A schoolteacher in rural Shanxi described a gathering of the Boxers in his area:

> In the autumn in the 7th month they gathered in great numbers at Jinci Temple, each holding a weapon and wearing a red head cloth, a red belt and a red scarf. They arrived in small groups, entered the temple of the Wutian God and when they had worshipped the god they paid their respects to the leader. The leader and his supporters acted as if they were drunk. Whenever there were several tens of thousands gathered, half adults and half children, they lined up and left, with two red flags carried in front of them bearing the words 'Support the Qing and destroy the foreigners; implement the Way on behalf of Heaven'. They did not disperse till the 8th month.

He goes on to describe some of the activities of another local Boxer group:

> On the 23rd of the 6th month the leader took his supporters to Sanxian village to attack the Catholics. There were a lot of Catholics in Sanxian, more than in other places, and the church was really magnificent. Many Catholics from neighbouring counties had taken refuge there and they defended the church strongly so that no one could take it. But the man known as His Honour Guan was passionate and determined. He repeated his attacks all day and he himself led from the front, climbing up the wall of the church compound where he was shot and fell, though not seriously enough to die. His supporters were bitterly angry and pushed the attack with all their force and on the third day they broke through. Then they massacred all the Catholics, men, women and children, killing several hundred people in total and leaving no survivors. All the church buildings were burned

down. The Boxer leader died of his injuries ten days later and three of his supporters were killed. At the beginning of the 7th month they scattered.[7]

There were very few foreigners in Shanxi and the neighbouring province of Inner Mongolia, about 140 all told, and almost all of them were killed during the uprising. A Christian who had escaped to Shanghai reported how two of them had died. Miss Whitchurch and Miss Sewell were missionaries stationed in a remote rural county. A crowd of Boxers came to their house and the two women sent a message to the magistrate asking him to disperse the crowd. He came and told them that his soldiers were to protect the Chinese, not them. After he left the crowd looted the house, stripped the women and beat them to death. Catholic communities had existed in Shanxi since the eighteenth century and Miss Whitchurch and Miss Sewell do not seem to have been an immediate threat to the local community. Why were these people so suddenly and savagely murdered? The reasons can be summed up as long-standing tensions with Catholics in village communities, fear of Western power, and the interaction in 1900 between a severe drought and high-court politics. In each of these factors the shifting relationship between cultural identity and national politics played an important role.

Christianity as a threat to the social order

In order to understand the problems Catholics posed in the villages we need to understand the nature of the relation between the Qing state and local communities, which was closely linked to the culturalist view of the world order. Late Qing magistrates governed large and populous counties with little administrative or military support. Direct state intervention in the villages was limited to the resolution of legal cases and the exaction of taxes. For the rest of the time the magistrates were dependent on local structures that drew their legitimacy from the state. Rural communities were organised by local leaders and power structures, such as crop watching or irrigation networks, legitimated through religious rituals. The leaders of an irrigation network might meet and feast in the temple of a local god, use the temple to store the stone steles on which the magistrate's legal decisions that confirmed their power were inscribed, and hold an annual festival with opera for the enjoyment of the god and local villagers. In order to do all these things local leaders had the right to levy money from the villagers, usually on the basis of the amount of land owned, and this right increased their power. This religiously based network was linked to the religious activities of the magistrate and the higher levels of the state. Thus the worship of local deities legitimated state power, while at the same time the state's rituals and beliefs legitimated the village social order.

However, during the late nineteenth century the new vision of the world order brought by the foreign powers gradually began to affect this social structure. In areas remote from the treaty ports, one of the most important ways in which this happened was change in the status of Christian communities and foreign missionaries. After the Treaty of Tianjin, which granted freedom of religious belief to Christians, some Christians began to refuse to pay village levies on the grounds that they were used to fund non-Christian religious rituals. Local leaders reacted angrily. In one Shanxi village when a Catholic called Li Xiangtai refused to pay the village levy, the village head, a man called Blind Cat Chang, took a hundred people to Li's home in the middle of the night, broke down the door and dragged Li to the temple, where he tried to force him to agree to pay a fine of 100,000 copper cash for temple repairs and an opera. When Li refused to hand over the money Blind Cat Chang had the Li family's 40 fruit trees cut down and sold. After that he cut down the fruit trees of anyone who was Catholic. All the parties in this dispute eventually appealed to the local magistrate, who supported the village head. This was, and continued to be, quite a common response despite the new treaty provisions. Magistrates worked, for the most part, not with a codified legal system but with commonly shared ideas of justice and morality. In the opinion of many magistrates Christianity was a heterodox religion and Christians were fortunate not to be punished for holding it; they certainly should not benefit from it. Magistrates were aware that to acquiesce to Catholic demands would strike at the legitimacy of the symbolic ties between local communities and the state.

In their judgements magistrates reformulated what had come to them as disputes over village power structures in broader, national terms. Thus the magistrate who examined Li Xiangtai asked, 'Why do you not act according to the ways of your former local temple?' To this Li replied, 'The church clearly bans this, so I now follow the temple [only] in matters concerning the public good.' The magistrate, seeing the power of the state threatened by the structures of the Catholic church, was furious at this reply and ordered Li to obey the temple organisation. Later he asked Li, 'Why do you people not respect the teachings of this country, but perversely believe in the heterodox teachings of the French religion?'[8] Here Christianity is explicitly linked to obedience to a foreign power.

In a similar Shanxi case in 1881 the magistrate asked Catholic church member Yang, 'You are a person of what country?' Yang replied, 'I am a person of the Qing.' To which the magistrate responded,

> If you are a person of the Qing dynasty then why are you following the foreign devils and their seditious religion? You didn't pay your opera money requested by the village and you were beaten. But how can you dare to bring a suit? Don't you know why Zuo Zongtang went to Beijing? In order to kill – to exterminate – the foreign devils. You certainly ought to pay the opera subscription. If you don't you won't

be allowed to live in the land of the Qing. You'll have to leave for a foreign country.[9]

The term used for both 'country' and 'dynasty' in this dialogue is *guo*, and the text shows how the use of this word was shifting: Yang replies that he is a subject of the Qing dynasty, while the magistrate refers to a choice between countries. The magistrate assumes a necessary association between local religious practice and nationality in a world of nation states. In other words, problems with cultural practices at the village level are beginning to be associated with political problems between the Qing and the foreign powers.

Fear of Western power

During this period knowledge of Western scientific and military power was also gradually spreading beyond the areas of direct Western influence. Imported arms were now in use by Chinese armies and were known to be extremely effective. But for many ordinary people the power of Westerners was exemplified in the work of Western doctors. Western techniques of surgery were rightly perceived as being dangerous, but powerful. A British doctor working in Shanxi in the 1880s found that many patients with eye problems came to him because of stories of the success of cataract operations. One woman of 47 who was completely cured had been dismissed from her job as a servant when she became blind and had twice attempted to drown herself in despair at her situation. With success stories of this kind it was not surprising that Chinese fraudsters and quacks were soon selling medicines they claimed they had acquired from the Westerners. However, almost all Western doctors were medical missionaries, and medical treatment was accompanied by fervent prayer and exhortations to the patient to thank the Christian god. For many people Western technology came to be associated with magic and ritual.

Western power was also understood in terms of magic and ritual because these were the terms commonly used by ordinary people to make sense of the incomprehensible. For many people Westerners were quintessentially other and strange, and therefore both frightening and potentially powerful. A jingle recorded in 1900 ran:

> The women are not chaste, the men are not worthy,
>   The devils are not the fruit of men.
> If you don't believe, please look carefully,
>   The devils' eyeballs emit blue light.[10]

Such ideas led to accusations of alien behaviour which took the form of the inversion of key Chinese ideas about the proper ordering of society. Westerners were regularly accused of not respecting familial relationships, and particularly of mother–son incest, the inversion of the primary Confucian relation of filial piety. When there was a serious drought in 1900, it was thought that this kind of immoral behaviour was disturbing the cosmos. A text posted in many places in Tianjin read:

> On account of the Protestant and Catholic religions the Buddhist gods are oppressed, and our sages thrust into the background. The law of Buddha is no longer respected, and the five relationships between monarch and minister, father and son, husband and wife, elder and younger brothers, and friends are disregarded. The anger of Heaven and Earth has been withheld from us. But Heaven is now sending down eight millions of spiritual soldiers to extirpate these foreign religions, and when this has been done there will be timely rain.[11]

In other words, it was being suggested to people that the inversion of moral behaviour practised by the Westerners was the primary cause of the serious drought, and only if the Westerners were exterminated would the drought be ended. Such attitudes associated the Westerners with power, but understood that power in terms of the earlier cultural order.

Fear of the power of Western technology combined with long-standing Chinese fears of the mutilation of the body to produce accusations that Western power was based on the removal of organs from Chinese bodies. In 1900 two Catholic nuns near Tianjin were killed by a crowd after rumours that they kidnapped children and then turned them over to church members to gouge out their hearts. A pamphlet distributed throughout Shanxi as a sort of chain letter said that foreign vessels seized at the coast had been found to contain quantities of human blood, eyes and nipples. The famous writer Lu Xun remembered how in the 1890s in his home village everybody, old and young, talked about how the foreign devils gouged out eyeballs to use in electricity and photography. He even remembered hearing an old lady explain that the reason the Westerners gouged out hearts was to melt down the fat into oil for lamps to go beneath the earth and find treasure, which was why foreigners were so rich. Boxer magic and spirit possession provided a solution to these kinds of magical and spiritual power. The widespread nature of these beliefs is indicated by the fact that even in the south of the country, where for political reasons provincial governments strictly suppressed the movement, churches were attacked, Christian property was burnt and there were rumours of foreign defeats by Boxer forces.

Fear of the foreigners was exacerbated in 1900 by the threat of drought. Across north China no rain fell in the planting season that year. This left farmers unemployed, with no crops to care for, deeply anxious and with time on their hands. As grain prices began to rise steeply the farmers stopped spending money and the crisis began to hit rural industries and country towns. Almost all adults could remember the drought of 1877 and 1878 and the famine that had followed. In those years men had sold their

wives and even their children and still died of starvation, and many more
had had to leave their homes as destitute refugees in a society where destitution almost always meant death. Drought was a fearsome thing. In 1900
people were already saying, 'more than half the people will die' or 'in the
great catastrophe seven out of ten will die'.[12] There were rumours that only
those who cooperated with the Boxers would escape. Drought exacerbated
tensions with Christians, because it was seen as a punishment for
immorality and prayers for rain required the sincere and public participation of the whole community. The magical techniques of the Westerners
also came under scrutiny and rumours spread that they were preventing the
rain not only by their immorality but also, for example, by standing naked
on the roofs of their houses fanning back the clouds.

Influence of court politics

High politics also played an important role in enabling and legitimating the
violence. The Chinese today refer to the events of 1900 not as the Boxer
Uprising but as the Invasion of the Eight Allied Armies. In doing so they
focus attention not on the rural attacks on foreigners and Catholics that
took place in the first part of the year, but on the Qing declaration of war
against the foreign powers in the summer. This declaration of war legitimated the Boxers' anti-foreign activities and thus expanded their scope, but
it also altered their nature.

Support for religiously inspired rural militias did not come naturally to a
government that had been putting down such rebellions for half a century.
The first response of the county and provincial authorities faced with the
mass murder of Catholic villagers, or Boxer troops demanding to be fed at
government expense, was to try to disperse the Boxer forces, distinguish the
leaders from those who had been drawn into the trouble against their better
judgement, execute the troublemakers and send the others back to their
homes. But these responses were countered by considerable support within
the government both for the Boxers' aims of punishing heterodox religion
and for using popular militias to fight the Western powers, an idea that still
had a hold over the imaginations of a certain faction within the court. The
result of these opposing forces within the court was that the central government vacillated and pursued contradictory policies. Yuan Shikai, the
governor of Shandong province, conducted a strong campaign against
Boxer groups and succeeded in preventing serious outbreaks; but the court
also issued an announcement that people drilling for self-defence were not
to be considered to be bandits, thus strengthening the hand of local officials
who did not want to suppress Boxer groups.

Meanwhile, the Western community in the treaty ports succeeded in
persuading the governments of the eight major foreign powers to announce
a military expedition against Beijing. In the face of this threat the debate at

court swung in favour of those who hoped to use the Boxers to drive out the foreign powers, and the court declared war on all the foreign powers simultaneously. The declaration of war instantly changed the potential costs of participation in Boxer groups, which had previously verged on the heterodox. Troops carried banners proclaiming 'United in harmony troop by imperial decree' or 'The righteous people by imperial decree; protect the Qing and destroy the foreigners!' Groups of Boxers began to gather in Beijing and Tianjin and fought alongside the imperial army in the siege of the foreign legations in Beijing and the foreign concessions in Tianjin. Fig. 3.2 is a contemporary populist depiction of the successes of the Boxer troops in an official military context. The text at the top of the picture tells how three generals in the Qing army ordered 5,000 Boxers to fight in the front line against the foreign troops. The illustration depicts the Boxers, with bare chests and legs and ferocious expressions, bringing the foreign soldiers they have captured to the Qing generals. In the background two soldiers from the regular army fire a cannon that appears to have sunk at least two of the foreign ships. In this context the Boxers are seen as integrated into the war declared by the court. However despite the declaration of war, there was still considerable dissension within the court, and high officials in the centre and south of the country concluded non-involvement pacts with the Western powers.

We should not imagine that because the Boxer movement was fed by rumours of mutilation and belief in the power of spirit possession, its participants were unaware of court politics. There were rumours that Li Hongzhang, who had negotiated the treaty that ceded Korea and Taiwan to Japan in 1895, had married his son to the daughter of the Japanese emperor, and a jingle heard in Shandong accused him of betraying the country. Similar stories and jingles had circulated a couple of years earlier about leading reformers, who were also unpopular: Kang Youwei, it was said, had been made into a saint by the foreign powers and the Guangxu emperor was accused of having converted to Christianity. Ordinary people were aware of the major trends and events of national politics and acted at least in part in response to them.

But it is clear from Boxer actions that the Western-inspired nationalism of the reformers was still alien to much of the population. In Beijing Boxers burnt down the Sino-Western Primary School established by the government. There was even a rumour that after the Christians were dead all students who read foreign books would be killed. Liang Shuming, a 7-year-old who had been sent to receive a Western-style education by his father, an official interested in Western reforms, was so frightened that he burnt all his English textbooks. A poster that circulated in the name of the Jade Emperor, an important folk deity, read: 'They spread heterodox religion everywhere, erect telegraph poles, build railways, don't believe in the teachings of the sages, profane the gods; their crimes are uncountable. I am exceedingly angry and will send forth great thunder.'[13]

Figure 3.2 'Qing troops victorious over the foreigners with the aid of the Boxers'
Source: British Museum

Across north China telegraph poles and railways were destroyed even as the foreign armies moved inland towards Beijing. Telegraph poles and railways had been promoted by the central government for the very purpose of repelling foreign invasion; they were rejected by a population whose sense of national identity was still closely linked to traditional culturalist ideas.

Popular opposition to the reform plans of the modern nationalists was exacerbated by the indemnity which the foreign powers imposed on China in the aftermath of the crisis. The foreign armies could not ultimately be defeated by the untrained Boxers or the troops of a government that was still vacillating in its response. They moved slowly inland, relieved the siege of the legations, took control of the city of Beijing, sacked the emperor's Summer Palace and blew up sections of the city wall. The emperor and the empress dowager fled west through Shanxi to Xian. Gradually news began to come through from the inland provinces, horrific stories of their flight told by the few foreigners who had escaped and bitter reports of the deaths of many others coming from Chinese converts. Some of the stories were so appalling that the missionary societies were actually accused in the treaty-port press of suppressing them in order to save people's feelings. Negotiations took place in an atmosphere of horror and rage and the peace settlement that resulted from them was punitive in the extreme. Its main features were the payment of a huge indemnity, which was still to be draining China's resources in the 1920s, and the punishment of all participants. The indemnity was to be raised initially mostly from the poor, drought-stricken counties of north China which had been at the heart of the uprising. The result was famine the following year. Punishment was to be meted out both to high officials who had supported the declaration of war and to the ordinary people who had joined Boxer groups. Meanwhile Christians who had lost property or livelihood during the uprising were to be recompensed, at just the same moment that their non-Christian neighbours were being fined and punished.

The Boxer settlement proved to the subjects of the Qing that the dynasty was now under foreign control. Hardly surprisingly there was considerable resistance to its implementation. In at least one part of Zhili there was a further uprising in which a county magistrate and several Qing soldiers were killed. The news of this uprising aroused strong feelings in neighbouring areas where many people shared with the rebels a strong sense of the basic rightness of the Boxer movement. One rural commentator wrote:

They have sent soldiers to oppress it and also told the local officials to implement the protection of foreigners and Christians. Now the uprising was caused entirely by those same foreigners' and Christians' extortion from the ordinary people, which the officials could not stop. And yet when the ordinary people oppose the priests of the foreign religion they are labelled rebels, and soldiers are used to suppress them: people's hearts do not agree to it, and even though there are incidents in which they kill officials or kill soldiers, they forgive them on several points. I fear that everyone in Zhili province will become a rebel.[14]

The outcome of the settlement was greatly increased opposition to the Qing dynasty, which was seen as having capitulated to the Western powers. The defeat was also associated with the reformers because the foreign governments had required that many of the most radical opponents of reform be executed and it was the reformers who now came to power and had the task of extracting the indemnity. Thus there was also a strong sense of antagonism towards those modern nationalists who, as promoters of westernising reforms, were seen as being in collaboration with the foreign powers.

Conclusion

The Western model of a world of independent states and international trade was in itself a threat to Chinese ideas of identity that were bound up with particular views of the position of the Chinese state in the world. In a court dominated by factional politics it was inevitable that these issues of identity would come to be affiliated with certain groups within the government. Paradoxically, during the course of the second half of the nineteenth century, contact with the West had the effect of strengthening the power of those within the government who were most committed to the idea of a culturalist world order. This took place at the same time that an increasingly powerful and wealthy class was developing in the treaty ports, which were beginning to act as a conduit for Western ideas of nationhood. The political tension between these two powerful lobbies set the stage for the disastrous Boxer Uprising of 1900. Much Western writing has depicted the Boxers as emblems of xenophobia. The fantastic rumours, the deaths of foreign missionaries and their children, the massacres of Catholics have all contributed to this picture. However the image of ignorant xenophobia underplays the awareness of high-level politics displayed by participants in the Boxer Uprising. Instead, I would argue that the widespread popular participation in the Boxer Uprising suggests the power of what Hobsbawm and others have referred to as 'proto-nationalism', and also the extent to which it differed from modern nationalism. Popular proto-nationalism of the late nineteenth century was not ignorant xenophobia; it was strongly opposed to foreign interference in China, which was relatively well known and understood. However, it differed from modern nationalism in that it was also radically opposed to the institutions of the modern state, which lay at the heart of modern nationalism.

Notes

1 Trans. in John K. Fairbank, *Trade and Diplomacy on the China Coast: The Opening of the Treaty Ports, 1842–1854* (Cambridge, MA: Harvard University Press, 1953), p. 12.
2 Ibid., p. 19.
3 Li Boyuan, *Modern Times: A Brief History of Enlightenment*, trans. Douglas Lancashire (Hong Kong: Research Centre for Translation, Chinese University of Hong Kong, [1997]), p. 117.
4 Quoted in David Pong, *Shen Pao-chen and China's Modernisation in the Nineteenth Century* (Cambridge: Cambridge University Press, 1994), p. 102.
5 Zhou Yueran, *Liushi huiyi* (Recollections at Sixty) (Shanghai: Taiping shuju, 1944), p. 86.
6 Benjamin Schwartz, *In Search of Wealth and Power: Yen Fu and the West* (Cambridge, MA: Harvard University Press, 1964), p. 19.
7 Liu Dapeng, *Jinci zhi* (Jinci Gazetteer) (Taiyuan: Shanxi renmin chubanshe, 1986), pp. 1048–9.
8 *Jiaowu jiao'an dang* (Archives of Religious Matters and Legal Cases) (Taibei: Zhongyang yanjiuyuan jindaishi yanjiusuo, 1974), series 1, vol. 2, p. 714.
9 Quoted in Roger R. Thompson, 'Cultural and Economic Imperialism and the Development of Chinese Nationalism in Shanxi Province, 1861–1911', American Historical Association Annual Meeting, Seattle, 1998.
10 Quoted in Li Wenhai and Liu Yangdong, 'Yihetuan yundong shiqi shehui xinli fenxi' (An analysis of common beliefs during the Boxer movement) in Zhongguo yihetuan yundongshi yanjiuhui (Committee for the Research of the History of the Chinese Boxer Movement) ed., *Yihetuan yu jindai Zhongguo shehui* (The Boxers and Modern Chinese Society) (Chengdu: Sichuan shehui kexue chubanshe, 1987), p. 22.
11 Quoted in Paul A. Cohen, *History in Three Keys: The Boxers as Event, Experience, and Myth* (New York: Columbia University Press, 1997), p. 84.
12 Quoted in Li Wenhai and Liu Yangdong, 'Yihetuan yundong shiqi shehui xinli fenxi', p. 6.
13 Quoted in ibid., p. 4.
14 Liu Dapeng, 'Tuixiangzhai riji (xuanlu)' (Diary for the study for retreat and contemplation (selections)) in *Yihetuan shiliao* (Historical Materials on the Boxers) (Beijing: Zhongguo shehui kexue chubanshe, 1982), vol. 2, p. 818.

4

The creation of modern nationalism

The utter failure of the Boxer movement, clearly demonstrated to all through the settlement that the foreign powers had extorted, swung the balance of power at court decisively in favour of the modernisers. Leading conservatives who had supported the Boxers were dead, disgraced or demoted. Meanwhile the modernising southern viceroys who had kept their areas out of the fighting had preserved the bases of their power. The central government now began to put in place many of the institutions of a modern nation. These institutions altered the way in which China was imagined, at least by those members of the elite who participated in them. Out of them grew a new class who were committed to modern nationalism and reform, and who promoted the creation of modern institutions. The late Qing reforms thus began the process of divorcing the Chinese nation from the passionate, but culturally defined, nationalism of the Boxers.

The Qing New Policies began with plans to reform the army and the education system. The creation of a modern army had been the basis of all the nineteenth-century efforts at reform, and from the late 1890s Yuan Shikai, originally in charge of military affairs under Li Hongzhang, had been creating a modern army. This was now expanded to include other forces and money was poured into military training. A modern army required an educated and mobilised citizenry, and education was second only to the military as the object of reform. The government ordered the establishment of new schools teaching Western learning and of educational associations to promote them. Military strength also required national wealth and this led to reforms in commercial matters. A commercial code was issued and merchants were encouraged to organise themselves into new chambers of commerce on the Western model, to help them to compete with Western business in China. Finally, in response to constant demands from those outside the bureaucracy for a greater say in decision-making, the court announced that it would move towards constitutional government. Initially this would involve the election of county assemblies from among the members of local elites, but later there would be provincial and national assemblies to advise the government. In this, as in the rest of the reforms, the central government looked to the successful example of Japan, where similar reforms had given great strength to the emperor and central government while at the same time enabling the state to compete effectively with the Western powers. These reforms were to alter many of the fundamental relationships within society and between society and the state, and were the means by which modern nationalism was tied into the structures of the state.

Education

The educational reforms promoted Western-style education and were rooted in innovations of the nineteenth century. Western-style education in China had begun with the missionary schools, which educated many of the early modernisers and reformers. But these schools and their students were on the margins of the social order. Concentrated on the southeast coast, they were physically peripheral in a state whose political heart was on the north China plain. Moreover, parents who chose to send their children to these schools were consigning them to a career that would be bounded by the world of the treaty ports. Since they had never studied the classics, boys who attended missionary schools could never hope to obtain posts in the bureaucracy; worse still, in a world that placed a very high value on knowledge of the classics, they would be unable to converse as equals with members of the bureaucratic elite. Consequently the mission schools were attended primarily by the children of the poor or impoverished who could not afford anything better. Western-style education had also been provided in a few official technical schools such as the Jiangnan Arsenal school and the Fuzhou Naval Dockyard school. But the products of these institutions too tended to be excluded from the centres of the bureaucracy. In general, education along Western lines had been regarded as a technical qualification for certain types of career, and though it had gradually become obvious that some people within the bureaucracy would need these skills, it was still basically a matter of training technical experts.

During the last years of the century there had also been some changes within the exam system and the academies that prepared students for its higher levels. In 1898 mathematics, which did have a history within China, was introduced into the exams, a move that was very unpopular with exam candidates. Then in 1902 the highly formulaic writing style known as the 'eight-legged essay' was replaced by policy essays. An essay topic set in the metropolitan exams of 1904 gives an indication of the differences between these new essays and the former strict emphasis on the Confucian classics. The question reads:

The establishment of new schools has three aims, namely to mould citizens, to create talent and to raise up industry. Since the citizens cannot stand up it is necessary to establish schools to teach them, so that they all have the virtue of kindness, hearts full of loyalty, the technical skills to support themselves and necessary knowledge, which is the same in all countries east and west, though Japan also emphasizes the spirit of militarism. This is education that moulds citizens. Discussion of the special areas of government, law, finance, and foreign affairs to prepare for official service is education that creates talent. The establishment of separate schools of agriculture, crafts, commerce and mining so that they may enrich the country and benefit the people is education that raises up industry. Which of these three is the most urgent policy?[1]

Although the candidates continued to answer such questions using the ideas and morality of the Confucian classics in which they had been trained, it is evident that the emphasis was on government policy options and particularly foreign affairs rather than on discussion of the classics as such. The question also suggests some of the government's aims in establishing new modern schools: to create good citizens, to train competent officials and to increase the nation's wealth. The aims of moulding good citizens and competent officials were very much the same as the aims of the traditional education system with its emphasis on morality and training for the bureaucracy. By contrast the third aim, that of increasing the nation's wealth, was entirely new for Chinese education, and relatively little emphasis was placed on this. The new education system was intended by the government primarily to train a new generation of potential officials.

State patriotism

The Boxer Uprising had been construed as the demonstration of the people's will both by those who encouraged it and by the modernisers who tried to prevent it. After the depressing finale of the 1901 settlement many inside and outside the government continued to believe in the importance of the people, but came to the conclusion that the people must be changed. The first aim of the Qing state when it encouraged local magistrates and provincial officials to establish schools teaching a modern Western curriculum was to transform the people, who tended to be viewed as a single unit, into loyal patriots. One of the primary-school textbooks issued at this time, which closely reflects the government's ideas, has a lesson that reads, 'Two brothers sing a song together. First they sing of loyalty to the monarch. Then they sing of love of country.' The teacher's manual explains that the image of brothers singing together is supposed to suggest the close relationship between loyalty and patriotism, which is the base of education for citizenship. The manual then provides an explanation that the teacher can give to the students of the words 'love', 'loyalty', 'country' and 'monarch':

He who loves the country must be loyal to the monarch. He who is loyal to the monarch must love the country. When one knows the close links between monarch and country, then loyalty to the monarch and love of country cannot be separated.[2]

The emphasis of the textbooks was to be on patriotism, but that patriotism was to be inseparable from loyalty to the emperor and thus the preservation of the existing political system.

The second aim of the government in establishing new schools was to train competent officials. Initially the main problem with this goal was that the government itself did not select the products of the modern schools as officials, but instead chose to employ those who had graduated from the examination system. This made sense, since success in the exams required a considerable degree of investment in the values and structures of the state, but the government's failure to appoint the graduates of modern schools to official positions greatly reduced the attractiveness of those schools in the eyes of parents. Few students attended the modern schools that were founded immediately after the Boxer crisis and those who did expected little in the way of general approval. In Guangzhou students at the first modern government school were accused either of being supporters of the ever-unpopular Kang Youwei or of being Christian converts. They were spat at in the streets and their friends and relatives urged them to leave the school.

It was soon obvious that the new schools could not compete with the traditional education system without further assistance and in 1905 the Qing government took a step that was to alter the course of the rest of the century: it abolished the examination system. In a country village in Shanxi, diarist Liu Dapeng recorded his feelings the day after he heard the news:

I woke at first light with my heart like dead ashes. I saw that all was vanity and there was nothing eternal. Only accumulated virtue lasts as long as Heaven and Earth, but it is not easy to accumulate virtue, and impossible without real achievements. During the day whenever I went out everyone I saw spoke about the end of the exam system, how it was very bad for the country and how there was no experience of the results of the new schools, so that no one knows what will become of customs and morals or how things will have changed in a few years. It is a sad and frightening step.[3]

The Shanxi villagers were right to worry about the impact of the ending of the system, though probably even they did not at this stage foresee all the momentous consequences of the change. By abolishing the examination system the government was in effect changing both the methods of selection of the country's top elite and the education system through which much of the population was socialised. It was inevitable that this would lead to political change.

The immediate effect of the abolition of the exam system was the creation of a great many new schools. The writer Guo Moruo, who grew up just outside Chengdu, the capital of Sichuan province, remembered how after the announcement two Western-style schools and a Western-style military academy were set up in Chengdu. In Shanxi a wealthy lineage which was very much ahead of the times had established its own modern primary school in 1903 and a girls' school in 1904 with classes in literature, mathematics and ethics; now it set up its own middle school with teachers of English and science. Across the country new schools were founded and old schools converted. Writers in journals were beginning to call for the education of women so that as 'virtuous wives and worthy mothers' they could train the next generation of citizens. But in practice the new schools were almost entirely for boys. In 1909 girls were less than 2 per cent of the total student body and education for girls remained to a large extent the province of foreign missionaries. Nevertheless, the ideas and morals of the new schools did later come to affect the way that both men and women were taught.

Nationalism and the new schools

In theory, the nature of the new schools was determined by central-government regulations about the syllabus. Sets of regulations were issued in 1903 and again in 1906. These restricted the amount of time to be spent in the traditional study of the Chinese classics, and introduced new subjects: history, geography, science, mathematics, physical exercise and music. Thus 1903 regulations included music as a part of physical exercise and explained that the songs should be 'composed of the military achievements and wars of the dynasty, praising the dead heroes of the past'.[4] Regulations like this assume, as does much of the secondary literature on the subject, that the newly established schools looked to the government for guidance and direction.

In fact, the nature of the new schools was initially determined not by the government regulations, but by the textbooks that were pouring out of the commercial publishing houses in Shanghai. Textbooks were important because very few of the schools were entirely new institutions; the vast majority took over the buildings and usually the personnel of existing schools and academies. Textbooks, which were relatively cheap and widely available, instructed both pupils and teachers in what constituted a modern school. In his account of growing up in rural Sichuan, Guo Moruo tells how his family school was transformed into a modern-style school when the teacher began to use the new textbooks and hung a map of Asia on the wall. Guo's younger sister and niece also joined the classes. However, in most respects the education given in the school remained the same as before: the same teacher continued to teach his pupils the Chinese classics alongside the lessons from the modern primer.

However, the authors and publishers of modern textbooks tended to come from that group of active westernisers who had already adopted Western ideologies that implied the necessity of changing the political system. Lu Feikui, who later made a fortune by anticipating the 1911 Revolution and cornering the market in republican textbooks, provides a good example of this. Lu had received a traditional education in Zhejiang, but in 1905 had opened a bookshop that sold revolutionary literature. As a result he had to flee to Shanghai, where he found employment working for a publishing firm writing primary-school textbooks for ethics and mathematics and running a teacher-training institute for another firm of textbook publishers. Men like Lu Feikui wrote textbooks that of necessity remained within the law; in a highly commercial world they did not actively promote revolution in their publications, but the kind of nationalism they promoted was not necessarily the state patriotism planned by the Qing. The government intended that nationalism should be focused around loyalty to the dynasty, as had been so successfully done in Japan, but loyalty to the emperor was only occasionally included in the textbooks as part of lessons on nationalism and even where this was done the role of the emperor often appeared to be secondary to that of the nation. Thus a 1907 primary-school Chinese-language textbook explains: 'The monarch is the head of the country. China's monarch is called an emperor.'[5] Although the emperor is the subject of this short lesson, his role is defined entirely in relation to the nation and it is China, not the emperor, that is clearly expected to be uppermost in the reader's imagination. Similarly, a patriotic song much used in schools during this period runs:

> For tens of thousands of years, the great empire of Asia!
> Lofty mountains crossing it raise the flag high; rivers and streams spread abroad the wave of civilisation.
> The four hundred million people are the descendants of the gods; the great land abounds in resources.
> Raise our Yellow Dragon Imperial Flag! Sing our Empire's song![6]

At first glance this song appears full of references to empire and thus to the dynasty. But a closer examination shows that the empire referred to is not the Qing empire, which had lasted a mere 300 or so years, but historical China embodied, as it traditionally was, in its mountains and streams and its 400 million people. In fact this song continued to be used under the republic simply by replacing the words 'Yellow Dragon Imperial Flag' with 'Five Colour Republican Flag' and 'our Empire's song' with 'our Republic's song'.

Patriotism and nationalism were major themes of many textbooks from first-year primary-school textbooks to more advanced volumes. An early lesson shows the difference between 'Chinese people' and 'foreign people'. The Chinese man wears a long gown and queue, while the foreigners wear European and Japanese dress. There were also many specific lessons on patriotism warning students, for example, that if they were to forget the country the present peaceful age would not last. Lessons about China's geography referred to China's 'subsidiary countries', the former tributary states of Burma, Vietnam and Korea, now all conquered by other countries, leaving China like a piece of meat ready to be cut up. Elsewhere students were urged to study to save China. Many textbooks included lessons on great cities such as Tianjin and Hankou, and lessons on the treaty ports often brought references to the evils of the treaties. A lesson on Tianjin described its railways and foreign concessions and the size of its trade. It then reminded the student that this was the first city to be attacked by the allied armies in 1900, and that after the peace treaty the city was handed back to the Chinese, but its defensive forts had been knocked down and the treaty specified that they were not to be rebuilt. There were also references to threats to China's natural resources, fears that it would be foreigners who would profit from China's coal or the gold (in lumps the size of a man's fist) to be found in Tibet. The thought of the profits foreigners would make from mining China's coal was painful.

In addition to the content of the texts, the whole idea of textbooks in the 'national language' or 'Chinese' was new and was driven by ideas of nationalism. As we have seen, during the nineteenth century the word *guo*, which is now conventionally translated as 'country', had the alternative meaning of 'dynasty'. Thus the Shanxi Catholic questioned about which 'country' he belonged to replied that he was 'a man of the Qing dynasty'. The period of the 1900s saw a decisive shift of this term towards the meaning of 'country' or 'nation'. Up until this time the term *guoyu*, which we now translate as 'national language' (or Mandarin Chinese), had referred not to the Chinese language at all, but to the Manchu, the language of the dynasty. The use of 'national language' (*guoyu*) to refer to Chinese on the covers of textbooks shows how fast the meaning of the term *guo* had shifted. Indeed, the very transfer of the primary meaning from 'dynasty' to 'country' in itself suggests the restructuring of loyalties that was in progress during this period. The authors of one early national language textbook, explaining why they had written it, recognised that not only did pronunciation differ between the south and north of the country, but even counties and prefectures had their own dialects. They hoped that by establishing a unified grammar, the textbook would begin the process of unifying the dialects – as had occurred in Japan, where, they claimed, the teaching of a single national language since the Meiji Restoration in the 1860s had resulted not only in the unification of the language but in the unification of customs and feelings. By such means the textbook authors endeavoured to build the institutions of nationalism from their base in Shanghai.

The new education system also promoted attitudes of civic responsibility that were considered problematic by the central government. Fig. 4.1, which is taken from an illustrated newspaper, shows a group of students handing out leaflets to wealthy merchants in the streets of Beijing in winter. The accompanying text informs us that the students have braved the freezing

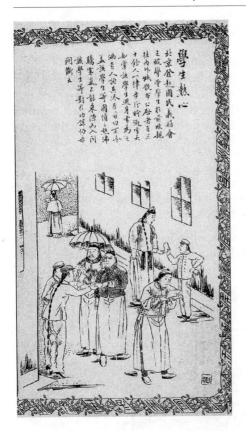

Figure 4.1 Students promoting
national bonds
Source: *Shenzhou huabao* (China
Illustrated Daily), 28 April 1909

winter weather to encourage people to make donations to the government. Such direct involvement of students in issues of government was unprecedented and not always acceptable. One primer tells a story of an old teacher who is on his way to the government offices to pay his taxes when his path is blocked by a crowd of people gathered round a newspaper seller. He berates the crowd:

> You folk reading some so-called newspaper. You've got lots of work of your own to do, but don't get on with it. And yet you seem to have plenty of time to spend managing public affairs and you even block the road.[7]

A sense that national politics should be the concern of the central government and not of the general population was certainly shared by much of that government. However, in this story the magistrate, who comes to hear of the incident, reprimands the old teacher, explaining that it is the duty of all citizens to be concerned for the country. Concern for the country was encouraged both by textbooks and by the aims of the whole new education system, but it was inevitable that it would lead to a threat to the government.

Nationalism and Confucian values

As well as through their immediate content, textbooks structured the learning experience through the type of behaviour they depicted and thus had a normalising influence on schoolchildren. Time in the new school was divided into terms and weeks, and the pupils were supposed to act together as a group, rather than individually in the fashion of the traditional schools. Fig. 4.2 is taken from a textbook and shows the beginning of term at a modern school. The text reads:

The beginning of term
It is the first day of term. We hang a national flag and a school flag. The teachers and pupils all begin their studies.

Another chapter in the same book tells pupils to enter the classroom when they hear the sound of a bell. Weeks marked by Sunday holidays were a

Figure 4.2 'The beginning of term'
Source: Zhu Shuren, *Chudeng xiaoxue guowen keben* (Primary-level Chinese Textbook). Shanghai: Zhongguo tushu gongsi, 1907, vol. 1, p. 3

particularly striking feature of the new schools, since in the past time had been divided primarily according to the frequencies of local markets and fairs. The new schools also prescribed a costume, and to an increasing extent an etiquette, that was very different from that expected of traditional scholars. Fig. 4.3 shows the teacher dressed in a long gown, but the pupil in a military-style jacket and trousers, which came to be the standard uniform for schoolboys. The boy does not kowtow, but simply bows, cap in hand, illustrating the very beginnings of a more egalitarian etiquette that went with values of freedom and equality which the textbooks also proclaimed. In an old-fashioned school the pupils were expected to kowtow both to the teacher and to the school's shrine to Confucius. The implications of this new egalitarian value system went far beyond questions of etiquette and struck at the heart of the Confucian moral order and its connection with the state.

The new schools continued to be unpopular among the general population even though some parents now felt impelled to send their children to them. Feelings of attachment to traditional culture of the sort exhibited during the Boxer uprising only go part of the way towards explaining this. The schools were also unpopular because they created new divisions both between the generations and between rich and poor. The new morality taught in the schools was often incomprehensible, and sometimes insulting, to those outside the system. The effects of this could be amusing: the novelist Li Boyuan, whose works were published in the newspapers at this period, tells the story of a young man educated in modern ideas who suddenly feels called upon to treat his servant with equality.

> When Jichuan asked repeatedly who was outside, the servant-boy walked into the room. Noticing that the boy showed the same fear

Figure 4.3 'Student and teacher bow' Source: Zhu Shuren, *Chudeng xiaoxue guowen keben* (Primary-level Chinese Textbook). Shanghai: Zhongguo tushu gongsi, 1907, vol. 1, p. 10b

that common people had for officials, Jichuan sighed and said: 'Stop going about as if you were afraid of me. You're a human being just as I am. The only difference is that you were born into a humble home, and that you're therefore a bit poorer, it's for this reason only that you're a servant. I happen to have a couple of coppers more than you, but you're the same kind of person as I am; you weren't born a slave. It doesn't follow that you should remain ignorant just because you are a slave and have to carry out your master's commands. I've recently read the biography of Wei Qing in the *History of the Han Dynasty*, and in it he says: 'Those born to slavery are satisfied simply to avoid a flogging!' Throughout history there have been great generals in China who have risen from the ranks of slaves. As slaves they thought of nothing but how to avoid a flogging, and had no ambition whatsoever to achieve anything great. Isn't that tragic? Now, as I look at you, a strapping lad, it's clear to me that there's no need for you to spend your whole life as a slave. The Tathāgata teaches that all beings are equal. If I were to try to explain to you the meaning of that equality, I'm afraid you wouldn't understand; but I would ask you, when you see me, not to maintain the distinction between master and servant.'[8]

The joke lies in the fact that the servant is completely bemused by this speech and doesn't know what to do.

But, while Li Boyuan and his audiences might laugh at the master who is as foolish and ignorant as his uncomprehending servant, part of the point of the joke lay in the fact that for many people this kind of situation was highly disturbing. Rumours circulated about the terrible effect of the new morality on family relations. Diarist Liu Dapeng in Shanxi reported the following story, which he had heard at a dinner in 1902:

Recently a certain Beijing official called Wang sent his son to travel abroad. Not ten days after he returned the son ordered a banquet for the following day saying he was inviting guests. The next day Wang asked what guests he was inviting. The son got down on his knees and begged a favour, 'Your son has one request, and he will only dare to rise if you permit it.' Wang said, 'What is your request?' His son said, 'What I ask today is that from now on my father will not act as a father to his son, but we shall be equal.' When Wang heard this request his face went grey and he had no words to reply, but there was already nothing he could do except obey his son's demand.[9]

The proper relations between father and son were the most basic level of Confucian morality. Whether or not this particular story is true, it is clear that people perceived the new values as threatening this basic morality. Gradually these threats grew closer to home, both physically and in terms of the ideas they represented. Less than two years later Liu heard a similar story but about the Shanxi county of Pingding not far from his home.

Moreover, in this case the young man concerned had not gone overseas, but had merely studied at the new Shanxi university. When he came back 'he did not treat his father as a father, but treated him on terms of equality. The people of the prefecture were astonished.'[10] Soon these ideas spread from the basic relation between father and son to the second relationship of the Confucian moral system, that between monarch and minister. Students at the modern schools were criticised for having 'no father and no monarch'. There were even stories that students in the Shanxi academies were talking of opposition to the Manchus. Traditional education had taken as its primary aim the inculcation of moral relationships. The most important of those relationships were those between father and son, and monarch and minister. Students who had absorbed the values of that education, as many did, lived their lives in the light of these values. To many Confucian scholars it was unsurprising that the learning of the barbarians would reverse the values of civilisation espoused by the Confucian centre.

The redefinition of basic values carried on by the new schools also created a gap between the generations. The writer Guo Moruo tells in his autobiography of a conversation he had with his elder brother, who was a student at a modern school and about to leave for Japan. His brother asked him whether he preferred girls to have bound or natural feet. Guo replied that he preferred natural feet. His brother was delighted and raised his voice as he said, 'Good, you are civilised. Big feet are civilised, bound feet are barbarous.' Unfortunately their father overheard them and was so furious at their having effectively criticised their ancestors that he reduced Guo's brother, then aged 30, to tears. In telling this story Guo denies that his father was reactionary and explains that the problem was a matter of differences between the generations. What we see is that between those generations an entire moral system was being redrawn so that such basic terms as civilised and barbarous were being entirely redefined.

At the same time as threatening common values the new schools began to increase the gap between rich and poor and especially between rich areas and poor areas. The new schools were much more expensive to establish than the traditional ones, since they needed a whole variety of equipment ranging from new textbooks to scientific equipment and specially trained teachers. Li Boyuan tells in his novel of a provincial governor wishing to establish a new school who is tricked by a visitor from Shanghai into handing over the huge sum of 20,000 ounces of silver for textbooks and scientific equipment. The canny visitor instantly siphons off 5,000 taels and sends the rest to his nephew in Shanghai to buy the books and equipment. Expenses of this kind were often increased by the use of imposing new Western-style buildings. Only the rich parts of the country, administrative capitals and the treaty ports could afford such expenditure and the increasing differentiation of these places from the rest of the country was marked by the westernisation of their outward appearance as the new buildings were constructed. However, even mediocre Western schools were expensive to fund and the cost was raised through high taxes laid by school boards on local communities and then by high fees that usually excluded the children of the poor.

Under these circumstances it is not surprising that the schools were unpopular. Local elites were seen as introducing heavy new taxes on the poor to pay for the maintenance of their own status while at the same time undermining basic moral values. Rumours give an idea of popular feeling: in Shanxi in 1904 it was rumoured that every three families would have to support a foreign teacher (a fabulous expense), and then in 1905 that all the children who entered a new school in one village would be sent abroad. Where there were disturbances, usually in opposition to increased taxation or higher food prices, the new schools were often burned down by angry mobs. In 1906 riots in Zhili brought on by the imposition of new taxes to pay for a police force ended in the destruction of the buildings of the county government and the burning of the locality's new school.

Meanwhile, for those students who did attend them, the schools provided little hope of a job. Few of the new graduates could be given jobs in an already overstaffed government and other employers were dubious of the new students with their strange ideas. The actual information – history, geography and science – that the students had learnt was just as useless as the Confucian classics, but carried a moral stigma. The following is part of a speech made by Zhang Jian, an enthusiastic founder and patron of the new schools, to a group of graduates of a vocational school in Beijing:

> There is something else that I would like to speak to you about today. You are at present studying in a commercial school, but later on after your graduation what will you in fact do? Will you profit from your title, discard what you have learned, and become officials? Or will you, making use of what you have learned, take up a career in commerce? If you choose the first alternative your studies will be of no use to you: your commercial studies will have as much value as the eight-legged essay. Yet I fear that you will not be capable of embarking on the career offered in the second alternative. I have observed the duties undertaken by apprentices in commercial firms: they offer cigarettes, pour tea, and obey the employer in every way. Could you do this? I fear the answer is no.[11]

Outside the treaty ports there were few opportunities for these unemployed and almost unemployable graduates. Many joined the modern army, an entirely new institution that asked for modern qualifications; many more who had been taught that they were the future of their country but could find no suitable employment began to think in terms of revolution.

Nationalism and revolutionary thought

At the same time as setting up the new schools, the Qing government began to send students abroad for advanced study. The aim was that the students would both bring back specific technical skills, for example the military sciences, and learn about Western culture so that they could return to China and help the state to face the challenge posed by the West. Initially a few candidates were chosen and persuaded to go; later exams were held to choose from among a large number of applicants. As the numbers being sent abroad by the state increased so did those who went abroad to study without financial help from the state. Some of these students went to Europe or America, but for most these countries were prohibitively expensive. The vast majority of students who went abroad, whether financed by their families or by the state, went to Japan.

The Japanese state had been engaged in modernisation along Western lines since the 1860s, when a section of the elite that had become increasingly dissatisfied with the policy of seclusion from the West adopted by the Tokugawa shoguns overthrew the Shogunate that had ruled Japan for several centuries and 'restored' the emperor, whose court had long been without real power. The new governing elite immediately began to research and then implement a series of policies designed to ensure that Japan had access to the sources of Western power, imitating the most up-to-date developments of the various European countries. These ranged from state-controlled universal primary education, constitutional monarchy and a German-based legal system to laws banning traditional hairstyles and encouraging the wearing of Western hats. In 1895 the Japanese militarily defeated and diplomatically outflanked China over the issue of Korea. Then in 1904 they fought and defeated Russia over the question of which country should have dominant influence in Manchuria. Although both these victories caused huge dismay in China, they were also a source of considerable admiration: the Japanese had proved that their westernising reforms enabled them to hold their own against a European power. Students were also attracted to Japan by the fact that living expenses and tuition fees were cheaper than in Western Europe or America, and the written language was relatively easy for Chinese students to learn. Chinese officials and students hoping to go abroad to study began to see Japan as an accessible model of development and a source of information about the West.

The first 13 officially sponsored Chinese students arrived in Japan in 1896 and by 1905 there were between 8,000 and 9,000 Chinese students studying there. Even though study was less costly in Japan than in Europe or America it was still expensive and most students came from wealthy backgrounds. This was obviously true for those whose families provided the funding for their stay. He Xiangning, later a prominent revolutionary, sold her dowry jewellery to finance her own studies and those of her husband.

The fact that her dowry jewellery was valuable enough to do this suggests the wealth of her background. She herself only learnt how to cook rice when the revolutionary Sun Yatsen asked her not to have a Japanese servant so he could hold secret meetings in their house. The same kind of economic background was also typical of those sent by the state. Many of those who passed the selection exams, or had the right connections to be chosen by officials without exams, came from wealthy and highly educated families. Chen Qimei, who later became Chiang Kaishek's earliest patron, was the son of a Zhejiang merchant and had been apprenticed to a pawnshop, a highly sought-after situation, and had begun to study English, before he was awarded a government scholarship to a military academy in Tokyo. In the early 1900s there were still few modern schools in China and most of those who went to Japan were the products of the old education system. Many already held old-style degrees, including such future revolutionaries as Xu Xilin and Huang Xing.

The ideology of race and nation

Political concerns were central for Chinese students in Japan. Very few studied technical scientific subjects, for which they were in any case poorly prepared. This was partly the result of the priorities of the officials who sent them and wanted subordinates, teachers for the new schools and officers for the new army. Similar career options, with a preference for employment in the civil bureaucracy, motivated those whose families paid for their studies. For those who chose their own courses, China's political problems seemed urgent and in need of political solutions. The famous author Lu Xun originally enrolled in a medical college, but left after a magic-lantern show of the war between Russia and Japan fought over Chinese Manchuria in 1904. During the show, Lu Xun's Japanese classmates cheered scenes of Chinese spies being executed by the Japanese. The combination of the scenes and the cheering drove Lu Xun to give up his medical career and embark on literature, with which he hoped to rouse the Chinese people to do something about their humiliating situation. As a result of these kinds of choice the students came face to face with European and Japanese writings about the nature of society and the state. Reading these had a great impact on their own understanding of the nation.

In addition, the students who arrived in Japan in the 1900s had to cope with the clash between the culturalism instilled by their initial training in China and the self-confidence of the Japanese society around them. Japanese did not conceive of their relationship with China in terms of China's traditional culturalism, and the Chinese students found that their achievements in many of the new subjects they had to study were well below those of their Japanese peers. At the same time they were members of China's elite suddenly set down in a very different society where their high status was no longer so apparent. Many Chinese students had moments when, like Lu Xun, they felt that Chinese as a group were being humiliated and became acutely aware of the differences between the two countries. It was not surprising that the intellectual questions that moved them most were those that related to ideas of national identity.

The great populariser of the new ideas was Liang Qichao, who had been a student of the radical Confucian reformer Kang Youwei and fled with him to Japan after the defeat of the Hundred Days' Reforms. There he learnt more about Western thought and wrote articles that presented the theories he had culled from his reading in a simple, easily understood language that helped make his ideas hugely influential. One of the concepts that Liang Qichao chose from the Western thought of the time and put at the heart of his own thinking was that of race and of competition between the races. The idea that the theory of evolution could be applied to groups of people was commonplace at the time and reflected a general tendency to extend Darwin's theories beyond the natural and into the social world – a trend that had also appealed to Yan Fu and had led him to translate Thomas Huxley's *Evolution and Ethics*. Part of the appeal of such ideas may have been that they put into words a subtle shift in Chinese ideas of identity that had been taking place since the late eighteenth century. At that time the efforts of the Qianlong emperor to preserve a separate Manchu people had the effect of shifting the basis of Manchu identity from cultural practices to inheritance. This emphasis on bloodline and heredity may well have been encouraged by the power of lineage institutions among the Han Chinese. Both the lineage and the idea of hereditary Manchu identity were to be central to the new understanding of national identity that developed in the 1900s. This used the idea of the Han Chinese being descendants of the Yellow Emperor, the mythical founder of the race, as a kind of lineage binding the whole Han people into a single family. At the same time the hereditary difference between Manchu and Han became a model for the difference between 'the Chinese' and all others, replacing the older concept of flexible boundaries based on degrees of acculturation.

However, to Liang Qichao this new sense of identity based on a racially constructed Han people was not a natural product of the times but a personal crusade. It was necessary, he said, to end the common idea that China was 'all under heaven' (*tianxia*) and create a new understanding of the importance of the country (*guojia*). Liang understood the evolution of peoples in arguments derived from the sociologist Herbert Spencer, who emphasised that the evolutionary process of selection worked between groups and that strength lay in cooperation within the group. Liang Qichao applied these arguments to all areas of Chinese life. Thus in an essay on the need for chambers of commerce he reminds his readers of the principle of survival of the fittest: in severe competition the superior win and the inferior are defeated, so in the end the superior will take power all over the world and the inferior will be destroyed. The superior are those who are strong and wise, and to be strong the Chinese need to unite in groups. Elsewhere he applies the argument directly to race, telling his readers that if China does not enter the struggle between the races then the whole race will be destroyed. In order for the Chinese to unite in this way a new morality is needed among the general population. To begin the process of creating this new morality Liang wrote a famous series of essays 'On a New People'. In these essays he argues that the country's strength depends on its people and that therefore China needs its people to have a sense of national unity. The need to renew the people was, of course, another product of the emphases of nineteenth-century Confucianism. However, Liang explicitly states that the morality that is needed to renew the people is no longer the old morality of the five relationships between father and son, brothers, husband and wife, monarch and minister, and between friends. These are relations between individuals. What is needed, Liang explains, is a new emphasis on the relationship between individuals and the collective: the family, society and the country. According to this new morality a man's duty to his country is just like a child's duty to his parents.

In order to express this new kind of identity Liang Qichao and others like him needed new words. The word for 'nation', *minzu*, was taken from Japanese, where it had been in use since the 1860s to translate the Western term. Up to about 1900 this term was used as the rough equivalent to 'tribe' and applied only to foreign peoples, being used, for example, in articles relating to the Arabs and Turks. However, after 1900 the word for nation rapidly came to be widely used in articles about China. Compounds meaning 'the Chinese nation' (*Zhonghua minzu, Zhongguo minzu*) also became common. Moreover, these terms soon developed very positive connotations. Liang Qichao explained that Europe's expansion since the sixteenth century was due to 'nationalism' (*minzuzhuyi*) and that this nationalism was a great and glorious idea. Other writers used the term in new histories of 'the Chinese nation'. The idea also became part of the burgeoning anti-Manchu thought of the time. Wang Jingwei, an infamous collaborator during World War II but at this time a patriot and revolutionary, defined the new term 'nation' as people who shared common blood, language, habitat, customs, religion, spirit and physical type. In these respects, he claimed, the Manchus were very different from the Han. The new vocabulary of the nation both reflected and helped to spread a sense of identity that was very different to the culturalism of the past with its emphasis on behaviour and customs.

Race, nation and revolutionary groups

The new ideas did not grow in a vacuum but were shaped and influenced by the political context. When in 1904 Japan fought Russia for dominance over Manchuria, Chinese students in Japan held a series of meetings which culminated in a decision to form a volunteer corps to assist the Chinese army in Manchuria. An activist speaking at one of these meetings explained, 'We simply have been aroused by the great principles of nationhood and have sworn to give our lives to ignite the determined spirit of our people.'[12]

The novelist Li Boyuan provides a satire on the meetings that led to the new student activism and on the new art of public speaking. The young men attending the meeting (which he sets in Shanghai rather than in Japan) find the organiser, Wei Bangxian, at the gate with his hands outstretched asking people for the entrance fee of 50 cents each. When Wei gets up to speak he begins:

> 'Gentlemen! Gentlemen! There is a crisis right before our eyes. Are you still not aware of it?'
> A shudder of alarm swept through the audience. Wei Bangxian continued: 'China, today, is like me – one body – whilst the eighteen provinces are like my head, arms and legs. The Japanese have occupied my head; the Germans have occupied my left shoulder; the French have occupied my right shoulder; the Russians have occupied my back, and the English my abdomen; then there is Italy which is riding my left leg and the United States which is astride my right leg. Alas! Alas! As you can see, my body has been divided up and occupied by all these people! Tell me, how can I continue to exist?'
> The audience burst into applause once more. Wei Bangxian closed his eyes, calmed himself, took a couple of deep breaths and continued: 'Gentlemen, gentlemen! In such times as we experience today, should we not think of organizing ourselves?. . . .'[13]

Wei then repeats his metaphor: if we organise the Japanese will not occupy my head, and so on, but when he gets to the end of this he is stuck and has nothing else to say, leaving the audience clapping to hide their embarrassment. Li Boyuan depicts the student radicals he satirises as venal (after the meeting they argue about how the fees are to be divided) and obsessed with simplistic images of the nation as a body. He also mocks the determination to form an organisation, which, following Liang Qichao and other influential commentators, had become the panacea of the time.

Given the combination of passionate commitment, criticism of government policy and complete inexperience, it is not surprising that Qing officials rejected the overtures of the students who travelled back from Japan to offer the assistance of their new organisation to the Chinese army in Manchuria. However, the result of the rejection was that members of the corps, finding themselves outside the structures of the government, turned it into an actively anti-dynastic organisation called the Association for National Military Education. In this new organisation we see the beginnings of the transformation of the new opinions and ideas into political action dedicated to the overthrow of the Qing government, now conceived of as the rule of an alien race. One of the members of the new organisation explained the reasons for its founding:

Under the yoke of the barbarian Manchus, our Han race may still hope for independence; crushed by the enlightened foreign powers, we face eternal slavery. Sitting by and waiting to be struck dead is not as good as dying with a struggle. This is why we have established the Association for National Military Education.[14]

The new idea of racial competition between the Han and Manchus was repeated in an identification tag used by members of the society which was a medal stamped with a picture of the Yellow Emperor on the one side and on the other the words, 'Our first Emperor forged five weapons to preside over the 100 clans. This is our ancestor; we submit to him our hearts and minds.'[15] As ancestor of the sage kings the Yellow Emperor was the ancestor of the Han people. The symbolism marks the importance of Han racial identity for the group's organisers. In this new organisation, and many other revolutionary groups like it, the new ideas of competition between races operated both as part of what motivated the students to take action and as a source of legitimation.

The political activities of student groups, motivated by these new ideas, were ultimately even more influential than the writings of such men as Liang Qichao. One of the most famous and influential events sparked by student political activities is known as the Subao case. The origin of the case was a pamphlet called *The Revolutionary Army*, by Zou Rong, a young man who had studied in Japan and had been a keen supporter of the attempts to form a student corps to resist Russian aggression. His co-defendant was a radical intellectual called Zhang Binglin who had published a very positive review of the pamphlet. *The Revolutionary Army* encapsulated the radical ideas of the time in their most extreme form. It begins:

Sweep away millennia of despotism in all its forms, throw off millennia of slavishness, annihilate the five million and more of the furry and horned Manchu race, cleanse ourselves of 260 years of harsh and unremitting pain, so that the soil of the Chinese subcontinent is made immaculate, and the descendants of the Yellow Emperor will all become Washingtons. Then they will return from the dead to life again, they will emerge from the Eighteen Levels of hell and rise to the Thirty Three Mansions of heaven, in all their magnificence and richness to arrive at their zenith, the unique and incomparable of goals – revolution. How sublime is revolution! How majestic![16]

The anti-Manchu rhetoric of the pamphlet included the long-standing complaints that Manchus filled official posts instead of better-qualified Han scholars, and that Han who did get official posts were not promoted. There were also references to the massacres that accompanied the Manchu invasion in the seventeenth century. Zou Rong told his readers that filial piety demanded that they avenge their ancestors who had been butchered by the Manchus. These too were ideas that had probably circulated in some circles, especially in the rich Yangzi delta area, throughout the dynasty. However Zou Rong combined these traditional charges with a complex racial model that was clearly imported from contemporary Western thought. Even the presentation of the model, which is laid out in Fig. 4.4, was an innovation in Chinese texts.

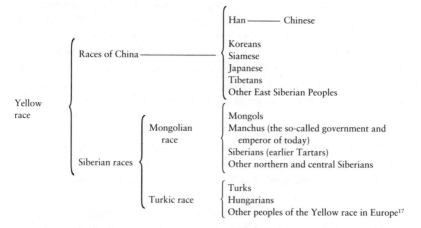

Figure 4.4 Zou Rong's model of the races of China
Source: Tsou Jung, *The Revolutionary Army: A Chinese Nationalist Tract of 1903*, trans. John Lust. The Hague: Mouton, 1968, p. 107

The diagram is a curious mixture of the influence of contemporary Western racial tabulations and Chinese culturalist traditions based on customs and ecology. Thus the Koreans, a former tributary state, are included among the races of China, while the nomadic peoples of the north are divided into a separate race. Zou Rong described the success of the Han race as illustrated by its expansion across China but declared dramatically that he would rather the whole race were killed than that its people should live happily under the Manchus. The pamphlet and Zhang Binglin's article praising it were published from the legal safety of the international concession in Shanghai. Unable to arrest the two men, the Qing state sued them for libel in the foreign-run Shanghai Mixed Court, which tried cases involving Chinese in Shanghai. The Qing pressed for heavy penalties, but in the end the judges sent Zou Rong to prison for two years and Zhang Binglin for three. Zou Rong died in prison shortly before his term ended but Zhang Binglin went on to become one of China's leading radical scholars. The case was widely reported in the newspapers and brought huge publicity to the radical cause. *The Revolutionary Army* was reprinted in Hong Kong, Singapore and Yokohama with 20 new editions recorded before the fall of the dynasty in 1911. Multiple editions of the book and newspaper reports of the legal case inevitably worked to spread the rhetoric of race and nation that Zou Rong had been promoting.

More publicity came from the violent deaths of radical activists, which were widely reported in the new newspapers. Several radicals lost their lives trying to assassinate leading Manchu figures or publicise their cause. In 1905 one Wu Yue went to the new Tianjin railway station intending to throw a bomb at five imperial commissioners who were being sent abroad to study foreign constitutions. Wu Yue had followed a classical education with study of foreign languages at the Jiangnan arsenal and further study at a modern-style high school. He had read Liang Qichao and then Zou Rong and had been moved by the Russian occupation of Manchuria. He had then met two other radicals who introduced him to their revolutionary organisation and taught him to make bombs. Unfortunately the bomb he was carrying at the railway station went off prematurely, killing him. The writings he left urged people to drive out the Manchus and resist the West and argued in favour of assassination.

Wu Yue's ideas were based on the Russian nihilists (whom he mentions) but probably also on traditional Chinese stories of heroic assassins. Chen Tianhua, who had introduced Wu Yue to revolutionary activities, came to prominence when he committed suicide by throwing himself into the sea during the student protests that followed the Japanese authorities' introduction of new regulations for Chinese students. A photograph of him published in a radical newspaper (Fig. 4.5) alongside his suicide note shows

相肖生先台星陳

Figure 4.5 Chen Tianhua
Source: *Minbao* 2, 1906

the unshaven head and shoulder-length hair with which he marked his opposition to the Manchus. In his suicide note he lamented that the only future he could conceive for himself was either to warn people of the danger to China as a journalist or to warn them through his death. People should study with all their strength to love their country and his suicide would force them to listen to this advice. With such dramatic actions, this generation of students brought their new ideology of nationalism to the forefront of political debate across the country.

At the same time, the passion of people like Chen Tianhua provided fertile ground for the growth of revolutionary groups. Some of these had already been in existence for several years, appealing primarily to Chinese living outside China or in the treaty ports. The two main organisations of this type were run by Sun Yatsen and Kang Youwei. Sun Yatsen, who was born in Guangdong and educated in Hawaii and Hong Kong, was a good example of the early generation of western-educated Chinese who found themselves simultaneously qualified for and excluded from government office. Like many members of this generation, Sun Yatsen had initially tried to influence the government from within, writing a letter to Li Hongzhang in which he recommended Western innovations and asked for employment. When this proposal was rejected Sun left China for Hawaii where he founded a group called the Revive China Society whose members took an oath to drive out the Manchus, revive China and found a government in which the people would cooperate. In 1895, in the aftermath of the loss of Korea, this group organised a revolutionary uprising in Guangzhou. This failed and Sun fled the country, ending up in London, where the Chinese embassy managed to kidnap him and hold him to be shipped back to China. He was rescued after the intervention of one of his former teachers from the medical college in Hong Kong, and spent two more years in Europe. Back in Asia in 1900 he organised an uprising to take place in Fujian, with the backing of the Japanese governor of Taiwan, who hoped to launch an invasion of Fujian if China was divided among the powers in the aftermath of the Boxer Uprising. Sun's uprising, which had the anti-Boxer slogan 'Protect the foreigners and exterminate the Manchus', failed after Tokyo blocked the Taiwan governor's plans. After the failure of his uprising Sun spent a lot of time touring Southeast Asia raising money for his projects from members of Chinese communities there. In this he came into conflict with Kang Youwei, who had fled China after the failure of the reform movement in 1898. Passionately loyal to the emperor who had been his patron, Kang Youwei organised a Protect the Emperor Society. Although the objective of this society was constitutional monarchy, in other respects the reforms it demanded and its methods were very much the same as those of Sun Yatsen. Kang Youwei's prestige as a top degree-holder and famous scholar made him a very effective fundraiser in the Chinese communities of Southeast Asia and this brought him into conflict with Sun Yatsen. Thus the two major organisations promoting radical political change spent much of their time during the 1900s fighting for the allegiance of the Chinese of Southeast Asia.

The bad relations between the two parties caused their adherents to exaggerate the differences between their ideologies. In fact the followers, and funders, of both organisations came from similar backgrounds and had similar aims; the strict distinction between 'reformers' and 'revolutionaries' that is often made is more a product of their internal politics than a reflection of the actual situation. However, the dramatic and well-publicised disputes between these two political parties had the effect of involving large numbers of ethnic Chinese in Southeast Asia in the politics of China. It is during this period that we see the development of the term 'Overseas Chinese' (*huaqiao*) to refer to ethnic Chinese living outside the Chinese state. The term implied that the Chinese communities abroad were sojourners whose primary loyalty was to their native homeland. At the same time the term defined that homeland as the Chinese nation state rather than, as had previously been the case, referring to ethnic Chinese primarily by their provinces of origin. The commitment of ethnic Chinese living in Southeast Asia and America to Chinese nationalist politics was to last through much of the twentieth century, when they continued to be important as funders of revolutionary and nationalist activities. One of the results of this was that Chinese nationalism was from an early stage pushed towards a definition of national identity that could encompass these groups. This introduced an emphasis on descent into the definition of national identity that fitted well with the racist ideas of many of the revolutionary groups.

The 1900s saw the development of a host of new student-based revolutionary organisations founded on these new ideas but competing with the organisations of both Kang Youwei and Sun Yatsen. Thus, for example, Huang Xing, who had been a member of the Association for National Military Education, founded a China Rise Society in 1903 and planned an uprising to coincide with the celebrations of the empress dowager's seventieth birthday. Sun Yatsen's relations with the students were limited since his Western education and appearance were a barrier even to these most radical members of the Chinese elite. When he was introduced to the community of Chinese students in Japan one of them later explained that his first impression of Sun was as an 'uncultured bandit'. Nevertheless Sun, who had extraordinary personal charisma, did win followers and succeeded in setting up a new organisation, known as the Chinese League, which was to act as an umbrella for the student groups. The members of this new organisation took an oath to 'drive out the Manchus, revive China, establish a Republic and equalise land rights'. The last clause shows the effects of Sun's recent reading in London, which had inspired him with socialist ideals in addition to his revolutionary ones, but the rest of the oath shows an emphasis he shared with the existing student groups on a racial identification of the Han and the establishment of a Han republic.

The Chinese League organised a series of unsuccessful uprisings in China (four in 1907 and two in 1908), but other student-based groups persisted. One of the most famous revolutionaries who operated outside Sun's umbrella organisation was Xu Xilin who, with the woman revolutionary Qiu Jin, planned an uprising to take place in Anhui and Zhejiang in 1907. Xu Xilin held a degree and was a member of a revolutionary group called the Restoration Society. This group had an oath similar to that sworn by members of Sun Yatsen's societies ('to restore the Han people to power and recover the land; to sacrifice oneself for the nation and to remain anonymous'), but this reflects the shared ideologies of the time rather than political ties. At his trial Xu was asked whether he was a member of Sun Yatsen's group, to which he replied that Sun was not fit to give him orders. Xu's response suggests the extent to which the revolutionary groups of the 1900s were united not by organisational ties but by a shared ideology that became popular during this period. That ideology, drawn from contemporary Western thought but accepting primarily those parts of that thought that seemed relevant to the experiences of the students who read it, emphasised race and heredity as a central feature of the nation.

Newspapers and the growth of public opinion

The ideologies of race and modern nationalism spread beyond the narrow circle of radical revolutionaries in large part because of the development of modern newspapers during this period. The most influential and successful newspapers were produced in the treaty ports but distributed across the country. They were financially viable because news itself was a valuable commodity. However, the news carried with it the ideas and attitudes of the journalists, many of whom were modernising intellectuals. Although the major newspapers were never as radical as the revolutionary student groups, they were drawing on the same range of ideas centred on nationalism and race.

Development of news and newspapers

Modern newspapers were a Western invention imported into China in the late nineteenth century. Previously most news had been generated by things people saw or heard. Refugees fleeing from famine or flood or rises in the price of silver would be noticed and reported to friends and neighbours. Travellers carried this news with them and told it to people they met along the road. Other forms of news interacted with this oral news network. Letters, gazettes and newspapers were carried by private carrying companies, often attached to banks or other businesses that had branches in different parts of the country. The speed at which such news travelled increased as the companies adopted the new forms of transport that were introduced in the course of the nineteenth century: steamboats from the 1860s, railways from the 1900s. From 1896 the foreign-run Imperial Maritime Customs established the Imperial Post Office, which gradually grew until it came to cover cities and towns across the country and was able to put the letter-carrying companies out of business. Government gazettes had existed for centuries, and had been widely read across the country from at least the fifteenth century. The original gazette was issued daily by one of the government offices in Beijing and consisted of the court diary for the day, followed by the complete text of imperial edicts issued that day and finally a section of memorials submitted to the emperor. Provincial officials and publishing houses employed copyists to make abridged versions which were sent out to the provinces and could be bought or rented in county towns. Although the gazettes were widely read and discussed, their impact was quite different from that of modern newspapers, for the gazettes were primarily a record of government decisions, whereas from the start the newspapers presented themselves as the organs of a new public opinion that lay outside the bounds of government.

Western-style newspapers began in China with the missionary press of the late nineteenth century. From its beginnings, much Protestant missionary work in China emphasised printing and distributing tracts. Newspapers and periodicals were developed as part of this process of spreading the gospel. There was also an English-language press in China, published by the members of the large foreign community for their own benefit. The best-known papers were the *North China Herald* published in Shanghai and the *South China Morning Post* published in Hong Kong. These were modern Western-style newspapers of the kind that had developed in Europe and America. They provided a model for Chinese-language newspapers and also became the main source for foreign news for the Chinese press. The first successful Chinese-language newspaper was founded in 1860 in Hong Kong and clearly grew out of this missionary tradition. The founder, Wang Tao, had been employed as an assistant to the Scottish missionary James Legge, who was engaged on the mammoth task of translating the entire corpus of the Chinese classics. Wang Tao worked for Legge for many years in Hong Kong, and later, after Legge's retirement, spent two years in Scotland assisting in the completion of the project. On his return to Hong Kong he founded a newspaper called *Sino-Foreign News*, which was commercially successful in Hong Kong. Wang Tao's connections with Westerners were long-standing and he was living in a British colony. His newspaper, and this was to be true of almost all the early newspapers, was deeply imbued with the new thought that called for the modernisation of China. Also typical of other early newspapers was the tendency to speak with the voice of those committed to modern nationalism, for both the authors and readers of such newspapers tended to be members of the new modernising community whose professions and training excluded them from the traditional cultural system and drew them towards modern nationalism.

The Chinese newspaper that achieved the largest circulation was the *Shenbao*, which was founded in 1872 by two English brothers, Frederick and Ernest Major, as a commercial venture. Frederick Major had already spent several years in trade in Shanghai and he started the newspaper at the suggestion of his Chinese comprador who had heard of the success of the Hong Kong Chinese-language newspapers. The commercial nature of the business is indicated by the fact that when Ernest Major branched out into book publishing he produced editions of standard examination texts. Thus the *Shenbao* did not have an explicit social or political agenda. An extract from the announcement printed in the first edition gives a sense of the newspaper's aims:

> The political situation of the empire, changing customs, important developments in foreign relations, prosperity and depression in business, and all that evokes surprise and astonishment and pleasure or refreshes the public ear, none of these things will be omitted. We shall apply our best efforts to convey only confirmable news, and without misrepresentation; also to make the news understandable. We shall not indulge in shallow or vainglorious talk, or write about ghosts or magic. Those interested in current affairs may get from our paper the gist of daily events, and those engaged in business will not be misled by any reports in our paper.[17]

The newspaper was initially sold largely on the telegraphic reports of major news items, but it also contained reprints of the *Peking Gazette*, prices for major commodities, business news and a variety of reports. Editorial control was in the hands of Chinese and as a commercial enterprise the paper reflected the needs and interests of its readers. As commercial ventures, the early Chinese newspapers addressed the concerns of the treaty-port world from which they had sprung. They reflected the interests of that world in modernisation and political reform, and in doing so came to be extremely influential.

The success of the early newspapers and the impact they had was dependent on changes in technology. In particular they were affected by the introduction of moveable type for printing Chinese and by the development of the international telegraphic network. These changes made printing cheaper and news more widely available and thus made it possible for news, and to some extent the new breed of newspapermen, to alter the way in which people understood the social and political context in which they lived. In the 1840s incidents between Chinese and Westerners in distant Guangdong were little known beyond the immediate local area; by the 1920s news of such incidents spread rapidly across the telegraphic network and politically active members of the elite could spread their opinions about the causes and implications through a huge array of national and local newspapers and periodicals.

Western printing techniques were introduced by missionary organisations in the nineteenth century and replaced woodblock printing, which was cheap but also slow and cumbersome. The most important innovations were the introduction of lithography and moveable type, both of which made it possible to print large editions to a much higher quality. A set of Chinese-character moveable type, which consists of one piece of metal cast to represent each character, was developed by the London Missionary Society. It meant that an evenly high-quality print could be achieved very fast when compared to the traditional method of engraving a block of wood. Moreover, the use of western-style printing machines meant that the metal could be used for a large print run without deteriorating.

Lithography was also introduced and came to be used not only in illustrated papers but also for cartoons, advertisements and, later, reproductions of photographs. Images of news events, personalities and even of new commodities helped to spread new views of the world beyond the intellectuals of the treaty ports. Fig. 4.6 is taken from an early illustrated

Figure 4.6 Newspaper illustration of a robbery in Nanjing
Source: *Tuhua ribao* (Pictorial Daily), 1909–10

newspaper and shows a robbery occurring in the treaty port of Nanjing. The text describes how a young man of good family got into a fight with the manager of a cinema and stole his watch. The illustration, which completely dominates the page, shows the beginning of the fight. However, the design of the illustration focuses attention on a series of imported Western innovations. Central to the picture is a large lamppost from which an electric lamp is hanging. Another electric light hangs over the entrance to the cinema. The cinema itself has a Cyrillic sign and advertises, 'Newly arrived foreign moving pictures'. The background architecture with its louvred shutters and classical style emphasised by the use of perspective is distinctively foreign. To the contemporary Chinese viewer, however, perhaps the most modern item of all would have been the rickshaw in which the young troublemaker arrived, which lies abandoned in the centre of the picture. The invention of the rickshaw was a result of the development of the rubber tyre, and rickshaws had only recently arrived in China. Altogether the picture presents the viewer with a vision of Nanjing that is both recognisable as everyday life and yet at the same time distinctively modern.

These technical developments in printing also made possible the greatly expanded circulations of the new newspapers compared with those of earlier news sheets and gazettes, and thus the spread of the images and ideas they promoted over a much wider area than the treaty ports in which they were developed.

The other important change driven by technology was the arrival of transcontinental telegraph lines from 1871 that connected Shanghai with Europe, first via Hong Kong and India, later overland via Vladivostock. Daily telegraphic communication with markets in London rapidly changed the way in which business was done in Shanghai. By tying Shanghai much more closely into world markets, the telegraph also made it necessary for people in Shanghai to follow world news. Moreover, it was soon obvious to the Qing government that internal telegraph lines were a military necessity. From 1881 Li Hongzhang began working with a Danish telegraph company to develop an internal Chinese network. The international cables were operated by commercial companies, while the cables inside China were operated by the Chinese Telegraph Administration, one of the most profitable of the self-strengthening enterprises of the period. By 1900 cables had been built across the country.

The existence of telegraphic news and the market for it encouraged the establishment of more newspapers. By 1909 in the provincial city of Chengdu you could buy any one of a total of 20 newspapers, ranging from the *Hong Kong Commercial Daily* and the *Shanghai Times* to the *Sichuan Official Gazette*. These were on sale in bookshops as well as being mailed to subscribers. The establishment of smaller local newspapers depended on this availability of news. Wu Yu, a radical scholar who edited a newspaper in Chengdu in 1911, got his news from letters from correspondents, telegrams from Beijing, Hubei and Shanghai, and by reprinting material from the range of other periodicals his office subscribed to, including the relatively conservative *Dagongbao*, the radical *Minlibao* and the *Eastern Miscellany*, an influential magazine issued by the textbook publisher the Commercial Press.

As in other countries, newspapers in China played an important role in the development of a sense of national identity. The existence of illustrated newspapers and telegraphic news combined to break down local and provincial barriers and create a sense of involvement with and concern for groups of people across the country. Fig. 4.7 is taken from an illustrated newspaper and shows famine victims in the province of Gansu. The newspaper in which this illustration was printed was published in Shanghai, many days' if not weeks' journey from Gansu. The famine victims are depicted in emotional detail: they are gaunt, dressed in rags and lean on sticks. A child pulls on the arm of an older man, presumably his father, who has collapsed to the ground. In the foreground another man crawls towards a rough wooden gate. Pictures like these were used to generate support for new famine-relief organisations that operated across the country. Thus the newspapers with the organisations they generated helped lay the ground for a new and more modern sense of national community.

Figure 4.7 Newspaper illustration of famine victims in Gansu
Source: *Shishibao* (Current Affairs Daily), 14 January 1908

Newspapers and the ideology of nationalism

However, newspapers also promoted the ideology of nationalism in a more immediate way. As early as the 1890s it was clear that newspapers could serve political aims. In 1896 Liang Qichao wrote an influential essay on the value of the periodical press in national affairs. In this he argued that newspapers should be used as an intermediary between the government and the people, to inform the government of the opinions of the people and the people of government policies. At the end of his article he listed what he thought were the proper aims of Chinese newspapers:

> To translate extensively news of all the world, so that readers may know the general condition of the nations and the causes of strength and prosperity or weakness and collapse, and thus be not like petty barbarian tribesmen regarding themselves as a mighty power, or like a frog sitting at the bottom of a well and expounding heaven and earth.
>
> To report in detail the new government measures in the several provinces, so that readers may know that the modern innovations actually do yield benefits; and also realize the difficulties of those in authority, and their aims. Then there will be few obstructionists.
>
> To delve into and fully expose details of important Sino-foreign problems, so that readers may understand that China is not established internationally, that because of internal disorganisation China is humiliated by other nations, and that because of our ignorance of international law we are duped by other nations; and thus to stimulate the new learning, and cause readers to give thought to purging the nation of its humiliations.
>
> To publish important books on political science and on the arts, so that readers may understand the sources and the applications of practical knowledge, and its constant progress; and thus relinquish the old examination system of study, the antiquarian scholarship and belletristics, and cease to take complacent pride in such learning.[18]

Thus newspapers are called upon to be the bearers of modern nationalism and political reform to an audience that is supposed to be largely unwilling to receive such ideas. Liang Qichao saw the newspaper as a mechanism for changing its readers. It was to emphasise knowledge relating to the nation in order to convince its readers of the benefits of reform.

During the Boxer crisis the *Shenbao* translated foreign news reports so literally that the Chinese army was referred to as 'the enemy'. Such a situation was unthinkable, even as an oversight, in the new politically motivated newspapers that sprang up in the 1900s. One of the best known of these was the *Shibao*, established in 1902 at the suggestion of Liang Qichao. Many of the newspaper's early journalists had studied in Japan, and their foreign experience influenced their writings. Another newspaper, the *Minlibao*, was run by Sun Yatsen and his supporters and promoted yet more radical views. Neither of these papers had a large enough circulation to make a profit, so both had to rely on subsidies from the political interests who had established them.

Much attention has been paid to the influence of newspapers, and especially the politically motivated newspapers of the 1900s, in altering the way people thought about the nation and society. Writers in these newspapers were affected by the old idea of a dichotomy between officials and people, and saw themselves as members of the people (*min*) criticising the government. Thus modern ideas of public opinion, formulated through the newspapers, followed on from long-standing efforts to give members of the elite who were not officials a greater voice in the development of government policy. By speaking of themselves as 'the people' the new journalists were emphasising the fact that they were outside the government. However, they were also committed to changing 'the people', that is to say the general population whom they saw as backward and ignorant. Using the word in these two different meanings they promoted the old idea of the people as being the base of the country, a manoeuvre that in the atmosphere of the 1900s was effectively a call for constitutional or republican government. In other words the Qing was displaced from its position at the centre of the state. Here again we see the redefinition of the word *guo* or 'country'. Liang Qichao wrote explicitly: 'In order for a dynasty to exist, there must first be a country. And while the country can change the quality of the dynasty, the dynasty cannot absorb the country.'[19] Thus the dynasty is made secondary to the country which preexisted it and which, in traditional culturalist style, cannot be changed or absorbed. This new language of nationalism was tied to earlier ideas of righteous elite opinion, and spread through the newspapers.

The army

Nationalism and a sense of citizenship were also closely tied to the promotion of a modern army. From the start the Qing reforms had been driven by the need to improve the military so that China could resist foreign imperialism. During the 1900s there was a huge enthusiasm for the military: at court the discussion was of training a modern army and outside the government people talked of militarism as an ideology. This view of the military was quite different from traditional negative attitudes towards soldiers, and the new vision of the nation as a people under arms was to be immensely influential over the course of the twentieth century.

The driving force behind the reforms of the nineteenth century had been the desire to build a strong army to defend the country against the Western powers. Early government attempts to import Western technology, such as the Jiangnan Arsenal and the Fuzhou Naval Dockyard, were aimed at reducing the need to import military equipment. After China's defeat by Japan in 1895 it was obvious that the European methods adopted in training the Japanese army were one of the causes of the Japanese victory. Thus one of the consequences of the defeat was the adoption of European methods of military organisation and training within the Chinese military. The reforms were initiated by officials with an interest in self-strengthening led by Zhang Zhidong in central China and Yuan Shikai in the north. These men did not try to alter the whole structure of the Chinese armed forces but instead began to build up units within the military that were trained on Western lines. As they grew these units came to be called the New Armies. They did not replace the existing armed forces, which continued alongside them. Some members of the New Armies were recruited from within the existing armed forces, but the majority were new to the army. The aim was to employ literate soldiers from respectable backgrounds. Indeed when Zhang Zhidong set up an academy for training officers in Wuhan, applicants had to be degree-holders, or prospective officials, or had to come from established gentry families.

The model for the New Armies was Germany, though to a large extent German arrangements were mediated through Japan, which had already adopted the German model. Germany was chosen because of the great military successes of the Prussian system in the nineteenth century. In Europe improvements in artillery resulting from the industrial revolution had made old-fashioned cavalry charges impossible. At the same time military strategists promoted the use of large numbers of men concentrated on particular points. Reacting to these kinds of changes the Prussian state had instituted conscription to the armed forces, replacing traditional professional soldiers. The aim was to recruit better-educated and disciplined men who served only for a limited period. These men were commanded by a corps of officers highly trained in military theory. In China, military primary schools were established in each province with secondary schools and officer-training colleges in the major cities. The highest levels of this officer-training system employed many Japanese and German staff and the government sent students to Japan to study in military academies there. Gradually the products of this new military education system began to take up positions within the New Armies while at the same time these forces were expanded by absorbing elements of other Qing forces. The growth of the New Armies created a powerful modern institution that was not fully integrated in the structures of the state. The nationalist ideals of many of its officers and men exacerbated this problem.

The ideology of militarism

Among the ideas that reached China from Europe and Japan were those of Herbert Spencer, who saw a struggle for survival between the nations in which war was a purifying element that eliminated the sickly and malformed. The term 'survival of the fittest', a slogan in which the term 'fittest' combines physical strength with moral right, was coined by Spencer. Drawing from these ideas writers began to call for a new military spirit that would enable China's armies to repel the European aggressors. The two key terms, endlessly repeated in these writings, were 'militarism' (*shangwu* – literally 'appreciation of martial values') and 'military citizenship' (*junguomin*). A new admiration for martial values was seen as being necessary because of the generally low view of the military in China. In the past military examinations and degrees had carried significantly lower status than those of the literary examination system, and Zeng Guofan, for example, preferred to recruit his officers from among the literary degree-holders. As for soldiers, a popular saying went, 'Good iron is not used for nails; good men do not become soldiers.'

By contrast, Westerners were seen as having a positive orientation towards the military. Articles in a radical magazine that circulated in Hubei in 1903 claimed that Westerners' appreciation of things military was demonstrated by the fact that they admired military heroes, painted pictures of battles and wrote martial poetry. Moreover, this militaristic ideology was spread beyond direct references to the army into the general population. Another writer in the same magazine informed his readers that all Germans read a book called *Our People Under Arms* and that all English people read *Robinson Crusoe*, which he claimed also promoted militarist ideas.

That these ideas were new and alien to many people is illustrated by a book of moral stories for young people published around this time. The author explains that he compiled it from his reading of history to provide examples of proper behaviour for the young. Chapters include the importance of studying, filial piety, brotherly love, the proper behaviour between husband and wife, friendship, etc. Each chapter consists of the author's comments on this particular virtue followed by extracts from traditional texts, which give outstanding examples of it. This works well enough for most of the chapters which concern traditional Confucian values, but when the author gets to his chapter on militarism he has a problem. In the introduction he writes of the individual's responsibility for his country and the necessity of discipline, obedience and patriotism. However the extracts he provides fail to illustrate these modern virtues: none of his texts concerns wars between nations, and most concern either clever strategists and scholars who, driven by poverty, entered the army and became famous generals, or examples of physical strength and skills. In the latter category is a story of a man who could jump into a well and then jump out again, an almost superhuman achievement. Ideas of military discipline and obedience were a product of the industrial revolution in the West and were new to China in the early twentieth century.

The emphasis on modern military virtues was even more obvious in discussions of military citizenship. Liang Qichao wrote that people should learn to prize military virtues so that the national spirit would become militaristic. He suggested that this should be done by instituting national military education for the whole population. State promotion of militarism was very obvious to Chinese living in Japan. One example noticed by many Chinese was the honour the Japanese state paid to those who died in wars for the imperial cause. In 1871 a shrine to them had been constructed in Tokyo under the aegis of the army and navy ministries. Sacrifices were held there every spring and autumn and the emperor frequently attended. The names of those who were to be honoured in the shrine were investigated by the government and the entry of a name was a privilege conferred by the emperor. Within the precinct was a Western-style brick building called the museum of arms in which were displayed the portraits of all the dead. By displaying large numbers of portraits the museum presented the individual soldier as a model for citizens, and reduced the sense of individual heroism. Chinese in Tokyo were impressed by the shrine and the sacrifices: Song Jiaoren, a radical visitor to Tokyo in 1905, attended the spring sacrifices at the shrine and commented approvingly, 'Ah! Should not those who offer their lives to defend the country be rewarded in this way!'[20] The establishment of a shrine to those who died in battle was only one of many possible ways to encourage the perception of the military as a model for ordinary people, but the approval of Chinese visitors suggests that they shared this goal.

The idea of military citizenship was elaborated in greater detail in a widely circulated and influential pamphlet by Cai E, who had been a student of Liang Qichao's in China and had later been sent to Japan to study in a military academy. He argues that a sense of military citizenship is essential to a modern state because of the pervasive competition between nations in an age of imperialism:

> Military citizenship flourished in Sparta in Greece and flooded the major powers of the modern age. In the West even women and children are deeply imbued with this ideology. This is because those countries use that ideology in the general education of their entire citizenry, and their citizens accept this ideology as their greatest lifelong duty. Imperialism is born of military citizenship. This is so because when the state's internal strength is fully developed, it cannot but expand beyond it.[21]

This view of world history goes beyond analysing the reasons for Western strength to accepting militarism as a necessary and positive development for China. Cai then analyses the reasons why China lacks this sense of military citizenship. These include the general tendency to look down on soldiers, a lack of physical training, poor weapons and even decadent music. This last may seem somewhat odd: it is drawn partly from the Confucian idea of the importance of rites and music, but in his justification Cai explains that in Japan, since the Meiji Restoration, music is taught in schools, as in the

West, and all the music is full of feelings of patriotism and militarism. Cai E is clearly looking for state intervention of the sort that the Japanese state had applied to alter people's attitudes towards the military and to create a militarised citizenry.

Physical training

One of the most important outcomes of militarist ideas of this sort was a new emphasis on physical fitness. This was linked to the goal of creating men who could act as soldiers in times of national need or under a conscription system (the citizen soldiers originally envisaged by the nineteenth-century Prussian state), and to the widespread use of metaphors that described the country as being like a human body. When the novelist Li Boyuan satirised the revolutionaries who used the clichéd image of China as a body that was being divided up, the metaphor implied the commonly held view that the strengthening of the physical body was in some way equivalent to the strengthening of the nation. At first most writers on militarism had been primarily concerned with the cultivation of a military spirit, but by the mid-1900s there was a shift towards the promotion of actual physical strength and fitness as a defining feature of the new military citizens.

The most immediate way of encouraging physical fitness was the introduction of physical exercise in schools. Initially this seemed very alien to people used to the strict formality and dignified movements expected of students in traditional schools. Many people dismissed sports in school as 'children's games' and despised both the teachers and the students who took part. Others were more surprised and amused. Guo Moruo recalls the beginning of physical exercise in a village school. The school was a modern one and the teacher, who was one of the first graduates of the local teacher-training college, introduced 'foreign exercises' for the students. The instructions for these were given in a strange gibberish, which many years later Guo Moruo found out was the Japanese for 'one, two, three' and other simple instructions. Since the physical-education teacher in the training college had been Japanese and had not troubled to translate his instructions, his pupil, the new village schoolteacher, treated the curious sounds as an essential part of the class. People found the whole performance fascinating and initially the students were watched by most of the local population.

Physical education almost always took the form of military drills, but this was only one of the means by which students were encouraged to act in a military style and with military discipline. Textbooks, which provided models for the modern schools, show children dressed as soldiers. Indeed, military-style clothing was frequently seen as the appropriate costume for pupils at modern schools. Fig. 4.3 shows a student in the short jacket and peaked cap of contemporary school uniform. The textbooks also encouraged drills and military games in schools. Fig. 4.8 is an illustration from a

Figure 4.8 'Playing at soldiers'
Source: Shen Yi and Dai
Kedun, *Gongheguo jiaokeshu
xin xiushen* (Republican
Textbook: New Ethics).
Shanghai: Shangwu
yinshuguan, 1912, vol. 4, p. 22

widely used series of ethics textbooks. It shows a group of boys playing at being soldiers, this time in more traditional clothing. The neat rows, identical postures and the position of the leader giving orders from the front suggest the discipline and uniformity of contemporary Western military drills. This is portrayed not as an organised school activity but as a children's game. Some of this rubbed off on the children: a girl who grew up in the 1900s remembers in her memoirs playing with a brother and cousin at being soldiers, marching round a flagpole they had erected in the garden.

In addition to military drills, Western-style sports were occasionally introduced, beginning in the nineteenth century in mission schools. These modern sports seemed even more foreign and strange than the military drills. Fig. 4.9 shows a running race as illustrated in a school textbook. The foreignness of the activity is immediately suggested by the use of perspective to depict the racecourse. A further glance shows the Western-style uniform of the teacher, and the jackets, shorts and socks of the four boys who are waiting to start. The contorted and uncomfortable postures of the boys are typical of illustrations of school sport during this period and make it unclear

Figure 4.9 'A running race'
Source: Shanxi guomin jiaokeshu bianji weiyuanhui ed., *Guomin xuexiao tongsu
guowen jiaokeshu* (Primary-school General Chinese Textbook). Taiyuan: Jinxin
shushe, 1924, vol. 3, p. 6

exactly what is going on. Other sports could seem equally incomprehensible: a Chinese official in Tianjin is said to have asked the British consul why he did not hire someone to play tennis for him.

As this probably apocryphal story suggests, Western-style physical exercises also involved a presentation of the self and particularly of the male body that was largely alien to the Chinese elite. One obvious example of this is inconvenience of the long gowns worn by elite men. The gowns were slit up the sides to allow some freedom of movement for the legs, but since the slit usually reached only just above the knee and the gown itself was narrow they were still quite restrictive (see Fig. 4.6). This was of course the point: such a gown was inconvenient for strenuous manual labour and could only be worn by those whose occupations did not require it. At first when Chinese students in mission schools took part in sports they continued to wear their long gowns. However later students, both in mission and in government schools, were encouraged to wear short jackets and trousers often in a military style. These allowed more freedom of movement but removed one of the scholar's traditional symbols of status. When these costumes were made required uniform for students in the Chinese department of Shanxi University it was said that several students left rather than wear the new uniforms.

The queue too could be an impediment to some forms of exercise. A student who studied in one of the missionary colleges in Shanghai remembered how in football matches students coiled their queues and pinned them on top of their heads (as labouring people did during the summer). But the energetic running brought the coils down, which made the spectators laugh, and there was no time to fix them back up. There was even a joke that one's queue whipping across an opponent's face should be a new foul. Similar problems occurred with military drill, as well as a general feeling that queues simply did not look right worn over the Western-style military uniforms. At first, like the football players, students simply pinned their queues up under their hats, but then some students, especially in military academies, began to cut theirs off. A primary-school textbook shows a mock battle depicted as taking place in a military academy (Fig. 4.10). In this picture the students have short hair, while all but two of the audience still have their queues. With the new hairstyles and clothing went a new sense of proper etiquette and therefore a new understanding of relations with others. A Manchu bannerman who had cut his queue while studying in a military academy and had to flee during the 1911 Revolution, recalled in his memoirs an interview with a senior official:

> After Fushou had sent his guest off, he summoned me to greet him in the main hall. I performed a full kowtow. Wearing military uniform and a military cap, I knelt on the ground and knocked my head on the floor: it was really neither the proper relationship nor the proper rituals.[22]

As we see in this story, the new ideal of physically strong and active citizens carried with it an ideology that undermined the old social order.

Figure 4.10 'A mock battle'
Source: Zhu Shuren, *Chudeng xiaoxue guowen keben* (Lower Primary School Chinese Textbook). Shanghai: Zhongguo tushu gongsi, 1907, vol. 4, p. 29

One of the results of the feeling that sports and drill were unacceptably foreign was the revitalisation and transformation of martial arts. During the nineteenth century the general opinion of martial arts was low. Martial-arts skills were associated with the lower classes and with types of popular religion usually condemned by elites. Certain areas and families were famous for their martial-arts skill, and in these areas members of the elite might occasionally take an interest in the physical techniques which they tended to combine with their own religious interests, for example in Daoist longevity practices. However, for the most part martial arts were seen as the preserve of the lower classes: one boy who learnt martial arts skills in the 1900s recalled that people thought of those who taught him as 'vagabonds selling their tricks'.[23] In addition to these problems, the common association of martial arts with the Boxers, widely condemned among the modernising elites during the 1900s, prevented much interest in the martial arts when physical exercise was first being promoted. However, the publication and dissemination of martial-arts manuals during the 1910s and 1920s brought knowledge that had previously been the property of certain individuals or groups into the public sphere. Wan Laisheng, who compiled a well-known manual, explained that he did so because he felt it was his duty as a citizen. At the same time Wan Laisheng's volume depicts the martial-arts skills in a very modern form: a series of photographs (in itself something of a printing innovation) show Wan performing the postures dressed in trousers and a striped singlet, in the style of contemporary European sportswear. In this new form, martial arts were justified in much the same terms as Western sport as bringing health and strength to the nation. Wan Laisheng quotes a saying: 'If one person practices the martial arts, he can protect his health; if one family practises the martial arts, they can strengthen the race.'[24]

Thus as martial arts were publicised they were also brought into the same realm as Western-style drills and sports. In the world of the treaty-port elites the two could even be combined, as happened at the Jingwu Athletic Association in Shanghai which offered swimming, ping-pong, roller-skating and photography alongside the martial arts, and where leaders were photographed performing martial arts in leopard-skin tunics. This kind of environment affected the way the martial arts were practised. When new schools for martial arts were established in the 1920s competitions for entry initially took the form of all-out fights, like the traditional folk entertainments of which the martial arts had been a part. However the fights were found to be too dangerous since, unlike most Western sports, martial arts had been designed primarily for killing. Instead the schools switched to judging the individual performance of the forms judged on a 10-point scale as in Western gymnastics. Through such changes the martial arts were dissociated from the Boxers and folk religious practice and the promoters of the new martial arts created something that was both Chinese and a modern sport. This change was marked by the removal of the word 'martial' from the name: the martial arts (*wushu*) were now to be called the 'national arts' (*guoshu*).

WOMEN

Western-style sports and Chinese martial arts were almost entirely the province of men, but the militarism of the 1900s also had a great impact on the lives of women. This was the time when women's education became popular. During the nineteenth century women's education had been the province of missionaries, and indeed missionary schools continued to be a very important part of women's education through the 1900s. The first Chinese-run girls' school was established in Shanghai in 1898. In 1902 the Commercial Press, leading from the front, began to publish special text-books for girls' schools. By 1907 there were 391 government girls' schools in the country with a total of over 11,000 pupils. This is obviously a very small number in a population conventionally estimated at the time as 400 million; nevertheless it marks the beginning of widespread education for women in China. This beginning was driven by the idea of women as 'worthy wives and good mothers', a phrase that occurs repeatedly in the writings of supporters of women's education. In this phrase and in the reformers' writings women are seen primarily in relation to men. Their role as worthy wives and good mothers was to support and most importantly to nurture and influence the new generation of military citizens.

Women's role as wives and mothers was seen to require some degree of physical strength in women just as military citizenship did in men. Thus the first goal of the reformers was the end of the custom of binding women's feet. Criticisms of foot binding had been a perennial if intermittent feature of elite writings, and indeed the Manchu Qing had once attempted to ban the custom, but it was so strongly entrenched as a marker of social status and ethnicity that such criticisms had little if any affect. Many of the Westerners who came to China in the nineteenth century were appalled by the custom and the pain and inconvenience it caused. Chinese-language magazines published by missionary organisations in the 1870s criticised foot binding as bad for women's health, harmful to family relations, a hindrance to women working and an impediment to church going. The missionaries began to form natural feet societies in places like Xiamen and Shanghai that were centres of their work. By the 1880s some Western-influenced Chinese in south China began to organise similar associations. The radical scholar Kang Youwei and a friend who had spent some time in America organised a natural feet society in their home town in 1883. Members, who were male heads of families, agreed that their wives, daughters and concubines should not continue to bind their feet. The inclusion of concubines suggests the extent to which this was an elite association. In 1897 Liang Qichao organised a similar but hugely successful association in Shanghai which drew its cachet by acting as a marriage club. Members promised that they would not bind their daughters' feet and their sons would marry only women with natural feet. Zhang Zhidong, a leading official, wrote a preface to the group's publicity materials, and the society was said to have 30,000 members. Around this time newspapers began to publish instructions for women who wished to unbind their feet, which was a very painful process, and to advertise medicines for it. Shops also began to sell shoes for women with unbound feet.

By the 1900s natural feet had become fashionable. Officials like Zhang Zhidong and Yuan Shikai gave their support; this was one change that the dynasty found easy to support. For the first time some parents outside the treaty ports began to question whether they should bind their daughters' feet. This questioning probably owed something to the fashion for a Western appearance, which is seen in the high collars and tight-fitting women's clothes of the time. But it was also due to the new ideas of inherited physique and genetics, which were connected with the popular theories of evolution and social Darwinism. It was thought that the mother's physical strength would directly affect the strength of the child. Liang Qichao believed that women who exercised during pregnancy would bear stronger children. Thus a nation of citizen soldiers required strong healthy women, and the end of foot binding as a widespread custom was seen as an essential part of that.

The army and modern education

Ideas of military citizenship changed social attitudes towards the relation between the individual and the state. This can be seen in the changing attitudes to physical exercise and self-presentation of members of the elite, but was also one of the immediate causes of the 1911 Revolution. Outside the treaty ports, a very high proportion of those who received a modern education were drawn into the army. This was partly the result of a deliberate policy of elite recruitment, which was particularly applied in the province of Hubei, where Governor General Zhang Zhidong had set a target of 50 per cent literacy for the common soldiers in the Hubei new army. Policies of elite recruitment interacted with the end of the examination system in 1905: education in the modern schools was more expensive than that for the traditional exams and was also slower. In addition graduates of the new schools often found themselves unemployed, having been trained to fill institutions and posts that did not yet exist. Education in military schools was shorter, cheaper and led to a secure position. Under these circumstances it is not surprising that the new military schools were heavily oversubscribed. In one Hunan county 500 young men, the vast majority of whom had graduated from higher primary schools or held lower-level degrees, took the exams for a single place offered to the county in the provincial military primary school in 1909.

A young man who entered a military primary school in Guangxi in southwest China during this period explained his motives:

> The time of the traditional examinations was past. Rather than sitting at home like a rotting log, it was better to seek a new way out by discarding literary studies for the military. Moreover the nation was weak and surrounded by waiting foreign powers, and its salvation depended on the military. Most important, it would not do to let the rare opportunity presented by the establishment of the New Army slip by.[25]

Here nationalist feelings are intricately bound up with personal career prospects that had been disrupted by the end of the examination system. Similar issues affected many of those who joined the ranks of the army, especially in Hubei where a special military primary school filled almost entirely from the ranks provided the possibility of advancement to the officer class, the equivalent of official status. As well as products of the new education system many traditional degree-holders entered the ranks in Hubei. One Hubei soldier said that 36 out of the 96 who joined the army along with him in a recruiting drive to his county had degrees. Another who joined in 1906 explained that after the ending of the examination system all the former examination students and candidates had to find alternative careers: 'Those whose family situations were good went to study abroad (mainly in Japan), those at the next level down took tests for local schools, and those without money entered the New Army as soldiers.'[26]

However, while nationalist feelings may have been mixed with career prospects, they nevertheless played an important role in the young men's decisions. A student who was studying in Japan at the time of the 1904 war between Russia and Japan over Manchuria, switched to a military academy. He remembered his naivety at the time: it was 'as if my own pursuit of military studies would directly influence whether or not the nation would survive'.[27] For other students nationalism and militarism could be used to justify choices made at least in part under economic pressures. This heavy investment in nationalism meant that soldiers had an interest in emphasising the importance of modern nationalism at the expense of other values.

Many students had been politically active before they entered the Qing army. It was claimed that one third of the Chinese students studying in Japan at the army officers' academy joined Sun Yatsen's Chinese League. These men then returned to commands or high-level teaching positions in the army in China. Moreover, the kind of modern-educated young men who joined the army, and especially those who joined the ranks, had a natural interest in political change since they tended to see themselves as members of an elite which should properly have access to power. In Hubei, where Zhang Zhidong's efforts had produced a new army with an especially high proportion of members from the traditional elites, the army was a hotbed of radical revolutionary societies. By 1911 it was said that between a quarter and a third of soldiers in the Hubei army were members of revolutionary societies. One day in the autumn of 1911 a bomb exploded accidentally at the headquarters of one of these revolutionary societies in Hankou. When police investigated the explosion they found, among other things, lists of all the society's members. Acting quickly the police arrested and executed three soldiers. Unknowingly the police had forced the hand of the revolutionary groups and by evening the revolution had begun.

Conclusion

The Qing government reforms of the 1900s fixed the shape of modern Chinese nationalism for much of the twentieth century. The reforms were radical and sudden; they have in fact been described as the 'new policy revolution'. They focused on the army and the education system in an attempt to create a new generation of citizens and officials who could resist the foreign threat. The centrality of the army in the reforms led to a state nationalism that was heavily imbued with militarism, while the emphasis on the education system gave rise to a generation of young people who had been taught radical new moral values which emphasised above all their duty to the Chinese nation state. However, the nationalism promoted by the reforms rapidly moved beyond the control of the Qing state with the spread of nationalist ideologies in the newspapers and the growth of revolutionary groups. Nationalism seemed essential to the efforts of the Qing state to face the Western threat, but the racist nature of the nationalist ideologies of the period meant that the promotion of nationalism had the effect of undermining the government of the non-Han Qing.

Notes

1 Liu Dapeng, *Tuixiangzhai riji* (Taiyuan: Shanxi renmin chubanshe, 1990), p. 134.
2 Quoted by Lau See-heng. D.Phil. thesis in progress, Oxford University.
3 Liu Dapeng, *Tuixiangzhai riji*, p. 146.
4 Quoted by Tsang Chiu-sam, *Nationalism in School Education in China* (Hong Kong: Progressive Education Publishers, 1967), p. 79.
5 Zhu Shuren ed., *Chudeng xiaoxue guowen keben* (Lower Primary School Chinese Textbook) (Shanghai: Zhongguo tushu gongsi, 1907), vol. 4, p. 2b.
6 Quoted in Zhou Kaiqing, *Xingzhi ji* (Collected essays on doing and knowing) (Taibei: Changliu banyuekan she, 1975), p. 81.
7 Huang Zhanyun et al. eds, *Chudeng xiaoxue guoyu jiaokeshu* (Primary School National Language Textbook) (Shanghai: Shangwu yinshuguan, 1907), vol. 3, pp. 15–16.
8 Li Boyuan, *Modern Times: A Brief History of Enlightenment* trans. Douglas Lancashire (Hong Kong: Research Centre for Translation, Chinese University of Hong Kong, 1996), p. 220.

9   Liu Dapeng, *Tuixiangzhai riji*, p. 138.
10   Ibid., p. 153.
11   Quoted in Marianne Bastid, *Educational Reform in Early Twentieth-Century China* (Ann Arbor: Center for Chinese Studies, University of Michigan, 1988), p. 143.
12   Quoted in Paula Harrell, *Sowing the Seeds of Change: Chinese Students, Japanese Teachers, 1895–1905* (Stanford: Stanford University Press, 1992), p. 135.
13   Li Boyuan, *Modern Times*, p. 172.
14   Quoted in Harrell, *Sowing the Seeds of Change*, p. 143.
15   Quoted in ibid.
16   Tsou Jung, *The Revolutionary Army: A Chinese Nationalist Tract of 1903*, trans. John Lust (The Hague: Mouton, 1968), p. 58.
17   Quoted in Roswell S. Britton, *The Chinese Periodical Press, 1800–1912* (Taipei: Ch'eng-wen Publishing Company, 1966), p. 65.
18   Quoted in ibid., pp. 89–90.
19   Quoted in Joan Judge, *Print and Politics: 'Shibao' and the Culture of Reform in Late Qing China* (Stanford: Stanford University Press, 1996), p. 59. I have altered her translation, replacing 'nation' with the more neutral 'country'.
20   Song Jiaoren, *Song Jiaoren riji* (The Diary of Song Jiaoren) (Changsha: Hunan renmin chubanshe, 1980), p. 60.
21   Cai E, *Cai E ji* (Collected works of Cai E) (Changsha: Hunan renmin chubanshe, 1983), pp. 19–20, passage trans. by David Faure.
22   Yiergenjuelo Tongpu, 'Fuzhou guangfu shiqi Manzu qiying nei de qingkuang' (The situation inside the Manchu banner garrison during the 1911 revolution in Fuzhou) *Jiangsu wenshi ziliao* (Jiangsu Historical Materials) 6 (1981 reprint).
23   Wan Laisheng, *Wushu huizong* (Collected Martial Arts) (Beijing: Zhongguo shudian, 1984), p. v.
24   Ibid., p. 4.
25   Quoted by Edward A. McCord, *The Power of the Gun: The Emergence of Modern Chinese Warlordism* (Berkeley: University of California Press, 1993), p. 53.
26   Quoted in ibid.
27   Quoted in ibid.

|5|

Ethnicity and modernity in the 1911 Revolution

The Wuchang Uprising that began the 1911 Revolution had its origins in the late Qing reforms. New ideas of loyalty to nation and race provided a rationale for overthrowing the dynasty, and this brought the students together with an older generation of modernisers who had become revolutionaries after failing to influence the government. Many of the students who shared these new ideas were driven by their poor career prospects to take jobs in the modern army that was being built up during the 1900s, and it was these men who were members of revolutionary groups which began the revolution. Once the revolution had begun it became necessary to decide how the new state would be structured. The nature of the state that people imagined was tied to their ideas of what they thought they were rebelling against, which took two very different forms: some people thought of themselves as participating in a revolution against the Manchu dynasty, while others saw the events as a revolution against foreign interference and westernising reforms. Each of these views of the revolution implied a different image of the new state.

The Han nation

Most revolutionary activists saw the revolution in racial terms as a contest between Han and Manchu. The Han Chinese were a nation and should have their own nation state. The new state that would be established after the revolution was imagined through opposition to the existing Manchu-dominated state. Since the Manchus were primarily involved in the central government in Beijing and were few in absolute numbers, this view implied that the goal of the revolution was a relatively limited restructuring of the highest levels of the government. Both the Western-inspired nationalism and the emphasis on the upper echelons of the government limited serious interest in these kinds of views to educated elites. These elites were, however, at the heart of the original Wuchang Uprising, and continued to play an important role in revolutionary thought.

A few days after the Wuchang Uprising the new revolutionary government in Wuchang decided to arrange a sacrifice to the spirits of Heaven, Earth and the Yellow Emperor. The sacrifice was suggested and organised by members of the revolutionary parties who had initiated the uprising. The chief actor was Li Yuanhong, the popular officer who had been compelled to lead the revolution. The ceremony was a strange mixture of ancient and modern, using the ancient form of sacrifice in which incense, wine and a yellow cow were offered, but with the participants dressed in military uniform, removing their caps to perform the kowtow. During the ceremonies a military anthem was played which was subsequently printed in a pro-revolutionary paper:

> Raise the Han, Raise the Han,
> Raise our great Han.
> The Han people love the mountains and rivers,
> How can they let thieves occupy them?
> Compatriots, work hard,
> Battle diligently forward,
> Kill all the barbarians,
> Raise the great Han.
>
> Raise the Han, Raise the Han,
> Raise our great Han.
> Destroy the Manchu, Destroy the Manchu,
> Destroy the thieving Manchu,
> The spirit of the Yellow Emperor
> Helps us to kill the thieves.
> Compatriots, work hard,
> March diligently forward,
> March to the north,
> Destroy the Manchu, Destroy the Manchu,
> Destroy the thieving Manchu.[1]

The song describes the revolution entirely in terms of conflict between Han and Manchu. The Yellow Emperor is invoked as the ancestor of the Han, and hence a provider of divine support for the Han, who are described as the rightful owners of the mountains and rivers, a conventional symbol of China as a geographic unit. The Manchus on the other hand are described as barbarians who have stolen that which rightly belongs to the Han. The goal of the revolution is to march north against the Manchu court in Beijing and destroy it.

The same ideas were expressed in the prayer Li Yuanhong intoned to the Yellow Emperor during the sacrifice:

On the 26th day of the 8th month of the 4609th year of the Yellow
Emperor, I, Li Yuanhong, military governor of the Hubei Army,
accompanied by all my troops, reverently honour the soul of the
Yellow Emperor with an animal sacrifice and wine. China, which the
Yellow Emperor bequeathed us, and the sacrifices to ancestors and
gods that he performed, have continued unbroken for more than four
thousand years, and have reached four million people. His virtue is
known around the globe. We repay him with sacrifices and our feeling.
But the foreign Manchu race has ruled for the last two hundred years,
so that our race has been troubled and has long thought to restore the
past. In the past we imitated the early martyrs and tasted wormwood
and gall for years. But this time as soon as we raised the flag of righteous rebellion we conquered Hubei in a morning, neighbouring cities
responded and we took the southeast in ten days. The people worked
together to exterminate the alien tribe and revive China. I humbly
request the support of the first emperor. Relying on our comrades'
vigorous advance we will achieve our goals and announce a constitution, which will enable us to keep up with every country in the world,
and cause our ancient country, which has already been civilised for
five thousand years, to become outstandingly glorious, so that our
sons and grandsons will preserve their prosperity forever. Only the
first emperor can see this.[2]

This prayer expresses both the ideology and the aspirations of the revolutionaries in Wuchang. The Yellow Emperor as ancestor of the Han people
replaces the Qing emperor in the date of the piece, a common practice in the
first months of the revolution. Against the image of the Yellow Emperor,
very much a symbol of the Han as defined by race and inheritance, is set the
vision of the Manchus as an 'alien tribe'. The modern idea of nationhood is
then linked to new ideas about China as being in competition with other
countries in the world and the call for constitutional government as a part
of that competition. These early symbols mark the racial nature of the revolution.

The alternative: a revolution against modernity

One of the first actions of the new revolutionary government was to
announce a ban on the wearing of the queue and the binding of women's
feet. The ban on foot binding had little immediate effect though it became
part of the rhetoric of the revolution. Queue cutting, however, was central
to the revolution, and was the first way in which the revolution affected
people in areas where there was no fighting. For the revolutionaries the
queue was a symbol of Manchu dominance, and thus of the subordination
of the Han by the Manchus. When Li Yuanhong ordered that queues should

be cut, he explained that he did so in order to revive the Han nation, root out the Manchus, build a republic and equalise human rights. Equalising human rights here refers to giving Han equal access to government positions, which had been blocked by the Manchus. In Wuchang soldiers were stationed at the city gates and on the major streets to forcibly cut the queues of passers by. In Fujian the new provincial governor ordered men to cut their queues, and, when he found that few did, ordered all government offices to hang notices forbidding anyone wearing a queue to enter. He then sent a notice to the officers of the provincial chamber of commerce, agricultural association and student association ordering them to cut their queues and to ensure that the leaders of their local branches did so too. Officials were told to see to it that they, their families and servants cut their queues on pain of dismissal.

For supporters of the revolution cutting off their queues was a demonstration of their support for the new order. In Wuzhou in Guangdong it was reported that 2,000 men cut their queues on the night that the town declared independence. However, military forces still fighting on behalf of the Qing continued to behead anyone found without a queue. For those who had cut their queues or had them forcibly cut, it was in their own interest to increase the numbers of those with short hair. Queue cutting spread rapidly through south and central China. Foreign observers on Hainan Island noticed that by the spring of 1912 there were almost no queues left. In many places this was achieved by soldiers and other rowdy young men taking to the streets and forcibly cutting queues. This led to frequent brawls and caused problems for the new local governments. For many men this violent change of their personal appearance so that they looked like the Westerners was highly problematic. A little boy whose queue was cut by his revolutionary father at this time remembered crying and refusing to go out for days. For those whose queues were cut in the street with crowds of mocking onlookers the experience was humiliating. One countryman who had his queue cut on a trip to the city was so mocked by his wife on his return that he committed suicide.

The countryman's attachment to his queue brings us to the alternative conception of the revolution as a Han Chinese movement not so much against the Manchus as against the westernising reforms that the Manchus had implemented. For many people the queue was a symbol not of Han subservience to the Manchus, but of their own identity as Chinese. When a man came back to Shanxi from Japan in the 1900s without his queue, a local schoolteacher commented, 'He has not only switched to wearing foreign clothes, but has also cut off his queue; although he is a Chinese he has almost become a barbarian.'[3] It was nearly 300 years since the Manchus had forcibly imposed the wearing of the queue and many people simply did not know about its Manchu origins. This is suggested by the fact that the writers of announcements ordering or encouraging the cutting of queues frequently felt it necessary to explain that the queue was not in fact a

Chinese custom. One from a county government in Shandong encouraged people to think of the characters in local operas:

> Be it known that from the Three Dynasties to the former Ming was all a time when men tied up their hair and wore caps. When you see this in an opera performance you will immediately realise that plaiting the hair dates only from the time when the Qing emperor entered the passes and enforced the change.[4]

Debate about the queue in Chinese communities in Southeast Asia in the 1900s also suggested that the queue was considered to be a sign of ethnic identity, with older generations complaining that among the young the queue was already the last sign of Chineseness in a group that had already been deeply influenced by non-Chinese customs.

There was also considerable popular opposition to short hair cut in Western styles. In Sichuan popular feeling against Western influence had overflowed into violence several months before the Wuchang Uprising. The origins of this violence lay in the reforms, which were seen as causing high taxes and being the result of foreign influence. The particular target of protesters was the new railway, which had been paid for by huge new taxes and was now to be taken over by the central government, which had raised the money through a large foreign loan. Posters sold in the streets of Chengdu included a cartoon of the sufferings of the Indians under British rule. Another showed figures representing Germany, England, the United States and France (the four powers behind the railway loan) seated at a table piled high with silver. Germany was saying, 'Let's open our mouths and gulp it down quickly. If we delay they may change their minds.' In front of the table were kneeling figures of four officials who had supported railway nationalisation, and written beneath them in large letters: 'Men of honour stand upon their feet. See these Chinese slaves abjectly prostrate worshipping the foreigner.'[5] Rumours suggested that the foreign powers had held a secret meeting in Paris to decide on the division of China. The posters and rumours in Sichuan reflected a widely shared fear of the foreign powers. This fear was tied to dislike of the Qing reforms, but was not necessarily anti-dynastic. Many people noticed that the streets of Sichuan at this time were pasted with slips of paper in front of which candles or incense were burning. The slips were printed to resemble an ancestral tablet dedicated to the late Guangxu emperor with a couple of sentences recalling his edicts in support of the provincial railway. People who honoured the Guangxu emperor with candles and incense showed that their grievances related to government policy rather than to the dynasty as such.

When the revolution broke out the form it took in Sichuan was explicitly anti-Western. The British consul described some of the leaders of the secret societies and other local groups who had thronged into the city after the declaration of independence from the Qing:

The picturesque appearance of these fantastically dressed braves and bandits, who crowded the principal thoroughfares, was heightened by the new style of dressing the hair in a top-knot adorned with silver ornaments; this coiffure was adopted in opposition to the queue cutting movement, the underlying idea being that while the wearers are no longer slaves of the Manchus, they have no desire to ape the foreigner by cutting off their hair.[6]

The new revolutionary governor promoted queue cutting and the unbinding of women's feet as well as other Western-influenced symbols such as the use of the solar calendar. This led to rumours that he had converted to Christianity and would ban people from worshipping at their household shrines. The governor was forced to issue an announcement claiming that queue cutting had nothing to do with the foreigners and he would not abolish sacrifices and incense. Again he explained that queues were a Manchu not a Chinese custom, but then called on people to wear their hair short rather than in the fashions of the Ming because short hair was now worn in the rest of the world. Less than a year later a Red Lantern sect uprising in Sichuan's second city, Chongqing, aimed to restore the Manchus and kill all foreigners and queueless Chinese.

Objections to short hair as a foreign custom were not limited to Sichuan. In Guilin in Guangxi province the revolutionaries who cut their hair were called 'monk heads'. There too many men adopted hairstyles drawn from local operatic depictions of the Ming dynasty and several men without queues were killed. Although for the revolutionaries the queue was seen as a symbol of racial subservience, for many people around the country cutting the queue and wearing short hair was a symbol of capitulation to the foreigners. These people resisted the Qing because of the unpopularity of the reforms. Their voices have been almost entirely lost to historians, most of whose sources were written by the revolutionaries. However, the popularity of hairstyles drawn from operatic depictions of the Ming suggests an alternative perception of the new state that was to replace the Qing as a revival of the Ming dynasty and the reaffirmation of native as opposed to foreign-influenced practices.

The linking of Han identity with modernity

The many ordinary people who supported the 1911 Revolution because they thought it would bring about a nativist state and an end to westernising policies were already out of touch with the views of the revolutionary leaders. For most of the revolutionaries the state that was to be constructed was a state that was both modern and dominated by the Han race. The great symbol of this new state was Sun Yatsen, who was appointed to be the first president of the new republic.

Sun Yatsen was in America when the Wuchang Uprising broke out and travelled on to Europe to try and encourage the European governments to support the new republic. Meanwhile in China negotiations were going on between the different revolutionary groups as to who was to lead the new state. The revolutionaries realised that much power still lay in the north, where several provinces still supported the Qing. There was considerable dispute among the different revolutionary groups since none of the hitherto more influential revolutionary leaders had actually been involved in events at Wuchang. Eventually they agreed to appoint Sun Yatsen as provisional president with Huang Xing, who had been a leader of radical student groups in Japan, as his deputy. Sun Yatsen was an attractive compromise because his political weakness meant that he would have little power to resist if others chose to force him out of the presidency. Having lived abroad for many years, he lacked a sufficiently influential power structure within the country. However, his Western education and long years of campaigning against the Manchu government made him the perfect symbol of the revolution as being both modern and racially Han.

Sun's inauguration was held in Nanjing, now declared the capital of the new republic, since Beijing was still in the hands of the Qing government. It took place on 1 January 1911 and the new government announced that henceforth the solar calendar would be adopted, making this the first day of the First Year of the Republic. The adoption of the solar calendar and this new year name later had the effect of making Sun's inauguration seem to be far more important than it appeared at the time. For it was clear then that the balance of power lay in the north. Yuan Shikai, the founder of the New Armies that had started the revolution, was still a Qing official and used the uprising to strengthen his own power over the dynasty. He sent part of his forces against the revolutionaries and eventually forced both the revolutionaries and the court into a compromise that was only partly acceptable to either: the emperor, still only a child, would abdicate and Sun Yatsen would resign from the presidency. Yuan Shikai himself would then bring the northern provinces and the rest of the Qing army over to the revolution. The price the revolutionaries were to pay was the acceptance of Yuan Shikai as the new president.

Shortly before his resignation Sun Yatsen took part in a sacrifice at the tomb of the first Ming emperor just outside Nanjing. The Ming had been the last native dynasty and the newspapers reported Sun's racial feeling with approval. A portrait of the Ming emperor was hung in the ruined halls of the tomb complex and offerings were set in front of it. As Sun Yatsen approached the portrait it was announced that the president of the Chinese republic had come to pay his respects to the great founder of the Chinese dynasty. Sun then made a speech that began with the words, '267 years after the fall of the Ming, the Republic of China has been established.'[7] In the speech he told a story of constant resistance by the Han people against the

Qing from the Taiping rebellion and the early revolutionaries (with a strong emphasis on the uprisings in which he himself had been involved) to the successful Wuchang Uprising. After the ceremony Sun was photographed alongside the portrait of the Ming emperor. Just as he had done at his inauguration, Sun Yatsen attempted to place himself and his own role at the centre of a historical narrative that had yet to be written. In doing so he placed the story of the battle between Manchu and Han races at the heart of the new republic. This view of China as a Han nation state has persisted at a popular level, despite considerable conflict with later official representations of the state.

National identity and the non-Han peoples

In many parts of the Qing empire the Han symbolism of the revolution was disturbing for large sections of the population. In some areas, especially in south China, Han identity was an important source of prestige and power in local politics, and the Han effectively constituted an elite class. To non-Han people in these places the rhetoric of 1911, with its emphasis on the rise of a racially defined Han people, was very threatening. In other areas violence and fighting between different communities was already frequent. This was especially true in the northwest, where Han villages were scattered among Muslim communities of various different types and in close proximity to the powerful alternative cultures of Tibet and Mongolia. Here too the perception of a rise in Han power ran the risk of increasing existing tensions.

For the non-Han peoples one of the most obvious signs of the Han affiliation of the revolution was the constant use of the character Han on revolutionary flags and banners. In Wuchang at the time of the uprising processions marched round the city headed by banners inscribed with the single word 'Han'. This was widely reported in the newspapers. In Sichuan a flag was widely used which was white with the word 'Han' written on it in red, surrounded by a black ring and 18 stars. In his memoirs, the author Ba Jin remembers his father making one of these for their household by printing a circle on a piece of white cloth using the edge of a bowl dipped in ink, and then writing in the character 'Han'. In Guiyang, in the autumn of 1911, it was reported that banners saying 'Revolution of the Great Han' flew from every home. Both Sichuan and Guiyang were areas with large non-Han minorities. In Yunnan, another similar area, people remember that the Muslim minority were afraid when they saw such flags.

Queue cutting, which was problematic for many people, was particularly so for non-Han. A radical activist from Inner Mongolia who studied at a special modern school for Mongols remembered how many of his classmates were beaten by the elders of their villages when they returned home after cutting off their queues at the school. Others wore false queues attached to their hats for their visits home. After 1912 the police frequently reported difficulties in enforcing regulations requiring queue cutting in non-Han districts. In Chengde, a city north of the great wall with large Mongol and Manchu populations, it was reported in 1914 that people were wearing their hair in all kinds of styles to avoid cutting their queues. The styles included bunches called 'cow and sheep horns' and plaits pinned to the top of the head ('turtle shell'), but also such modern-sounding fashions as three plaits to represent the three separate powers of the constitution or five plaits, known as 'the five-nation republic'. In 1914 the police conducted a survey in Beijing prior to a campaign to get men to cut their queues: they found that the numbers of men still wearing queues varied from 92 per cent in one district to 39 per cent in another. The district where 92 per cent were still wearing their queues was in the area around the former imperial palace inhabited mainly by Manchus, while the lowest proportion of queues came from an area that was predominantly Han.

However, not all Manchus refused to cut their queues. In some areas where the Manchus were in a minority and there was already a high degree of acculturation, many Manchus cut off their queues and assimilated, vanishing from the record as a separate ethnic group. Given the violent anti-Manchu rhetoric of 1911 and the stories of massacres of Manchu communities, especially in the northwest, this was not surprising. The extent of the fear is revealed by recorded statistics of Manchus resident in Taiyuan, the capital of Shanxi province. Before the revolution in 1911 there were between 2,500 and 3,000 registered Manchus in Taiyuan. By 1953 this had dropped to 451. Although some of these changes are due to population movements it is also clear that some people whose families continued to remember a sense of Manchu identity registered as Han in the years after 1911. The process by which this happened is suggested by the story of the author Xiao Qian, who was a Mongol. Xiao Qian was born in 1910 and grew up in Beijing. From his childhood he knew that his father, who died before his birth, had been a Mongol, because the family had an ancestral shrine with a carved figure of a herdsman and a genealogy in Mongol script. But at school Xiao Qian quickly observed that his Muslim classmates were chased and bullied, and even boys with southern accents were called 'barbarian'. So he filled in his ethnicity as Han on all official forms until 1956 when he was accused of being a rightist and had to think of crimes to confess. After that he wrote 'Mongol', but much later in his autobiography he commented that he still felt that it was truer to call him a Han. Xiao Qian's story shows how easy it was for the highly assimilated Manchu and Mongol communities living in the predominantly Han parts of China to shift to a Han identity. It also suggests some of the forces that pulled them towards this.

Han ethnicity and the collapse of the Qing empire:
Xinjiang, Mongolia and Tibet

Thus within the provinces of China proper members of some highly acculturated non-Han communities were assimilating rapidly with the Han Chinese. However, for Manchuria, Mongolia, Xinjiang and Tibet, the non-Han dependencies of the Qing empire, quite different pressures were active. Qing policy towards these areas had emphasised the separation of their communities from those of the Han, with bans on immigration, intermarriage and even the learning of the Chinese language. In practice, the effectiveness of these policies depended on geographical and economic factors. The increasing cultivation of the soya bean in Manchuria from the eighteenth century had meant that the government was unable to prevent large-scale immigration by Chinese farmers, mostly from Shandong province. By 1911 only a small proportion of the population of Manchuria was non-Han. Thus although Manchuria remained loyal to the Qing until the abdication of the emperor, the process of the 1911 revolution there was not significantly different from that of much of north China. The same was true of Xinjiang, which did not have such a large Han population. By the late nineteenth century the rise of Han power in the central bureaucracy and the need to make the province financially self-sustaining had resulted in assimilationist policies being adopted. Han Chinese were encouraged to settle. An increasing proportion of the territory was governed through the regular Chinese bureaucracy and Chinese education was promoted. In 1911 ethnic fighting broke out as a result of the revolution but ultimate control over the province went to a Han Chinese army officer, Yang Zengxin.

In Mongolia and Tibet, however, the immediate effects of the revolution were very different. Visitors to northern Mongolia in the late nineteenth and early twentieth centuries were invariably struck by the terrible poverty they saw. Historical accounts record the problems caused by the huge debts owed by many Mongol banners to Chinese bankers and traders, and the frequent brawls between Chinese merchants and groups of Mongols. These problems were exacerbated by the ending of salaries from the Qing government to the banner princes when the Qing state began to run short of money after the Taiping Rebellion. At the same time an ever-larger proportion of taxes was being collected in silver rather than in kind. The result of this, in an economy based on annual sales of animals, was the increase of debts to Chinese shops and moneylenders. Some of these debts were owed by individuals, but banner princes also borrowed money and then passed the debts on to their banners, leaving many rural communities in a state of chronic indebtedness. By the 1900s northern Mongolia was already suffering from a serious breakdown of social order that resulted in widespread destitution and banditry. The problems of the people of northern Mongolia were increased by the Qing reforms, which reached Mongolia in 1909. Having

seen the gradual removal of its tributary states, the Qing was determined to
tie its non-Han dependencies more closely to the centre and to strengthen
the border with Russia. This meant a stronger administrative framework:
the idea of dividing Mongolia into provinces was suggested but never put
into action. However, as had happened in Xinjiang, other policies were put
in place that would diminish the territory's separation from the rest of the
Qing empire. The ban on intermarriage between Chinese, Manchus and
Mongols was lifted; Mongols were permitted, and even encouraged, to
study Chinese; and colonisation by Han farmers was encouraged. It was
evident to the Mongolian elite that these policies would change both the
ecology and the social structure of the region. In 1910 members of the
Mongolian elite sent a mission to the Russian court. The aim of the mission
was to solicit Russian support for opposition to the reforms and especially
to oppose the training of soldiers, the establishment of a school, the conversion of land use from herding to agriculture and, above all, the increased
taxes.

In this situation the Wuchang Uprising and the declarations of independence by the Chinese provinces that followed provided a welcome
opportunity for the Mongolian elite. In the autumn of 1911, well before the
Qing abdication, which did not take place till February 1912, the
Jebtsundamba Khutuktu, the most powerful Mongol incarnation, was
enthroned as emperor of a new Mongol state. The new state was justified in
terms of the rejection of the Manchu dynasty by the Han. The following is
part of the declaration made at the time of the enthronement:

> Originally Mongolia was not part of China, but because it followed
> the Qing royal house from the first day, it owes that house a great
> debt. Mongolia has absolutely no connection at all with China.
> Consequently, today when the Qing court has been destroyed,
> Mongolia has no natural connection with China and should be inde-
> pendent.[8]

The emphatic nature of this statement is more apparent when we realise that
the Mongolian language had no term for China that included Mongolia,
Tibet and Manchuria. The term for China, '*kitad*', referred not to the whole
territory of the Qing empire, but to the home of the Han people. From the
first, Han Chinese were aware of developments in Mongolia and their implications for the new Republic of China. Chinese newspaper reports of the
enthronement of the Jebtsundamba Khutuktu emphasise the symbols
through which the Mongols claimed independence from the Chinese state.
These included a new Mongolian flag to be flown by Han as well as
Mongols on ceremonial occasions. There were also rules about costume:
officials were to wear Western styles, but ordinary people should wear
Mongol styles. According to Chinese newspaper reports, Chinese styles
were not permitted and the shops selling them were to be closed down.

Although the heart of the new Mongol state was Urga in northern

Mongolia, its existence threatened Chinese control over areas of Inner Mongolia, where several banners applied to join the new state. The leaders of one Inner Mongolian banner that applied to join the new state in the autumn of 1912 explained their reasoning as follows:

> Since the 29th year of the Guangxu emperor [1903], the Chinese farmers have occupied most of our native land. The newly established government of President Yuan Shikai has replaced our military standard with a five-coloured standard. Because the Chinese government ordered the Mongols to cut off their pigtails and change the tops of the hats of their high-ranking officials, in addition to the fact that we have been intermingling with the Chinese farmers, we, the Mongols of Tsakhar tribe, have distorted our real character and identity. Oppressed by these harsh conditions, 2,248 people in 496 households of our one banner would like to submit to you.[9]

Here symbolic changes such as the adoption of a new national flag and the queue-cutting edicts are combined with social problems caused by Han immigration to create a sense of the threat to the banner's Mongol identity. In practice, despite such applications from banners further south, Mongolian independence was limited to northern Mongolia. This was due to the delicate balance of the Russian and Japanese spheres of influence in the area. Northern Mongolia was recognised as part of the Russian sphere, whereas southern Mongolia was part of the Japanese sphere of influence centred in Manchuria. Neither Russia nor Japan was willing at this time to unsettle these boundaries, and thus neither could interfere too actively in the affairs of the new Mongolian state and its relationship with Beijing.

Foreign spheres of influence were also an influential factor in the situation in Tibet. Here the powers involved were Russia and Britain, which feared the establishment of Tibet as a Russian protectorate on the border of its Indian empire. Matters were complicated by the fact that the British administration in India pursued a much more aggressive policy towards Tibet than the Foreign Office in London was prepared to back up in its diplomatic dealings with China. In 1904 the British administration in India actually initiated a military expedition, led by Francis Younghusband, in which British troops entered Lhasa. The Dalai Lama fled to Mongolia and the British troops forced members of the Tibetan government to sign a treaty making Tibet a British protectorate. However, the lack of the agreement of either the Dalai Lama or the Chinese government invalidated this treaty and it was rejected by London. Then in 1908 the Qing reforms began to affect Tibet. The Manchu governor in Lhasa set about establishing a new army, schools and a military academy, and promoting changes in agricultural practices. As in Mongolia, these policies were unpopular. Then in 1910 and 1911 the Qing general Zhao Erfeng conducted a successful military campaign to enforce the submission of the remote and inaccessible area of eastern Tibet. This too was accompanied by reforms ranging from the abolition of corvée labour and the establishment of inns to the introduction of school officials, and modern mining and tanning companies. This time the Dalai Lama fled to India as the Chinese forces advanced.

However, the successful advance of the Qing forces was ended by the revolution of 1911 and General Zhao Erfeng, who was famous for his brutality and unpopular with his subordinates, was beheaded in eastern Tibet. In Lhasa the Chinese garrison deposed the Manchu governor and there was fighting in which Tibetans were involved on both sides. Eventually a truce was arranged and all the Chinese soldiers left via India. By this time the Dalai Lama had returned and in 1913 he declared Tibet to be independent. His government then embarked on its own modernising reforms, employing Japanese and British advisors, reforming the penal system, introducing salaries for officials and creating a new army. Meanwhile the British government continued its diplomatic attempts to make Tibet a British protectorate and to prevent Russian influence.

The five-nation republic

Han Chinese nationalism had been in large part inspired by opposition to the loss of the territories that had been in some way dependent on the Qing empire. This nationalism had led to the antipathy between Manchu and Han that made the new republic so alarming to the non-Han areas of that empire. The news of Mongolia's declaration of independence so soon after the Wuchang Uprising brought home to the revolutionary leaders the problematic nature of this racial nationalism. By the time of Sun Yatsen's inauguration republican leaders were already speaking of a five-nation republic of Han, Manchu, Mongol, Tibetan and Muslim. The formula was supposed to distinguish the revolutionary leaders' fraternal feelings towards Manchus, Mongols, Tibetans and Muslims as members of the new republic from their oft-repeated hatred for the Manchu rulers. The importance of the former Qing dependencies is obvious from the fact that the non-Han peoples of southern China are entirely ignored by this formulation.

The idea of China as a five-nation republic was spread in part through the new five-colour national flag that was adopted in 1912. The flag is depicted in the centre of Fig. 5.1. (The characters on it give the colours of the stripes.) An examination of its adoption shows how ideas about the new republic were shifting at this point. In most areas of the country the flags used at the time of the revolution itself had just been white cloths, symbolising the cleansing of the government. These had soon been replaced by the banners bearing the character 'Han', which were so obviously problematic for the non-Han peoples. If China was to be a Han state, as these flags and many of the revolutionaries so blatantly claimed, then other races were by definition excluded. However there were also other flags, which had been designed by various revolutionary groups to represent their aspirations for

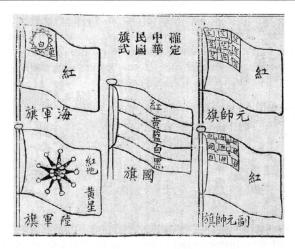

Figure 5.1 Flags of the Republic of China
Source: *Shenbao*, 8 December 1911, p. 14.

the new republic. One of these flags, which had been used by the revolutionaries in Wuchang, became particularly widespread during 1911 and was put forward as a possible national flag in 1912. It is seen in the bottom left corner of Fig. 5.1 and consisted of 18 black stars arranged in a large star shape on a red ground. The Hubei revolutionary who designed the flag claimed that the stars represented the revolutionary groups affiliated with his own, but in practice the stars were interpreted as representing the 18 provinces. This interpretation was strengthened by the fact that the words 'province' (*sheng*) and 'star' (*xing*) sound the same in many Chinese dialects. However, as many people pointed out in the National Assembly debate over which flag should be adopted, the 18 provinces were the provinces of China proper and excluded Manchuria, Xinjiang, Mongolia, Tibet and Qinghai. The idea of this flag as representing the revolutionaries' aim of Han dominance is also suggested by the fact that it was used in Sichuan province with the character 'Han' written in the central circle of stars.

The five-colour flag that was finally adopted was first used by the revolutionaries in Shanghai, where it was compared with the French and Russian tricolours. As this suggests, it was seen as being very obviously modern and Western. Indeed, in Sichuan there were objections that the foreign design implied that the country was going to be handed over to the foreign powers. The flag was adopted as a national flag after a debate in the National Assembly at which it was agreed that the five colours represented the five races of the republic (as well as the five colours and five constant virtues of Confucianism) and thus the flag represented the spirit of the country. One newspaper at the time explained that the colours referred to areas: red stood for China, yellow for Manchuria, blue for Mongolia, white for the north-

west and black for Siberia. But this report also notes that students say that
the colours refer not to areas but to races: red to the Han, yellow the
Manchus, blue the Mongols, white the Muslims and black the Tibetans. The
idea of the colours representing races was reinforced through patriotic songs
published in textbooks:

> Look, look at the national flag shining in the air;
> The five bright colours have shaken East Asia.
> Look, look at the national flag divided into colours;
> Red, yellow, blue, white and black
> Represent our Han, Manchu, Mongol, Hui and Tibetan.
> May we make innumerable Five Colour Flags,
> Their rays shining everywhere.[10]

Despite the apparent equality between the races suggested by this formulation, considerable emphasis was placed on getting the colours the right way
round with the red stripe representing the Han at the top of the flag. In
Shanghai the Chamber of Commerce complained about shops whose flags
had the stripes in the wrong order. A physical-exercise textbook published
in 1922 even instructed the teacher to make sure that the flag was folded
and put away with the red stripe at the top.

As well as being referred to in the national flag, which became a regular
feature of many celebrations, the five races were also mentioned in the
national anthem that was selected in 1915. This ran:

> China stands strong in the universe
> And expands in all directions.
> The people of China come from the Kunlun Peaks.
> The rivers, streams and huge mountains never end.
> The five races of the Republic began in the days of Yao.
> A hundred thousand ten thousand years![11]

This anthem was commonly enough sung in schools for men writing in the
1970s to remember it. It is noticeable that it puts the new idea of China as
consisting of five races back into the mists of ancient history with the refer-
ence to the mythical emperor Yao.

It was typical of Yuan Shikai to push through the adoption of a national
flag and anthem that replaced images of Han domination with those of the
five-nation republic. Yuan Shikai's inauguration was unlike that of Li
Yuanhong, whose ceremonies had centred on the Yellow Emperor, and of
Sun Yatsen, who had used the language of five nations but nevertheless
maintained a structure and formalities that were exclusively Han and
modern. Yuan Shikai, who despite his recent poor relations with the court
had long been a high official in the Manchu government, did not have any
great antipathy towards the Manchus as a race. He was also heavily
involved in the world of power politics and diplomacy and thus concerned
with the threat the revolution posed to the unity of the Qing empire. His

inauguration as president in the spring of 1912 was meant to provide an image of the new republic that would help repair the damage done by the 1911 Revolution. He therefore played down the Han elements of the republic and emphasised its modernity. The date was no longer given from the birth of the Yellow Emperor, but from the beginning of the republic and according to the Western solar calendar. Foreign dignitaries were invited and although several did not attend because their governments had not yet recognised the new state, their presence was nevertheless recorded in reports of the event. Lists of participants included not only representatives of the 18 provinces of China, as at Sun Yatsen's inauguration, but also the generals of the Manchu, Mongol and Han banners of the former Qing army and representatives of the Manchu, Mongol, Hui and Tibetan gentry. Most participants wore uniform or Western suits and among these the yellow robes of the Mongolian and Tibetan lamas who took part were strikingly visible. During the course of the ceremony the lamas presented strips of cloth, a traditional central Asian gift of welcome, to the new president. The oath Yuan Shikai swore reflected this emphasis on the republic as modern rather than Han:

> Since the Republic has been established, many works now have to be performed. I shall endeavour faithfully to develop the Republic, to sweep away the disadvantages attached to absolute monarchy, to observe the laws of the constitution, to increase the welfare of the country, to cement together a strong nation, which shall embrace all five races. When the National Assembly elects a permanent President, I shall retire. This I swear before the Chinese Republic.[12]

This new presentation of the modern republic had a great impact on the way the nation was understood, especially by governing elites. Initially the impact was felt in two areas, firstly in the kinds of relations republican governments tried to conduct with Mongolia and Tibet, and secondly in the government's attitude towards traditional Han culture. Mongolia and Tibet were now represented in the government in Beijing, with, for example, seats in the National Assembly for their delegates. On the first anniversary of the Wuchang Uprising it was even reported that a Tibetan incarnation and lamas had taken part in a ceremony for revolutionary martyrs in Beijing. At the same time there was an attempt to reassure the Mongolians and Tibetans that they would maintain the autonomy that they had had under the Qing, and would not be drawn into the system of Chinese provinces as the Qing reforms had threatened. To make this point there was separate legislation even for their activities in Beijing: special laws decreed the formal costume and etiquette appropriate for Mongol, Hui and Tibetan princes. For example, the rules covering a meeting between Mongol, Hui and Tibetan leaders and the president specified a bow to the president, which the president would then return, thus preserving a degree of equality, though the president had the right to sit down first. The Jebtsundamba Khutuktu was to be allowed to wear his religious robes and was to bow three times and present a strip of cloth in the Central Asian style. The fact that the National Assembly felt it necessary to enact such laws suggests that the republican state was attempting to create a self-image that could include the non-Han Qing dependencies.

The Han Chinese elite also attempted to promote changes in customs in the non-Han areas that would link them symbolically to the new state. So when the Astronomical Bureau in Beijing issued a new calendar in Beijing, the Shanghai newspaper the *Shenbao* urged the government to make sure it was spread to Mongolia and Tibet, 'to illustrate the unification of the central government's commands'.[13] Similarly, Han officials applied for rewards for banner leaders who promoted queue cutting among the Mongol tribes. And when the governor of Suiyuan mobilised a group of Mongol leaders from his area to travel to Beijing to read a letter of congratulation to Yuan Shikai, he was delighted to find the delegation rewarded with titles and gifts and escorted to Beijing station by a military band. When representatives of the Chinese, Russian and Mongolian governments met in 1914 to discuss the status of Mongolia, the Chinese government were particularly concerned with symbolic changes, demanding that the Mongols stop using the terms 'emperor' (*huangdi*) and 'country' (*guo*) and give up the use of a separate reign title to date years. Thus Mongolia and Tibet were symbolically incorporated into the new republican state, even as they were moving beyond its control.

Today, Tibet and Inner Mongolia are part of the People's Republic of China, while northern or outer Mongolia is an independent state. The difference is not related to the sense of identity of either the Mongols or the Tibetans, both of whom might plausibly be called historical nations which had been incorporated within the Qing empire. Nor is it related to the attitudes or sense of identity of the Han Chinese, who had grown to regard both territories as part of a Chinese state. Instead the difference of status is the result of great-power politics during the period between the fall of the Qing and the establishment of a strong central government in China in 1949. In 1919 northern Mongolia was invaded by Chinese warlord forces. These were then driven out by White Russian forces coming in from the north. The White Russians in their turn were defeated by Soviet Russian troops who re-established the former constitutional monarchy of the Jebtsundamba Khutuktu in 1921. From this time onwards, Soviet troops were stationed in northern Mongolia and the country was largely dominated by the USSR. In Tibet, British diplomatic intervention continued to play a role in the western part of the country round Lhasa. However the primary British concern continued to be with the Russian threat to India, rather than with the degree of central Chinese authority. Meanwhile eastern Tibet fought against control by either Lhasa or Beijing. British imperial manoeuvring in Asia may have prevented the feared establishment of a Tibetan state controlled by Russia, but the decline of the British empire left the way open for a reassertion of Chinese authority at a later date.

Conclusion

During the revolution of 1911 the tension that had previously existed between Han culturalism and the Manchu empire was transformed into one of the features of the modern Chinese state. The revolution was driven by a Han Chinese nationalism that asserted the importance of racial and cultural differences between Han and Manchus. It was inevitable that the image of the new republican state produced by such an ideology would exclude the non-Han parts of the Qing empire. However, lying behind Han Chinese nationalism was the battle against the foreign powers and a determination to maintain the borders of the Chinese state, that is to say the Qing empire. The conflict between these two aspects of nationalism has lain at the heart of modern Chinese nationalism ever since. The events of 1911 and 1912 also hint at the new link between Han Chinese identity and modernity that was to be central to the new state's efforts to impose a unified nationalist ideology. It is to that link that the next chapter turns.

Notes

1 *Minlibao*, 25 October 1911.
2 Hu Shian, *Geming shijian* (True Sights of the Revolution) (Wuchang: Da Han chubanshe, 1912), p. 45.
3 Liu Dapeng, *Tuixiangzhai riji*, p. 169.
4 *Dagongbao*, 21 May 1912, p. 3.1a.
5 *North China Herald*, 9 September 1911, p. 635.
6 Public Record Office, London, FO 228/1838, Chengtu 2/12.
7 Sun Zhongshan, *Sun Zhongshan quanji* (Complete Works of Sun Yatsen) (Beijing: Zhonghua shuju, 1982), p. 95.
8 Translation adapted from Urgunge Onon and Derrick Pritchatt, *Asia's First Modern Revolution: Mongolia Proclaims its Independence in 1911* (Leiden: E.J. Brill, 1989), p. 40.
9 Quoted ibid., p. 37.
10 Hua Hangchen, *Xin jiaoyu changge ji* (Collected Songs for New Education) (Shanghai: Shangwu yinshuguan, 1914), p. 24.
11 Zhou Kaiqing, *Xingzhi ji* (Collected Essays on Doing and Knowing) (Taibei: Changlin banyuekan she, 1975) p. 83.
12 *North China Herald*, 16 March 1912.
13 *Shenbao*, 23 April 1912, p. 2.

6

Nation, modernity and class

The 1910s and 1920s saw rising nationalism and changing ideas of the nation, but this took place alongside the breakdown of unified government. In practice, after 1916 the government in Beijing had little control over the Chinese provinces, let alone northern Mongolia and Tibet. The centralised state the republic had inherited from the Qing dynasty began to disintegrate into competing regional blocs. Yuan Shikai had been able to hold the provinces together because of the strong personal relationships he had created when he was building the new army under the Qing. After his death in 1916 the weakness of the Beijing government was exacerbated by the corruption of its primary representative and legislative body, the National Assembly. Electoral politics and the open espousal of parties were morally problematic for old-fashioned Confucians who believed in an appointed meritocracy. The open corruption of the members of the National Assembly, who seemed willing to sell the presidency to the highest bidder, did nothing to alleviate such worries. Although the Beijing government continued to be recognised by the foreign powers, at home it gradually lost all claim to legitimacy. And as Beijing's authority declined, real power shifted to the rulers of the provinces. These were mostly men who had risen to power during the 1911 Revolution and who had gained control of the province's armed forces. They subsequently came to be known as warlords, a term that was first used against them in campaigns for the reestablishment of a single national government and can be misleading; several had reputations as modernisers or even radicals. Meanwhile large parts of China's major cities, including Shanghai, Hong Kong, Tianjin and Wuhan, were controlled by foreign colonial powers. Warlord rule, colonial power and a powerless central government set the context for the development of nationalism.

In this time of political disorder, new images of the nation were created by ordinary people and the ways in which they defined themselves as citizens of the new republic. The idea of the new state as a five-nation republic played an important part in the creation of these images since Han dominance of the new republic now came to be legitimised by the idea that the Han were more modern than the other races. Finding legitimacy for Han rule in modernity came naturally to the revolutionaries. A Tianjin news-paper explained the reasons for this:

> Many of the giants of the revolution have been abroad, and become accustomed to straw boaters, leather shoes, and woollen and down clothes. The people who most like to use foreign goods are invariably the politicians, who all copy each other, and who think that if they don't do this they won't be able to stand beside the modern men.[1]

Indeed, in 1912 westernising modernity was highly fashionable and reached beyond the revolutionaries and politicians. The same article complains that anyone who can afford it has bought a Western suit of clothes and those who cannot are buying imported straw boaters. A woman who wrote in her memoirs about her wedding in Anhui in 1912 remembered that she had had a trousseau entirely in 'Han dynasty' styles (which were a source of huge curiosity to onlookers and were never used again) while her husband wore a Western-style suit.

These kinds of ideas lay behind the adoption in 1912 of Western styles as formal dress for Chinese. Fig. 6.1 is taken from the government's own regulations for costume. While the full formal dress and the first type of regular formal dress are obviously entirely drawn from Western styles, the man shown in a traditional long gown and jacket is also wearing a bowler hat. Moreover this costume was often worn with Western-style leather shoes. The costumes were drawn from styles commonly worn immediately after the revolution, when, for example, a Hunan town decided that formal costume for officials should include felt hat, leather shoes and a short woollen jacket. Similarly, the Sichuan provincial government required its officials to doff their hats and bow, an action that was entirely alien to traditional modes of greeting. Like so many other aspects of nationalism, knowledge of these practices was spread by the modern schools. In 1917 a British official touring a remote part of Yunnan in search of opium growing was put up in part of the local temple which had been converted into a school and saw on the wall a print of ceremonial garments including top hats, bowler hats and frock coats.

Through new customs and practices, ranging from short hair for men to celebrating national holidays, people across the country presented them-selves as citizens. The choices they made when they did so affected how citizens were perceived and thus how the republic, literally the 'citizens' country' (*minguo*), was perceived. However the cost of presenting the Han as exemplars of modernity in the five-nation republic was that many aspects of Han culture were delegitimated. Thus the republic demanded the use of the solar calendar and the modern national holidays that went with it as a sign of legitimacy, but most people preferred to continue to use the lunar calendar and the old festivals. Attempts to discourage the celebration of the

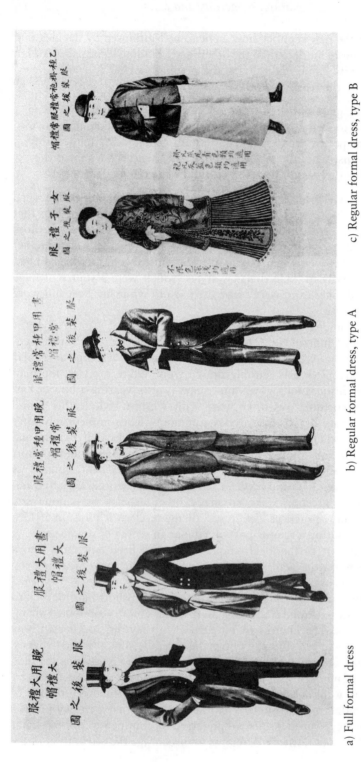

a) Full formal dress

b) Regular formal dress, type A

c) Regular formal dress, type B

Figure 6.1 Formal dress as specified by law in 1912.
Source: No 2 Archives, Nanjing

lunar new year were particularly unpopular (and unsuccessful). A British newspaper published in Shanghai commented of the solar calendar that, 'Only people with short hair and foreign hats really believe it effective.'[2] A Shanxi schoolteacher who kept a diary and intensely disliked the new government wrote that the fact that people continued to celebrate the festivals of the old calendar showed that they did not agree with the revolution, which he referred to as a rebellion. The elision of Han Chinese identity with Western-style modernity exacerbated the growing differences between popular and elite cultures and senses of identity.

Clothing and etiquette

In 1912 Western clothes were the height of fashion and had been declared by the government to be official formal dress for the country. Photographs of the National Assembly taken that year show rows of men in greatcoats and felt hats. One of the results of this official enthusiasm was that Western dress came to be considered the appropriate dress for formal public occasions. So, for example, many people thought it appropriate to wear Western dress to enter a government office. Textbooks published after 1912 show teachers no longer in long gowns but in Western suits and ties, while the pupils now all wear trousers and short jackets. In Fig. 6.2, which shows a teacher and pupils engaged in the distinctively republican activity of bowing to the national flag, both pupils and teacher wear Western-style jackets and trousers.

Figure 6.2 'The teacher leads us in making a bow to the national flag'
Source: Shanxi guomin jiaokeshu bianji weiyuanhui, ed., *Guomin xuexiao tongsu guowen jiaokeshu* (Primary School General Chinese Textbook). Taiyuan: Jinxin shushe, 1924, vol. 4, p. 29

But in many places this Western costume still looked very strange. In one town in northern Jiangsu when the leader of a new troupe of actors performing the new spoken dramas arrived in the town wearing a Western suit and leather shoes and carrying a cane, all the children followed him. Similar astonishment at full Western dress is depicted in Lu Xun's famous satire on the 1911 Revolution, *The Story of Ah Q*, in which a character who assumes Western dress is described as a 'fake foreign devil'. After 1912 the fashion for full Western dress declined. Many officials wore jacket and gown, but with felt hat and sometimes leather shoes as seen in Fig. 6.3, an illustration taken from a textbook published in the 1920s in the rather conservative province of Shanxi. It accompanies a lesson on the Mid-Autumn Festival and shows a man and two boys standing in front of a table at which offerings have been set and admiring the moon. One of the boys is in military-style school uniform with a tightly buttoned jacket and peaked cap, thus identifying the family as one with an interest in modernity. The man may seem to be dressed in traditional Chinese costume, but is in fact wearing the combination of jacket, gown and felt hat that marked the modern citizen. The adoption of these elements of Western dress marked the larger group of those interested in modernisation, and the combination

Figure 6.3 'Looking at the moon in the Mid-Autumn Festival'
Source: Shanxi guomin jiaokeshu bianji weiyuanhui, ed., *Guomin xuexiao tongsu guowen jiaokeshu* (Primary School General Chinese Textbook). Taiyuan: Jinxin shushe, 1924, vol. 4, p. 12

eventually came to be seen as 'the accepted insignia of provincial officialdom'.[3] A columnist for the English-language *North China Herald*
noticed that in his town a soft felt hat and a large foreign cut overcoat
marked out a class of young men who had the time and the education to
take an interest in national affairs.

However, as the political order collapsed, the association of the jacket,
gown and hat with officialdom became more negative. For many years the
long gown and especially the jacket worn over it, which was seen as a
Manchu item, were unacceptable costume for members of radical groups.
Feng Yuxiang, a provincial leader with left-wing inclinations who was ambi-
tious of a national role in the 1920s, ensured that during this period neither
he nor his followers ever appeared in public in jacket and gown. Instead he
was photographed in the short padded jacket and trousers worn by his soldiers. For those who wished to present themselves as civilians the Zhongshan
suit provided the most acceptable alternative. The suit was named after Sun
Yatsen, whose trademark garment it was and who was subsequently said to
have invented it. (Zhongshan is the form of Sun Yatsen's name most commonly used in Chinese.) The textbook illustration (Fig. 6.4) shows a man
with a moustache, very much like Sun himself. At first the suit was usually
made of imported woollen cloth and the buttons, pockets and styling suggest Western influence. It was also clearly influenced by army uniforms and
the general enthusiasm for things military in the 1900s when it was first
worn. Despite its foreign style and fabric the Zhongshan suit was promoted
as being both Chinese and modern. It remained the dominant garment of
China's political elite, as is suggested to us by the fact that it is known in
English as the 'Mao suit'. Thus although the wearing of full Western dress
declined in the years after the 1911 Revolution, Western-influenced styles
continued to be an important part of the self-presentation of those who considered themselves to be the citizens of the new republic.

With the new costume went new ways of holding oneself or moving and
new manners. A new system of etiquette was legally decreed by the Beijing
government under Yuan Shikai. This replaced the great variety of different
greetings current under the Qing with a set of simple variations on doffing
the hat and bowing. Under the Qing when two men met possible greetings
ranged from a full kowtow (kneeling on the floor three times and knocking
the head on the ground three times each time one knelt – a show of respect
reserved for the emperor) to a simple raising of the joined hands. These
different greetings showed different status relationships between the two
people. Republican etiquette drew on contemporary Western manners to be
more egalitarian. The new Western style of bow with the arms at the sides
was introduced (*see* Fig. 5.3), and the most elaborate formality, for example
on meeting the president, was merely to remove one's hat and bow three
times. In practice on many occasions, such as funerals or expressing one's
respects to one's parents, people felt that just bowing was insufficient. A
Hangzhou headmaster, who was later to lose his job because of his radical

Figure 6.4 'This is a perfect kind of clothing'
Source: Jiang Jinfu, *Xin Zhonghua shehui keben* (New China Textbook on
Society). Shanghai: Zhonghua shuju, 1927

ideas, wrote a letter home to his brother in 1918 in which he asked his
brother to kowtow to their parents on his behalf. Different etiquette was
also appropriate to different occasions. A Manchu woman who grew up in
Beijing remembered being taught by her parents to perform old-fashioned
forms of greeting to some of her parents' friends, but to bow in the modern
style to modern Han Chinese. The use of the bow for official occasions and
among people with modernising ideas created both a feeling of equality and
a sense of community. A much stronger sense of community was created by
the handshake. Grasping one's friend's hand had previously been a gesture
of intimacy and affection. Now the introduction of handshaking in the
Western style as a modern custom created a feeling of community among
those who practised it. This was a very limited group, as people continued
to feel that the handshake was a gesture appropriate for intimacy. Women
in China today still very seldom shake hands, and the custom only spread to

the countryside in the 1950s. Here again we see the way in which new customs considered appropriate for republican citizens worked to form a relatively exclusive group of members of the urban elite.

However, not only gestures changed; even the way people held themselves was altered by the 1911 Revolution. Even today in China people stand, sit, walk or gesture in styles different from those customary in Europe and America. These differences were much greater in the early twentieth century when they were also closely connected to the type of clothes people wore. In the nineteenth century elite men were supposed to walk or stand with their shoulders slightly bent looking at the ground. A woman who was a servant to an official family in the 1900s remembered how surprised her master was to find that her face was pockmarked from smallpox. She told the story to illustrate what a proper man he was, that she could live in his house for several months without him ever looking at her face. This slightly hunched, downward-looking posture can be seen in the teacher shown in Fig. 4.3. The emphasis from the 1900s on military drill, Western sports and the adoption of Western dress for men all worked to shift Chinese men towards the more upright outward-looking Western presentation. Fig. 6.5

Figure 6.5 The young Chiang Kaishek
Source: No 2 Archives

Time

People could also show that they considered themselves as citizens of the republic by the way they divided up time. Fixing a new calendar was traditionally the act of a new dynasty, and under the Qing there were severe penalties for privately published calendars. The Republican government had declared that the new state would follow the solar calendar in use in Western countries and that the years, which had previously been numbered according to the reign title of the emperor, would now be numbered from the beginning of the republic. Thus the fourth year of the Xuantong emperor (1911), calculated using the lunar calendar, would be followed by the first year of the republic (1912), calculated using the solar calendar. In practice people already used a variety of different calendars for different purposes and the solar calendar was added to these. So, for example, many farming activities and also the grave-sweeping festival Qingming were timed according to the phases of the solar year (though not according to the Western solar calendar). Other important festivals, such as New Year, the Dragon Boat Festival and the Mid-Autumn Festival (also the settlement dates for debts) were calculated according to the calendar of lunar months.

Now the Western solar calendar was added to this with its own cycle of festivals related to the new republic. At the beginning these consisted only of the solar New Year, the anniversary of the Wuchang Uprising, which was celebrated as National Day, and occasionally the anniversary of the date the revolution had begun in one's own province. Later other major political events were commemorated according to this new solar calendar. Thus 25 December, the date on which Sun Yatsen and his supporters launched an uprising against Yuan Shikai in 1914, was commemorated and is still celebrated as Constitution Day in Taiwan. The idea of a seven-day week with a

every family in the city celebrates it. For us not to do so would look sort of bad.'[6] The explanation suggests the extent to which participation in National Day activities was both an urban phenomenon (the sceptical grandfather is depicted as a countryman) and connected to higher status within the urban environment. This meant that National Day activities were sometimes used to lay claim to status and by groups who were often denied it. So, for example, one year Shanghai rickshaw pullers, who had not been invited to take part as a group in the major processions, decorated a mission hall with national flags and portraits of the president. When the newspapers describe who is taking part in these events they use the traditional division of society into scholars, farmers, artisans and merchants. However, they add various modern groups to this classification: the military, police or newspapermen. Until the 1920s farmers and artisans are seldom described as participating. In other words, the citizens of the republic who are representing the nation are the modern urban elite.

Women as citizens

Women occasionally took part in National Day ceremonies as a group. This was a radical departure from Qing views of women as being properly excluded from politics. The Empress Dowager Cixi, who was effectively the highest authority in the land for almost 40 years, nevertheless had to communicate with officials through a screen that marked her separation from them. By contrast, from the very beginning of the 1911 Revolution the participation of women in the creation of the republic was regarded as legitimate and proper. In 1911 some Shanghai women were recorded as having donated jewellery to the revolutionary cause at a public meeting. Similarly a set of memoirs about the Jiangsu town of Yangzhou records that one of the notable differences in local affairs after the revolution was that a woman, the headmistress of the local girls' school, publicly visited the local government buildings.

The ways in which women marked themselves as citizens of the new republic were, however, different from those of men. While men cut off their queues, women were supposed to have natural feet. One of the first acts of the military government that was set up in Wuchang immediately after the uprising in 1911 was to ban foot binding:

> Be it known that foot binding is a bad custom which is a barrier to women's health. The body is greatly harmed, and the connection of this with the race is no small one. Now the Republic has been founded and it is appropriate to reform all areas. Men all cut their queues, and women too should arise. How can the mothers of citizens follow without considering? We hereby order the unbinding of feet, let all obey.[7]

Initially bans like this had little effect. For women who already had bound feet unbinding was painful and few people expected this. Girls whose feet were in the process of being bound were at an age when they were usually sequestered from society and spent almost all their time within the family home. The slow response to the policy meant that government campaigns continued through the 1910s and 1920s. A folk song collected in Shanxi in the 1960s recalls memories of this period:

> Now the Republic has been around for five or six years,
> The provincial capital has sent down two commissioners,
> One tells people not to wear their queues,
> One tells people not to bind their feet,
> They post up a notice in the street.[8]

Campaigns like this one driven by the warlord Yan Xishan both pushed forward and reflected changes in customs that were already taking place. A Cantonese traveller to Shanxi in the 1920s was astonished to see so many women with bound feet, because in Guangdong the practice was already rare among the younger generation. Even in north China foot binding was rapidly diminishing. Observation of elderly women in China today suggests that few women born in the 1920s had their feet bound. This confirms a survey made in one north China county in 1929 where it was found that 99 per cent of the women born before 1890 had their feet bound. A slight drop took place for girls who grew up in the 1900s, but for those who reached the age of 7 in the years immediately following the 1911 revolution the figure was only 60 per cent and by the 1920s foot binding had completely vanished for young girls.

Natural feet were very much a marker of the modern woman and writers often note the noisy clattering of modern young women in their leather shoes. Like men, modern women were also marked by their new Western-influenced style of clothing. Fig. 6.6, which is taken from a set of pictures of beautiful women made in the 1920s, shows a very modern young woman speaking on the telephone while her maid leans over her. The maid wears a jacket and trousers, relatively conventional garb for young women. The mistress wears a modern jacket and skirt to go with the Western-style furniture and telephone. Like her maid she has bare wrists and ankles. Her costume is very different from traditional women's clothes which completely covered the body. Traditionally, skirts were the preserve of wealthy married women and were worn over trousers which ensured that the legs would be fully covered. For many people the new fashion of wearing a jacket and skirt without trousers beneath seemed shocking. However it was this costume that was the symbol of the modern woman. One young woman who ran away from home at the age of 15 in 1919 with the help of a radical magazine, remembered that her first act was to have a jacket and skirt made instead of her conventional jacket and trousers. Putting this on made her feel 'like a soldier putting on his uniform hastily

Figure 6.6 One of Du Yu's portraits of a hundred beauties
Source: Dan Duyu and Xu Zhiyan, *Duyu baimei tu xuji* (Duyu's Portraits
of a Hundred Beauties, 2nd collection). Shanghai: Xinmin tushuguan xiongdi
gongsi, 1923

before going into battle'.[9] A friend then helped her undo her long plaits and
pin her hair up in a bun, which was the style conventionally worn by
married women, and which she felt symbolised her struggle against conven-
tion. When she later attended a girls' school the school uniform was in
precisely this style: skirt and jacket, leather shoes and hair pinned up in a
bun. This costume, which was a symbol of political commitment as well as
modern style, identified the wearer as an active citizen of the republic.

As women moved towards greater involvement in public life they also
began to wear fashions that made them appear more like men. The first of
these was the man's long gown, first adapted by women in the early 1920s.
This garment (the *cheongsam* or *qipao*) initially reflected Western women's
fashions of the 1920s, which emphasised a simple shape and straight lines,
but was later influenced by changes in Western fashion and became increasingly fitted and feminine. Fig. 6.7 shows two young women dressed in

Figure 6.7 Kwong Sang Hong
advertising calendar, 1930

fashionable gowns as depicted on a 1930 calendar advertising cosmetics. Roundels at either side display the company's trademark: two girls dressed in the knee-length jackets and full trousers that were the appropriate garb of young women at an earlier date. The two women in the centre of the calendar, however, wear the latest fashions: their hair is permed, they have high heels and wear straight knee-length dresses with high collars and elbow-length sleeves. The fitted style of the new fashion is emphasised by the women's posture, which brings out the curve of the hips and the swelling of the breasts. However, when it was first worn in the 1920s the new gown was longer, was cut very straight and was seen as the adoption of men's dress by women.

A similar process occurred with women's hairstyles, again following both Western fashion and revolutionary commitment. During the Qing dynasty women had not usually cut their hair. Cutting the hair was not only seen, as for men, as causing damage to the body one had received from one's parents, but was also thought to be unlucky since it was associated with the barren fate of a shaven-headed Buddhist nun. However, during the 1920s many women, especially those who had been educated, did begin to cut their hair short. In this they were following contemporary Western fashions for bobbed hair, but also claiming revolutionary commitment and similarity with men who had cut off their queues during the revolution. The writer Ding Ling, who cut off her queue in 1919 along with many of her class-mates, remembered going home afterwards to an unsympathetic uncle and aunt. Her uncle merely snorted and said, 'Huh! You are good at playing, you've even lost your tail.' Her aunt however berated her with unfilial behaviour in harming the body she had received from her parents. Ding Ling then turned on her uncle and said, 'You lost your tail long ago. If you can, why can't I?'[10]

These changes in women's lives reversed the previous symbolism of status. Traditionally wealthy women had led lives largely restricted to the domestic sphere, while poor women who had to work for their living were out in the streets except in the short period between puberty and marriage. In Chengdu in the 1900s common women's occupations included collecting firewood, selling ornaments, telling fortunes and pulling teeth. Women peddlers were particularly common because only they could enter the women's quarters of upper-class homes. However this scenario was reversed in the great trading cities of the early twentieth century where women of the urban elite had natural feet and walked freely through the streets. A woman from an inland area who visited Hong Kong in the 1900s was astonished to see women going freely through the streets, whereas in her hometown only servants and working women could do that. With women as with men, the modern customs that marked out the republican citizens were by and large restricted to urban elites.

Conclusion

By wearing Western-style clothes, conducting themselves according to a new Western-influenced system of etiquette, using the solar calendar and accepting the political involvement of women, a new modernising elite marked themselves as citizens of the Chinese nation state. In many places, especially inland rural areas, the new customs were unpopular. In these places feelings of national identity had been expressed in the Boxer Uprising and the revolution of 1911 through antipathy to Western customs. In addi-tion, the republican political settlement had brought about the collapse of the central order alongside increases in taxation to fund modernising projects and the military build-up that accompanied the devolution of power to the provinces. It was not surprising that practices that redefined national identity, shifting it away from what was familiar and widely acceptable to modern and apparently un-Chinese forms, would be unpop-ular. Moreover, people could see that the new customs were part of the creation of an exclusive new modernising elite who held power at the expense of others. The new customs had come to define an exclusive community of modern citizens, composed largely of members of the urban elite. In their minds their modern customs made them representatives of the Chinese nation, and thus gave them the legitimacy to transform the nation in their image.

Notes

1 *Dagongbao*, 1 June 1912, p. 3.
2 *North China Herald*, 4 May 1912, p. 307.
3 PRO FO 228 /2008, Ichang 36/17 p. 8.
4 Jing Hengyi, *Jing Hengyi riji* (The Diary of Jing Hengyi) (Hangzhou: Zhejiang guji chubanshe, 1984), p. 1.
5 Chinese Second National Archives, Nanjing. 1001.5525.
6 *Shengjing shibao* (Shengjing Times), 10 October 1926.
7 Yan Changhong, *Zhongguo jindai shehui fengsu shi* (A History of Social Customs in Modern China) (Hangzhou: Zhejiang renmin chubanshe, 1992), p. 229.
8 *Zhongguo minjian gequ jicheng: Shanxi juan* (Chinese Folk Song Collection: Shanxi Volume) (Beijing: Renmin yinyue chubanshe, 1990), p. 787.
9 Chow Chung-cheng, *The Lotus Pool of Memory* (London: Michael Joseph, 1961), p. 149.
10 Ding Ling, *Wode tongsheng* (My Childhood) (Tianjin: Xinlei chubanshe, 1980), p. 77.

PART
III

NATIONALISM AND IMPERIALISM

|7|

The growth of nationalism as an ideology

By the 1920s features of modern nationalism, such as the wearing of Western-style clothing or the celebration of National Day, were status symbols for certain segments of the urban population. But even while the symbols of citizenship and modern nationalism had become the property of an urban elite, the lifestyles and attitudes that defined that elite were beginning to spread. The ideology of modern nationalism, which was part of this bundle of attitudes and practices, was also promoted by the expanding modern education system. In this chapter we will look at how the ideology of nationalism spread both among and beyond the urban elite and was ultimately institutionalised through the establishment of the Nationalist Party.

Looking back at the textbooks and reformist journalism of the 1900s, we find that calls for freedom and equality were invariably accompanied by an emphasis on patriotism as a virtue. Liang Qichao and others argued that feelings of nationalism were essential if a country was to survive in the bitter struggle between nations. Moreover, from the 1900s there had been demonstrations and protests that used the rhetoric of nationalism. The best known of these early nationalist movements was the boycott that took place in 1905 in response to American immigration laws that discriminated against Chinese. The Qing government had refused to renew its immigration treaty with the United States and its position was supported by a boycott of American goods, which took place in many cities and lasted for several months. The boycott was clearly in the government's interest, but was not organised by officials. In the north, which supplied few of the country's immigrants, the boycott became involved with the movement to recover certain economic concessions that had been sold to foreign business consortia. The gentlemen of the Tianjin chamber of commerce recorded their opinion in response to a letter urging them to support efforts to get back a concession that had been given to a Belgian company to build the city's new tramline:

> Recently we have read the newspapers on the two subjects of opposing the American treaty and the tramcars. Since we are aware of people's feelings and have considered the strength of public opinion and how our country has been roused to anger, we will immediately make it a special issue.[1]

But despite nationalistic rhetoric of this kind, most of the popular action against the new tram lines seems to have been motivated by anger at street accidents in which the trams were involved and by fear and resentment at the economic changes caused by the arrival of the trams.

Student nationalism: the May 4th Movement of 1919

Nationalist rhetoric did not become a major motivating factor for action for a large community in China until the 1920s, and the foundations of this change were laid by the May 4th Movement of 1919. During the 1910s the increasing threat from Japan was a major source of Chinese resentment, partly because Japan was not a major power and also because the Japanese had historically not been respected by the Chinese. Then in 1914 Japan joined World War I on the Allied side and sent troops to occupy the Shandong port city of Qingdao, which was a German concession. Shortly afterwards the Japanese presented a set of demands to Yuan Shikai, the Chinese president, which included recognition of a Japanese sphere of influence and the employment of Japanese advisors by the government. During the negotiations that followed, Yuan Shikai strengthened his hand by gradually leaking the demands to the press and using the consequent outcry against the Japanese. Coming so soon after the Japanese invasion of Qingdao, these events caused an outpouring of patriotic feeling in the newspapers, but most people assumed that when the war ended in Europe the foreign powers would return Qingdao to China. This idea was encouraged by the fact that the Beijing government had officially entered the war on the Allied side. However, at the Versailles Peace Conference it emerged that the Allied powers had already secretly agreed to support Japan, and, far worse, that when the Beijing government was concluding a set of loans from the Japanese in 1918, minister Zhang Zongxiang had accepted in writing Japan's position in Shandong. Consequently, the foreign powers agreed to the transfer of Qingdao to Japan. Uproar followed in China, where the dispute focused on the largely symbolic issue of whether or not the country should sign the final treaty. On 3 May 1919 rumours spread through Beijing that Zhang Zongxiang, who had bungled so catastrophically in negotiating the Japanese loans, was to be sent to replace one of China's delegates to the Versailles Conference. In what looked like an impending crisis, Beijing students, who had been planning a patriotic protest march for 7 May, the anniversary of Japan's demands to Yuan Shikai, decided to bring it forward to the following day.

For several years Beijing University had been providing an institutional base for the articulation of radical and nationalist views. The chancellor, Cai Yuanpei, commanded considerable personal prestige and used this to appoint many of the most important figures in the debate over modernisation to posts within the university: Chen Duxiu, later a founding member of the Communist Party, became dean of letters; Lu Xun, one of China's most famous and most radical modern writers, joined the Chinese department. Other major figures whom Cai employed included Hu Shi, who had received a doctorate in philosophy in America, and whose experiences there had made him the country's most prominent promoter of liberalism, and Li Dazhao, who was to become one of the founding figures of the Communist Party and who, as chief librarian, supported an assortment of radical young employees including Mao Zedong. There were also members of staff who held equally extreme reactionary views, such as Gu Hongming, who had studied in Glasgow and occasionally wrote pastiche Scottish ballads for the English-language press, wore a queue and was an ardent monarchist. Beijing University thus provided institutional support for a radicalisation of the debate about cultural and political change. It was no surprise when its teachers and students took a leading role in the demonstrations against the Treaty of Versailles.

On 4 May a large number of students marched through the streets of the city. The slogans they carried give a sense of their demands: 'Return our Qingdao!' 'China has been sentenced to death!' 'Boycott Japanese goods!' 'Protect our country's soil!' 'China belongs to the Chinese!' 'Down with the traitors!' At first the demonstration was orderly, but in the evening it descended into violence as a group of students set fire to the house of a prominent politician and beat up Zhang Zongxiang, who was staying there. When several students were arrested, further protests followed. The demonstrations were carried by the telegraph and the modern newspapers and quickly spread beyond Beijing to Shanghai, but also to the major cities of the interior. Across the country student associations organised marches and sent small groups of their members to give lectures in the streets. The protests spread beyond the students, and for several weeks some shops in the major cities did no business, and there were strikes in factories. The actions of the strike organisers and shop owners suggest that the patriotic rhetoric had begun to have an appeal beyond the Beijing students.

That nationalism as an idea should have some appeal in the major cities is not surprising when we consider the extent to which it had informed the education system of the 1900s. The radical Chen Duxiu, writing in June as the demonstrations were beginning to wind down, recognised both its influence and its problems. In an article entitled 'Should we really love the country?', he answered his own question with the emphatic statement:

What we love is the country in which the people take their patriotism
to oppose oppression by the people; it is not the country in which the
government uses the people's patriotism to oppress other people.

What we love is the country in which the country plans for the
prosperity of its people and not a country in which the people act as a
sacrifice for the country.[2]

The article is clearly much influenced by European questioning of patriotism
in the aftermath of the Great War and Chen's voice was one of very few
raised against patriotism, but it does point out the ease with which people
could be manipulated through patriotic rhetoric.

At least in part as a result of the student protests, the Chinese delegates
eventually refused to sign the Treaty of Versailles. This made no difference
to practical position of Qingdao, but it did cause the government to lose
face. Such a reversal was only possible because of the extreme weakness of
the so-called national government in Beijing. To many onlookers the
successful protests demonstrated the desperate need for a source of legitimacy for the government, and the power of the idea of nationalism to fulfill
that role. Another important result of the protests was the effect they had on
the student participants. A large group of students, especially those at
Beijing University, was fired by their success with a sense of community and
political involvement. This was to be the origin of a new generation of the
top political elite. Up to this time most high political positions had been held
by people whose successful careers had begun during the Qing. As the time
since the fall of the dynasty lengthened and the early republican institutions
were gradually discredited by failure, these people were slowly retiring from
power. During the 1920s a new group was entering politics, most of whose
members had received a primarily modern education. For many of this
group, which was to dominate China till the 1980s, the nationalism of the
May 4th Movement was a formative personal experience.

Cultural change

The nationalist movement of 1919 was also associated with a series of
radical attacks on the values and morality of the imperial state. Since the
1900s the official education system had stressed the new values of freedom
and equality. These had both social and political implications. The traditional family was structured around ideas of hierarchy that paralleled the
hierarchies of the government and the state. The classical family relationships between father and son, husband and wife, and older and younger
brothers were all strictly hierarchical relationships that were seen as being
parallel to the relationship between an emperor and his minister. When children who had been educated in the modern system grew to adulthood in the
1910s they felt that their education in the values of freedom and equality

clashed with their subservient position in the family. The result of this generational crisis was a series of attacks on Confucianism as an ideology and particularly on the virtue of filial piety. For filial piety was not only the central virtue of the Confucian classics, but also, in its demand for complete obedience to parents, the moral value most oppressive to the young men reading and writing these articles.

An article by Chen Duxiu entitled 'The way of Confucius and modern life' provides an example of the kind of arguments that were being made against Confucianism at this time. Chen Duxiu lists a whole series of ways in which Confucian ideals are incompatible with modern life. This is his paragraph on the incompatibility of Confucianism and political parties:

> Modern constitutional countries, whether they are monarchies or republics, all have political parties. Those who throw themselves into the life of political parties all have a spirit of independent belief and each does what is right for him. Sons do not have to be the same as fathers; wives do not have to be the same as husbands. For example, the Confucians teach the righteousness of filial piety and of a woman following her husband – for three years after a parent's death one should not change from his way; a woman follows her father and husband, and also follows her son. – How can they themselves choose their party in a neutral way?[3]

Criticisms of Confucian values of this kind were supported by a systematic attack on the Confucian system and its relationship to traditional political structures, made by a Chengdu scholar called Wu Yu who had studied in Japan in the 1900s. Wu Yu came from a much older generation than most of the radicals of the 1910s, and his strong condemnation of Confucian values had grown out of his own family situation: he refers to his father in his diary as 'the old devil'. At the time the revolution broke out in 1911 he was engaged in a legal case against his father on the question of how much money he should receive as maintenance. Wu Yu was both a scholar and a member of the elite among whom lavish displays of filial piety were required by accepted morality; even to bring such a case required considerable temerity. He had begun to develop a written critique of Confucianism in the 1900s, but his work did not come to widespread notice until the late 1910s. In it he argued that the paternalism of Confucianism was in itself a basis for despotism. In other words, since filial piety was the basis of loyalty to the emperor, Confucian morality effectively prevented the people from rebellion against the despotism under which they lived. Wu Yu's work created uproar in 1916 because it appealed to the younger generation who had received a modern education and who realised that the values they had imbibed were in conflict with those of the society in which they lived.

Wu Yu's emphasis on the role of moral values in structuring society was in itself the product of his Confucian education. However, the consequence of this line of thought was a violent attack on Confucian morals. Reformers attacked everything from arranged marriages to funeral customs. However, they continued to see these in a political context. Although it has been argued that the May 4th Movement was as much about cultural change as about anti-Japanese nationalism, the driving force behind that cultural change was nationalism. The reformers hoped to change the lives and morals of their fellow citizens with the intent that this would make China a stronger and more powerful country. So it was essential that they should reach beyond the narrow circle of the educated elite and begin to influence the majority of the population.

Central to the movement for cultural change were efforts to alter the language, and particularly the written language, so that the highly educated intellectuals of institutions like Beijing University could communicate more easily with ordinary people. Efforts to simplify the written language to make it easier for ordinary people were hardly new: as well as widespread missionary romanisation of Chinese dialects for the illiterate, several simplified writing systems had been designed by Chinese as early as the 1890s. The famous anarchist Wu Zhihui had even used his version to communicate with his previously illiterate wife when he was studying in France in the 1900s. The contribution of the May 4th Movement to this cause was an attempt to create a literary language that would more closely reflect patterns of everyday speech. Hu Shi, one of the leaders of the movement, explained his aims as follows:

> My purpose in the 'Constructive Revolution in Chinese Literature' is simply to suggest the creation of 'a literature in the national language and a national language suitable for literature.' Our aim in the literary revolution is merely to create in China a literature in the national language. A national language may be established only after we have produced a literature in the national language; and the national language may be considered a genuine national language only after we have established a national language suitable for literature.[4]

In a country whose spoken language was divided into dialects, some of which were as different from one another as the various European languages are, and whose written texts dealt with this problem by the use of structures and vocabulary significantly different from any spoken forms, this was no easy task.

The major contribution of the May 4th Movement was in fact the creation of a new written style based on the vernacular language. Hu Shi saw the origins of this style not in the high literature of the past but in novels, which had previously been regarded as a rather lowly form of literature. The contemporary popular novels of the period, by writers known as the Mandarin Duck and Butterfly School because of their sentimental references to these romantic species, but which also included adventure stories, tales of scandal in high places and detective stories, were in direct competition with the new vernacular literature and were roundly condemned.

Instead Hu Shi and others looked back to the elite fiction of the eighteenth century, and particularly to *The Dream of the Red Chamber*, long beloved of Chinese readers but now reevaluated as a major work of literature. However, the new vernacular literature was not as popular as the Mandarin Duck and Butterfly novels. This was partly a problem of style, since the writers seeking a new vernacular style were mostly heavily influenced by Western prose, and this made their language seem strange to many readers. So, for example, influenced by the contemporary Western idea that uninflected languages were primitive, they introduced written forms that differentiated 'he', 'she' and 'it', despite the fact that there was no such differentiation in the spoken language. Moreover, although much of their literature was sympathetic to the problems of the poor, its expected readers were clearly members of the elite who sympathised with the poor, not the poor themselves. Popular audiences continued to prefer butterfly novels that allowed them to enjoy descriptions of stylish modern behaviour, but confirmed the popular distrust of this by having the more traditional characters turn out to be the more reliable.

Attempts to create a national spoken language were even less effective. There had been calls for a national spoken language since the 1900s and the textbook publishers had produced a variety of primers, but these did not deal with the problem of how the written characters they gave were to be pronounced. In 1913 a conference on the unification of pronunciation was organised by the Ministry of Education. This resulted in a stalemate on the question of which dialect should be used as the basis for the new national pronunciation, which was resolved by giving each province one vote. Thus Mandarin, a version of the dialect of north China, was chosen as the national language, a decision much resented by speakers of southern dialects who claimed that the north China dialect lacked sufficient tonal distinctions. When eventually a dictionary of the new national language was published in 1919 at the height of the May 4th Movement it was found that the writers had included various ancient distinctions no longer found in Mandarin and other peculiarities. While these may have been intended to appease the southerners, the result was that the only person who could be found who was able to make the pronunciations suggested in the dictionary was a man named Zhao Yuanren who had been trained in linguistics and phonetics in America. He made a set of records of how the language should sound, but, as he himself joked, for 10 years he was its only speaker, and in the end he became a leading member of the campaign against these implausible pronunciations and in favour of the use of the Beijing dialect.

The Beijing government published edicts requiring the new national language to be taught in schools, but the division of the country into competing regional blocks meant that there was little incentive for the provincial governments to promote it. Indeed, as classical Chinese declined, dialect literature flourished during this period. The new interest in writing that would reach ordinary people inspired attempts to create vernacular styles that would reflect various spoken dialects. Meanwhile, for the first time in many centuries, provincial government was for the most part in the hands of natives of the province concerned. No longer transferred around the country by a central government, there was inevitably a tendency for officials to conduct their government in the dominant dialect of the province.

The result of this lack of government interest was that most promotion of Mandarin was by the two largest publishing houses in Shanghai, China Bookstore and the Commercial Press. Both publishers had grown alongside the modern education system and had made much of their money from the school textbooks they published. In towns and villages as far away as Shanxi province children learnt their lessons from these textbooks published in Shanghai. The business was both profitable and highly competitive. The sale of a whole new range of national-language textbooks provided a golden opportunity for each of the publishers to increase its market share. Both China Bookstore and the Commercial Press published dictionaries of pronunciation, teaching materials and publicity materials for the new national language. They even organised public associations, such as the National Language Promotion Society established by the head of the China Bookstore. This society organised classes in the new phonetic writing systems which were needed to convey the national pronunciation. There were also speech competitions and courses for schoolteachers. China Bookstore reported that more than 3,000 people had taken part in such activities in one year, while the Commercial Press claimed to have taught between 2,000 and 3,000 schoolteachers over four years by sending teachers to branch stores across the country. At the same time the two publishing houses held frequent sales of their new textbooks. The vernacular movement had increased interest in these efforts to produce a national spoken language, but the fact that its promotion was left to commercial operations suggests the limits of language-reform efforts during this period. During the 1920s political figures who were not particularly able linguists still needed interpreters when they gave speeches away from their own dialect area. Neither a national literature nor a national language had yet been created.

Working-class nationalism: the May 30th Movement of 1925

The first nationalist movement to involve large numbers of people outside the educated elite took place not in Beijing but in Shanghai. Shanghai's position at the mouth of the Yangzi River made it the greatest of the treaty ports. The Shanghai waterfront and the International Concession and French Concession behind it had developed into a modern city with Western-style architecture, paved streets and even street lighting. A writer who grew up in Beijing and visited Shanghai for the first time in 1928 remembered:

> I'd read about Shanghai's foreign settlement, but now I saw it with my own eyes. I'd never seen so many tall buildings, or *any* as tall as this, for that matter. Some had domes and some had steeples; some were Victorian, others rococo. There were neon advertisements in all colours of the rainbow and line after line of automobiles crawling down the river embankment road.[5]

Physical surroundings like these reminded every Chinese visitor that this was a foreign city, and by 1935 the city's residents included 10,000 Britons, 20,000 Japanese, 3,000 White Russian refugees, 2,000 Americans and 1,000 Germans. Nevertheless this large foreign population formed less than 1 per cent of the population of the International Concession, without even counting the vast numbers of Chinese who lived in the industrial areas of the city, which were mostly under the administration of the surrounding Chinese counties.

Many of the Chinese residents were drawn into the city to work in its factories, some of them owned by the British, but most by Japanese or Chinese industrialists. World War I saw a boom in Shanghai's industry as factories in Europe were put out of action or converted to making war materiel. In the same period warlord wars and natural disasters drove many families from their homes in rural areas. Many of these refugees ended up in Shanghai where they worked as petty traders or unskilled labourers. Such people lived in a very different world from the glamorous areas of the foreign concessions, even though that world was intricately tied to the concessions. A Chinese YMCA investigator reported in 1931 on the shanty-town housing where many of these recent immigrants lived:

> The house with six inmates – father, mother, and four children – occupies a space of about ten feet by fourteen feet. The roof, built of bamboo matting and straw, now in a dilapidated state, lined underneath with soot and cobwebs, lets in water even in a shower. The walls, riddled with holes, are caving in and afford no privacy and no protection against cold and storms. There is no flooring. Everything rests on an uneven mud floor. There is no drainage and no lavatory. The home is surrounded by garbage heaps and cesspools. One's throat becomes inflamed in this neighbourhood in ten minutes. On rainy days water contaminated by refuse and manure enters and floods the house up to a depth of several inches . . . In this particular working community there are nearly four hundred such 'homes'.[6]

Others who came from more prosperous backgrounds or had managed to move their families a little up the social ladder lived in solidly built, but crowded, tenements. All these workers were members of a new social class that had been created by the rapid development of modern industry.

In the summer of 1925 large numbers of workers in Shanghai participated in political strikes motivated by nationalism. Why did they do so and
what do their actions tell us about the spread of nationalism as an ideology?
The strikes began with the death of a mill worker called Gu Zhenghong in
a strike at a Japanese-owned mill. The striking workers who had been
locked out broke into the mill and began smashing the machines. Japanese
guards opened fire on them and Gu was killed. The strike had begun with
unskilled cotton-mill workers and Gu's death brought out many more in
sympathy strikes in other mills. On 30 May a large march of workers and
students took place in the city. By now the protests had spread beyond the
striking mill workers and many of the marchers were better-educated
workers with more secure jobs and students protesting not only at Gu's
death but at Gu's death as a symbol of foreign imperialist power in the city.
As the procession advanced on a British police station in the international
settlement, the police officer lost his nerve and ordered his men to fire into
the crowd. In the ensuing chaos 10 people were killed and 50 injured.

UNSKILLED LABOURERS

The demonstration of 30 May and the strikes that led up to it show the
participation of workers in nationalist activities. The strikes first broke out
among unskilled mill workers. Mill workers, like dock workers and rickshaw pullers, led a life dominated by the insecurity of their work. An
unskilled worker could easily be sacked and replaced; many factory jobs, for
example in silk reeling, were seasonal, with the factories working only for as
long as the relevant crop was available; factories also laid off unskilled
workers in large numbers in times of recession. So the people who took
these jobs were usually recent immigrants, forced to leave home by disasters
ranging from family poverty, to the death of the family's main wage earner,
to widespread flooding or warfare. For them Shanghai provided a possibility of life for the destitute.

Like other immigrants, many unskilled workers found themselves jobs
through connections with other people in Shanghai from their hometowns.
Some young people came to Shanghai jobs directly from the countryside,
hired from their parents as contract labourers. One cotton worker explained
how this worked:

> I'm from Subei. I lived in a village as a child . . . We were very poor.
> When I was thirteen a labour contractor from Shanghai came to our
> village to recruit children as contract workers. He said, 'Shanghai is a
> wonderful place. You can eat good rice as well as fish and meat. You
> can live in a Western-style house and make money.' So many parents
> in the countryside agreed to let their children go off as contract
> workers.[7]

Obviously contract labour of this type was something only to be thought of by the poor, but equally obviously the riches of Shanghai were part of the allure. The contract effectively sold the girl to the contractor for a certain period of time. A typical contract might run:

> The undersigned, X, because of present economic difficulties, on this day wishes to hire out his daughter, Y, to recruiting agent of name Z, who will take her to work in a cotton mill in Shanghai. The hiring payment will be [$30] for a period of three years. The money will be paid in three annual instalments of [$10], to be paid in March of each year.
>
> From the time she enters the factory, the girl will owe full obedience to the recruiting agent, and must not violate his instructions. In the event of her abscondence or death, the undersigned takes full responsibility. If she should fall ill, the recruiting agent will be responsible. Throughout the three-year contracted period, the girl will be clothed and fed by the recruiting agent. If any working time is lost, the girl will have to make it up at the end of the contracted period. After the contract expires, the recruiting agent has no further responsibility for the girl.
>
> I hereby agree to this.[8]

The terms of the contract, with their emphasis on obedience, hugely increased the dependence of the girl on the recruiting agent.

One of the results of this dependence of unskilled workers on foremen and forewomen, contractors and recruiters was the strength of the city's underworld gangs in the control of labour. These gangs had begun in the nineteenth century with the control of the opium trade, and had expanded into controlling the labour market. Foremen and women were often members of gangs, which meant that the gang leaders had the potential to control much of the workforce. Although the gangs were costly and ultimately controlled people through violence, they nevertheless made it possible for workers to strike effectively, where collective action was in their interest. At the top of the hierarchy the gangs were closely connected with the Shanghai establishment. For several years the administration of the French Concession was knowingly using the gangs to police the underworld, thus consolidating the power of the gangs, who then allowed the French administrators to cream off part of the profits of the illegal opium trade.

Because of the control the gangs had over unskilled workers, attempts by political parties to influence the behaviour of the workers usually had to be conducted through the gangs. As socialist ideologies became popular after the May 4th Movement students from the left-wing Shanghai University began to try and mobilise labour by working through the gangs. However, the young radicals with their modern ideas faced an uphill task in trying to adapt to this world. Most unskilled women workers questioned by a sociologist in 1933 still thought free marriages were shameful and connected them with scandalous stories of promiscuous or immoral behaviour. The differences in ideas were part of widely different cultural attitudes. One woman worker recalled the first time she met the communist organiser Deng Zhongxia:

> I had come back from the night shift, so I was already in bed. Deng Zhongxia sat on my bed, patted me and said, 'Young girl, did you work the night shift?' I was scared to death – no man had ever come in like that and talked to me. What was he doing sitting on my bed? At that time women were not supposed to talk to men![9]

Unskilled workers were hard to draw into ideologically motivated activity, and much of their participation in the May 30th Movement was mediated through the powerful gangs.

The massacre of demonstrators by British police was followed by an unprecedented strike by workers across the city that lasted until the middle of August. This is one of the most famous examples of nationalist political action taken by Chinese workers, but it is surprising that most workers could have afforded to go on strike for so long. While there was undoubtedly resentment against managers, and especially foreign managers, the strike could only be sustained because of the support of the newly formed Shanghai General Labour Union, whose leader formally joined the Green Gang and brought in the power of the gangs to police the strike. Even so the strike would have been impossible without the support of the elite Chinese Chamber of Commerce which provided strike pay. As one cotton-mill worker remembered that summer:

> Some students came to our factory. We didn't know they were Communists. All we knew was that they had come to help us workers. They told us to strike and promised they'd provide enough money for us to survive during the work stoppage. We were delighted by this news so we went on strike. Every two weeks we could pick up our pay.[10]

Given the monotonous nature of the work, the long hours and a history of strikes and disputes it becomes more obvious why workers offered strike pay should agree to leave their jobs.

SKILLED WORKERS

Whatever the motivation of some of the strikers, there were also many people who felt passionately about the fact that Chinese could be shot by foreign police in their own country. Shortly after the massacre a man called Liu Guangquan committed suicide. Liu had received some basic education and had then been employed as a clerk in the army. From there he moved into the Shanghai police and then into a transport company. After he heard the news of the massacre he wept ceaselessly. He was a poor drinker, but took to drinking heavily. On the morning of 7 June he got up and read the newspaper, which made him weep. Looking very pale he went to the water-front where he boarded one of the small steam ferries that carried passengers across the river. Halfway across he leapt overboard, shouting, 'Love the country! I call on my countrymen with my death.'[11] He was unable to swim and attempts to rescue him failed. Afterwards it was found that he had left a suicide note in which he protested against the May 30th killings and wrote that his soul would pursue the warlords, in the traditional vengeful manner of the soul of a suicide. In an obituary the *Shenbao* news-paper commented that though Liu Guangquan had not studied much since childhood he had a good knowledge of the most important ideas promoted by the education system. His death and other similar suicides suggest the new power of modern nationalism to move and spur to action people who were very far from being members of the upper elite.

Descriptions of the May 30th demonstrations suggest that most of the workers who took part came from the most highly educated class of urban workers. A postal worker who took part on that day remembered that his group included wood carvers, railway workers, carpenters, clerks in cloth-ing stores and workers in foreign companies. These people were workers, but workers of a very different type from the dead mill-hand Gu Zhenghong; several were members of the Communist Party. They are perhaps most eas-ily described as those who wore the long gowns that were the mark of the literate scholar, but had to work for a living and did so in jobs that made it unlikely that they would ever make a lot of money but did enable a man to support a family. A 1930 survey found that among printers at the Commercial Press the husband provided 97 per cent of the family income. By contrast among factory workers in a cotton-mill district husbands pro-vided on average only 26 per cent of family income. Most of these skilled workers were also literate: a survey of male silk weavers from east Zhejiang found that 30 per cent of them had graduated from middle schools, and a further 40 per cent from primary schools, and that 95 per cent of them were literate. These men were performing skilled jobs in modern factories.

As a group these workers tended to feel that they had been deprived of education for economic reasons, and this made them both conscious of their status as literate people and at the same time often resentful of the student classes. They aspired to the modernity of the students, wearing Western-style clothing and leather shoes, going to the new cinemas and occasionally eating foreign food. This was the audience for the Butterfly literature, the circulation of which expanded greatly in the 1920s. Unlike previous gener-ations, for whom books were an expensive luxury, the better-off members of the Shanghai working class could afford the new cheaply printed enter-tainment literature. This allowed them to explore the new modern lifestyles through fictional stories of such quintessentially modern characters as girl students, while often reaffirming traditional values. Magazines, films, cartoons and the pictorial press also developed to appeal to this audience, as well as the so-called 'mosquito newspapers' – single sheets sold for a cent and containing serialised fiction, gossip and anecdotes.

Magazines aimed at this audience promoted images of modernity that were drawn from the cultural ideology of the May 4th Movement, emphasising, for example, the nuclear family based on love between husband and wife. The hugely popular *Life Weekly* praised Nationalist Party leader Chiang Kaishek and his wife Song Meiling for using the English terms 'darling' and 'dear' to each other. The magazine also urged its readers to win financial independence from their extended families by marrying later in life. Its picture of the nuclear family included the pretty, feminine, but also educated wife at home looking after and teaching the children, and a family life centred around dinner when the husband came home from work. Readers' letters to *Life Weekly* told stories of unhappiness at marriages arranged by senior family members, and offered support to those who hoped to break with their families. Much advertising also promoted the nuclear family. Milk, for example, which had not traditionally been drunk in China, was promoted as a feature of the nuclear family life. Similarly the Sanyou Company, which sold linen and home furnishings, created a display room on Nanjing Road, Shanghai's main shopping street, which was laid out and furnished as an entire modern home. The home was designed for a nuclear family and laid out with rooms furnished as a dining room, bedroom, study and kitchen, very unlike the more flexible organisation of traditional compounds.

Nationalism became part of this modern image in campaigns to buy Chinese rather than imported goods. So, for example, in 1925 Nanyang Tobacco tried to undercut the market leader British American Tobacco with an advertising campaign that presented Nanyang brands as a patriotic choice. After his death in 1925, Sun Yatsen's image was used to sell Nanyang cigarettes with brand names like Zhongshan designed to display the patriotism of the smoker. Fig. 7.1 shows an advertisement for one of these. Sun is depicted on the packaging of the cigarettes and there are stone busts of him on either side of the picture. The writing on the the bases of the busts quotes two of his most famous slogans calling on people to promote national products and take back national rights. On the columns above the busts are the closing lines from his political testament: 'The revolution is not yet complete, my comrades must still be diligent.' The advertisement was published on National Day and images of Sun Yatsen are mixed with other nationalist symbols: the five-colour national flag hangs in the background and the words 'Celebrate National Day' are written on paper lanterns. Sun Yatsen's name was also used to sell tinned olives, Sun Yatsen memorial spectacles (with 'Zhongshan' engraved on the bridge) and even a foreign patent medicine, Dr Williams' Pink Pills for Pale People, which advertised using a picture of Sun flanked by his wife, Song Qingling, and his political

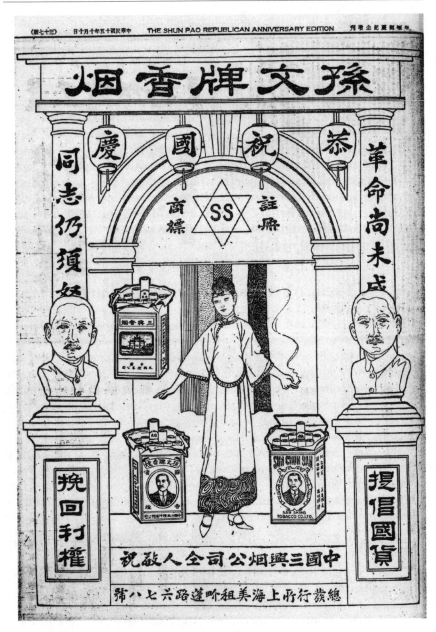

Figure 7.1 Nanyang Tobacco advertisement for National Day, 1925
Source: *Shenbao*, 10 October 1926, p. 37.

heir, Chiang Kaishek. People were being urged to display their patriotism by buying and using certain goods, and the success of the various national-products movements, at least during the course of the campaign, suggests that this appeal could be effective for a mass audience.

As well as expressing nationalism through consumer culture, some workers were directly involved in politics. As the profits of trade and industry expanded in the 1910s so did protest activity, and much of this was led by better-paid workers in more secure jobs. These workers tended to have strong communities forged by occupational and native-place organisations. They struck for wage increases and also for the freedom to organise in various forms. Li Lisan, a printer who headed the city's general labour union and was at the forefront of the May 30th strikes, provides a clear example of the politicisation of such workers during this period. As they became increasingly politically active Shanghai workers began to take an interest in the political parties.

The growth of the Nationalist Party

As a result of the May 4th Movement students across the country had set up groups to study a whole variety of different possible ideologies. Anarchism was a leading contender, but there was also interest in socialism, guild socialism, anarcho-syndicalism and Marxism. These ideologies brought with them an interest in joining organisations that could help promote them. The period saw the rapid growth of the Nationalist Party and of interest in Sun Yatsen's rather mixed ideology known as the Three People's Principles. (These were nationalism, democracy and people's livelihood, so-called because the character for 'people' is included in each of the Chinese terms.) The motivation of some of the new members of the Nationalist Party can be gauged from answers to the question 'Why do you wish to enter this school?' on the application form for entry into the party's military academy. Answers included:

> 'My intention is to seek military knowledge in order to bring prosperity to my country and people.'
> 'Because society is in a bad way I wish to receive mental training in an ideology for saving the country.'
> 'I wish to transform the country.'
> 'Because our country's soldiers are no use I have specially come to study military matters in order to rescue the country.'[12]

In these responses, which are typical, the applicants emphasise the connection between nationalism and commitment to the party. Applicants to the party's military academy were some of the most committed of the new nationalists, and more general enthusiasm for an ideological solution to political problems led to the rapid growth of Sun Yatsen's political party, now known as the Nationalist Party (literally 'citizens' party', *guomin-dang*).

Between 1920 and 1925 the Nationalist Party was transformed from one of a series of revolutionary groups focused on Sun Yatsen to an instrument of modern mass politics. Sun's first revolutionary group had been formed in the 1890s in response to China's defeat in the war against Japan over Korea. He was a charismatic leader and as his ideas changed and the political situation shifted he formed and reformed the political groups he led. Thus, for example, the alliance of revolutionary groups under Sun's leadership known as the Chinese League, which was active in the period immediately before the 1911 Revolution, was changed in 1912 into the Nationalist Party. However, this party moved away from Sun as its other leaders sought power within the structures of the new republic. In 1913 Sun dissolved the Nationalist Party and formed a new Revolutionary Party, whose members had to swear an oath of personal loyalty to Sun. Then, following the death of Yuan Shikai in 1916, Sun moved to Guangzhou where, with the support of some members of the National Assembly, he claimed to be the leader of a legitimate national government. In line with this claim, he created a new Nationalist Party in 1920. Sun's fame as one of the earliest and most radical revolutionaries of the last years of the Qing, as well as his charisma, personal honesty, passionate belief in his own ideals and exclusion from any real power made this new Nationalist Party an attractive cause for the many young people who shared both his commitment to the nation and his status as an outsider in the contest for national power.

However Sun's position in Guangzhou was far from secure. While he claimed to be the rightful president of all of China, real power in the city shifted between Chen Jiongming, the man chosen as the provincial governor of Guangdong in 1912, and the military forces from Yunnan and Guangxi whom Sun had invited into the city to balance Chen's power. Since Sun's own position in the city was dependent on them he was unable to control these armies. Thus, although Sun's power in Guangzhou was based on his claim to the rest of China, it was also a factor in the city's warlord politics and it was hardly surprising that Sun was by no means popular in the city. The British Colonial Office reported that:

> Sun is now regarded by all classes in Canton as an avenging wolf, devouring the fat and blood of the people in order to sustain his obsession that he is destined to be the saviour of the country. He is being used by the mercenary Yunnanese troops, who have no object by plunder, and, in his name, there has been established in Canton a system of extortion astonishing even for China.[13]

The British Colonial Office was by no means unbiased in its view of Sun, who was regarded as being exceptionally opposed to the foreign presence in China, but this particular comment reflects a view that was widely shared in the Guangzhou area.

Since Sun claimed to be the national president, he also laid claim to Guangzhou's rich customs revenues which were at this time handed over, under the aegis of the foreign powers, to the government in Beijing. One of a series of crises over this question blew up in 1922 when Sun threatened to seize the customs revenue and the foreign powers sent in more than a dozen gunboats to protect the customs offices. After this Sun declared that if the Western powers would not help him he would accept aid from the Soviet Union. Sun's rhetoric of opposition to the foreign presence exacerbated the difficulties of his relationship with the foreign powers. In fact the weakness of Sun's position in Guangzhou made it almost inevitable that he would accept aid from any source that was willing, but the friction with the Western powers over the customs revenue ensured that it would be the Soviet Union who supplied that aid. Soviet policy was to work towards a national revolution in China which would overthrow foreign imperialism. The Comintern advisors who came to Guangzhou provided loans to support Sun's government and assisted in the establishment of a new Nationalist Party military academy that would train an officer corps and thus free Sun from reliance on the unsavoury Yunnan armies. The new military academy was also intended to enrol young nationalists and to train them in ideological commitment as well as military skills. The form of that ideological commitment was the most important of the Soviet advisors' contributions to the Nationalist Party.

The alliance with the Soviet Union produced a new political language through which China's political problems could be understood and linked to the socialist ideologies that were so popular with students. This Marxist language included the terminology of labour, unions and feudalism, but the ideas that had the most profound impact on conceptions of the nation were those of Lenin concerning the link between imperialism and capitalism. Lenin had argued that in order to support their own capitalists, imperialist governments prevented the development of production in colonies and semi-colonies by supporting the holding of power by groups opposed to progress. This was interpreted in relation to China's current situation to mean that the foreign powers, the imperialists, were supporting 'warlords', a group whose very name defined them as concerned only with the military perpetuation of their power. The idea of a link between imperialism and warlords was simple to understand and seemed to explain almost all of China's problems. It justified the overthrow of warlord power by progressive forces in society, in other words the Nationalist Party. There were problems: both 'imperialism' and 'warlord' were new terms and their meanings were not necessarily immediately apparent. In the official Nationalist interpretations of this period 'warlord' refers only to militarists supported by the foreign powers, but as the term was popularised it increasingly referred to all militarists. Moreover, both 'imperialist' and 'warlord' were used more often as insults than as objective types. However, the new language did provide a new way of thinking about the causes of regional conflict and through that a justification for the idea that a campaign against the foreign powers would solve the nation's problems. The vocabulary of imperialism and warlordism eventually spread far beyond the narrow confines of Nationalist Party members and came to influence the way a whole generation thought about nationalism and about their country. This was partly through the spread of written materials such as newspapers and pamphlets issued by the party, but was also the result of events during which large crowds assembled, slogans were shouted, speeches were made and the party's new ideology became simplified and at the same time accessible to many more people. The most important of these events was the Nationalist Party's Northern Expedition, as a result of which the party came to national power, but the groundwork was laid in 1925 with the death of Sun Yatsen and the May 30th demonstrations.

Sun Yatsen died in Beijing. He had gone there to take part in negotiations with the northern regional powers over national unification. He had continued to work through a long and painful illness and by doing so had probably caused his death. In addition his will revealed that he had died penniless, leaving his young wife nothing but the contents of his house in Shanghai. These facts, which were widely publicised, combined with his recent record of fiery speeches against the foreign powers, contributed to the outpouring of popular grief that followed his death. In Guangzhou, Sun Yatsen had been part of the balance of power between regional militarists, and local people had condemned his policies; but in the rest of China he had remained a symbol of commitment to the revolutionary cause and the circumstances of his death reinforced such views. As he lay ill in Beijing crowds gathered outside the house where he was staying, and photographs of his funeral procession a few days later show people climbing up trees and onto the tops of cars to see over the seething crowds to where the coffin was carried along on the shoulders of his disciples. Written accounts of the funeral describe the packed streets in the centre of Beijing and the press of people pushing forward to try to touch the coffin. The funeral procession and the various memorial ceremonies were accompanied by shouted slogans: 'Down with imperialism!', 'Down with warlords!'

Similar scenes were repeated throughout the country. In Wuhan in central China, a reporter for an English-language newspaper reported scathingly on the mourning, which he called 'a perfect epidemic of tears and lamentation'. He described one of the many young men making open-air speeches in the park, using the occasion to bring up the issues of imperialism and nationalism:

> The speaker was very excited. He spoke quickly and in a high rasping voice. His points were heartily applauded by the crowd. At each pause, when after having made a point, the speaker paused to indulge in a little expectoration, his listeners showed their appreciation with loud applause.[14]

This appreciative audience was listening to an account of how foreigners were coming to China and getting rich by robbing and cheating the Chinese. The account was combined with attacks on the existence of the foreign concessions, the unequal treaties, foreign control of the Maritime Customs revenues and the continued payment of the Boxer Indemnity. Pamphlets were distributed throughout the city on similar subjects. The dramatic displays of the funeral and the huge number of local memorial services, many of which were also reported in detail in the press, brought home to many people the formula of opposition to imperialism and warlordism and its connection with Sun.

As well as promoting the ideology that lay behind the Nationalist Party claim to power, many of the commemorative meetings were also used to encourage people to join the party or to give them a sense of commitment to it. Thus in Nanjing a volume issued to go with one large commemorative meeting ended with a rousing call to action:

> Each one of us present at this meeting should make a decision to remember Sun's testament, to recognise his ideology and achievements, to study the revolutionary spirit that he displayed over forty years, and should swear to struggle to the end for the people's benefit. How are we to struggle? By joining the revolutionary Chinese National Party and expanding its force among the people.[15]

Thus the ceremonies surrounding Sun's death laid a foundation of popular support for the Nationalist Party and its simple and attractive campaign against imperialism and warlordism that stretched well beyond the party's base in Guangdong.

Conclusion

The campaign to expand Nationalist Party membership in the aftermath of Sun Yatsen's death coincided with strikes in Shanghai and the May 30th Movement. While most Nationalist Party members were still either students or members of the urban elite who had been inspired by the nationalism of 1919, the May 30th Movement appealed to a much broader segment of the population. Both the May 4th and May 30th Movements were signs of the growing appeal of nationalism. However, the rhetoric of nationalism was now heavily influenced by political ideology. The introduction of the vocabulary of imperialism and warlordism influenced the way in which the events in Shanghai in the summer of 1925 were understood. Looking at them we see that nationalism was already beginning to be shaped by the dominant political party, a process that was to intensify in the years that followed and continue until the 1980s.

Notes

1   *Tianjin shanghui dang'an huibian* (Collected Archives of the Tianjin Chamber of Commerce) (Tianjin: Tianjin renmin chubanshe, 1989), p. 2254.
2   Chen Duxiu, *Duxiu wencun* (Collected Essays of Chen Duxiu) (Shanghai: Yadong tushuguan, 1922), vol. 1, pp. 430–2.
3   Ibid., vol. 1, p. 118.
4   Quoted in Chow Tse-tung, *The May Fourth Movement: Intellectual Revolution in Modern China* (Cambridge MA: Harvard University Press, 1964), p. 277.
5   Hsiao Ch'ien, *Traveller Without a Map* (Stanford: Stanford University Press, 1990), p. 45.
6   Frederic Wakeman, *Policing Shanghai 1927–1937* (Berkeley: University of California Press, 1995), pp. 87–8.
7   Elizabeth J. Perry, *Shanghai on Strike: The Politics of Chinese Labour* (Stanford: Stanford University Press, 1993), p. 56.
8   Emily Honig, *Sisters and Strangers: Women in the Shanghai Cotton Mills, 1919–1949* (Stanford: Stanford University Press, 1986), pp. 99–100.
9   Ibid., pp. 207–8.
10 Perry, *Shanghai on Strike*, p. 83.
11 *Shenbao*, 10 June 1925, p. 14.
12 Second Historical Archives, Nanjing. 230.110.
13 Quoted in Stephanie Po-yin Chung, *Chinese Business Groups in Hong Kong and Political Change in South China, 1900–25* (Basingstoke: Macmillan, 1998), p. 93.
14 *North China Herald*, 25 April 1925, p. 133.
15 Nanjing zhuidao Sun Zhongshan xiansheng dahui, ed., *Zhuidao Sun Zhongshan xiansheng tekan* (Special Publication Mourning Mr Sun Yatsen; 1925).

8

Nationalism and the party state

The rise of political parties changed the nature of Chinese nationalism. Since the appearance of modern nationalism in the late nineteenth century, it had been conceived of as something separate from politics. This attitude drew on a traditional distrust for political factions and had been encouraged by the school textbooks of the 1900s, which carefully distinguished between patriotism and loyalty to the emperor. After the fall of the Qing dynasty and the disintegration of the Republican state the split between politics and nationalism became clearer still. As in Japan during the same period, nationalism was seen as a virtue set apart from, and above, the increasingly murky world of politics. The shift that then occurred with the rise of political parties during the 1920s was similar to the one that Hobsbawm, looking at the growth of nationalism in Europe during a somewhat earlier period, observed between state patriotism and nationalism. Nationalism changed from being a form of attachment to the state to being an attachment to a particular version of that state. In China that shift was associated with the rise to power of the Nationalist Party.

The rise of the party state

Sun Yatsen's death in 1925 left leaderless a party that had been formed round its leader. In addition, the Nationalist Party's alliance with the Soviet Union had involved great changes in ideology, which had been pushed through successfully only because of the loyalty of the central leadership to Sun. The result was that Sun's death was followed by a series of disputes over the leadership, involving, among other things, an assassination case in which one potential candidate died and another was discredited through the implication of his association with the assassin. The man who emerged from this struggle as party leader was Chiang Kaishek, the head of the party's newly formed military academy. Shortly after he took power in the party Chiang launched a military expedition north from Guangdong in an attempt to gain control of the country. At first there seemed little chance that such an expedition would succeed in the face of the huge armies of the northern militarists, which were even then fighting each other on the North China Plain. Indeed, for the first few months of the expedition the national newspapers hardly mentioned Chiang's forces. But gradually it became clear that Chiang Kaishek and his National Revolutionary Army were achieving much more than people had thought possible for such a small force, and that the reason lay in the ideological commitment of the troops and the existence of a considerable segment of the population who shared that ideology and supported the expedition's aims.

Ideologically committed troops and the existence of specialised propaganda units within the army ensured that the ideas and goals of the expedition were well publicised. All sections of the army set out from Guangzhou with publicity materials: printed sheets of slogans to shout, portraits of Sun Yatsen, copies of Sun's political testament in which he urged his followers to complete the revolution, flags, posters and booklets explaining the party's ideas. These were intended to be reprinted in towns and cities along the way. A British missionary in Hunan reported that soldiers were out on the street corners lecturing even before the army had settled down in the city. Many observers noticed how when the Nationalist army arrived in a town or city the walls would be covered with illustrated posters. According to the *North China Herald* correspondent in Changsha, 'Never before has the city been so billed, placarded, circularized or so snowed under with showers of leaflets.'[1]

It has often been argued that the Northern Expedition succeeded as a result of this propaganda, and particularly as a result of the mobilisation of peasants, women and other groups by communists and other left-wing elements within the Nationalist Party. However, the success of these activities depended on the receptiveness of the audience. Why were so many people so eager to support the Nationalist army? It is clear that, far from being the result of Nationalist propaganda, popular enthusiasm often preceded the arrival of the army. In Beijing the population was said to have been up all night making flags the day before the Nationalist takeover. Indeed, observers described the disappointment on the faces of the students who had gone out with their flags to welcome the arriving troops, when instead of the victorious army they expected they saw tired, bedraggled men with seedy ponies and shabby equipment. As well as welcoming the Nationalist troops, many people took the initiative in spreading Nationalist ideas and publicity before the army arrived. In Hangzhou excited young men and women were said to have mobbed the Bureau of Education where there was a stash of printed propaganda materials and paper flags which they hoped to be allowed to distribute; the soldiers of the Nationalist army

did not arrive until some hours later. Much of the propaganda was commercially printed by firms wishing to take advantage of the new market among
the enthusiastic promoters of Nationalist ideas. Clearly there were considerable numbers of people, especially in the cities, who shared the stated
ideals of the Nationalist army and were eager to help bring the party to
power.

But it was only a section of the population that shared this enthusiasm.
For many people Nationalist Party propaganda was irrelevant and incomprehensible. A good sense of the different attitudes of urban east coast elites
and north China villagers is given by the diary of Ou Zhenhua, a military
officer who took part in the expedition. As he marched with his men
through the villages of the north China plain, Ou Zhenhua noticed that
about half the men still had queues and almost all wore either gowns or
traditional jackets. Even in the county towns one seldom saw a man in
Western dress or a young girl in the street. He commented:

> When I read public documents or write they always come in to visit me
> with their heads lowered and do not know whether to go or stay.
> When I talk with them about the affairs of the party-nation, they do
> not know what kind of thing the nation is; when I talk with them
> about party affairs, they also do not recognise what kind of business
> party affairs are. The cause of their ignorance is really that few people
> leave the village and not many study.[2]

Ou Zhenhua spent the anniversary of the 1911 Revolution that year in the
Jiangsu county town of Liyang. His soldiers organised a celebratory meeting
and the local officials had flowers and leaves arranged on the gates of the
county offices, but there were no processions or other activities. Ou
Zhenhua felt that this showed the weakness of the people's patriotic feelings. Ou Zhenhua is a sympathetic reporter of the customs and responses of
the people of the towns and villages he passed through with the expedition,
but like many of those who supported the revolution he shares a perception
of the nation and nationalism that excludes those who do not participate in
the forms of modern nationalism. The creation of the new politicised
nationalism was to increase this gap that separated modern nationalism
from traditional forms of allegiance to the Chinese state.

Symbols of the party state

The Nationalist Party's propaganda presented a quite new view of the
Chinese nation, one in which the spirit of the nation was embodied in the
Nationalist Party and the Nationalist Party represented the nation to the
people. A new term, 'the party nation' (*dangguo*), which was much used at
this time, implied that the nation was defined conceptually and even
geographically through its allegiance to the party. It was this binding

together of nation and party that laid the foundation for the identification of nationalism with support for party rule, whether Nationalist or later Communist, which has been such an important feature of Chinese nationalism in subsequent years.

The difference between the images of the nation promoted by the Northern Expedition and those that had existed previously is well illustrated by the change to the national flag. Since 1912 the national flag of the republic had been the five-colour flag consisting of five bands representing the five different peoples of the Chinese empire. This flag was widely used on patriotic occasions, ranging from official National Day celebrations to anti-government demonstrations, and its use had given it a strong association with nationalism. It was not associated with any particular government grouping or policy. Indeed, in an environment where politics was frequently condemned as corrupt and immoral, part of the attraction of the five-colour flag as a national symbol lay in its emptiness of political meaning: the flag presented the nation as something above and beyond politics. This situation was reversed by the Northern Expedition when the first sign of a town going over to the Nationalist Party was the hanging of a new blue and white flag. This new flag, which showed a white sun in a blue sky, was both the flag of the Nationalist Party and the new flag of the Chinese nation. It was also very much Sun Yatsen's personal symbol: it had been designed by his friend Lu Haodong, who had died clasping it in an early uprising, and in 1912 Sun had unsuccessfully proposed it as the national flag. He himself had continued to use it as the flag of his Nationalist Party and had used the same design on a red ground as the national flag. This latter version can be seen in the upper left-hand corner of Fig. 5.1, which shows a selection of flags in use in 1911. The two flags were usually flown and depicted together, marking yet more firmly the point that the party was now to be coterminous with the nation. As Northern Expedition soldiers hung blue sky white sun flags over the towns they arrived in they were marking their demand for people to recognise the party as the embodiment of the nation.

NATIONAL GOVERNMENT

The Nationalist army eventually reached central China and in 1928 the party, under the leadership of Chiang Kaishek, established a national government in Nanjing. The new government was weak and the provincial military powers were still major players on the political scene. However, the fact that it claimed to be a national, rather than merely a provincial or regional government, distinguished the Nanjing government from these other political forces and made it possible for it to claim a certain degree of hegemony. This was despite the fact that initially the government in Nanjing controlled little more than the two provinces of Jiangsu and Zhejiang.

The city of Nanjing had been the capital of the country in the fifteenth century. Since then it had gradually declined in wealth and influence. As the capital of the Taiping Heavenly Kingdom it was the scene of serious fighting in the 1860s and much of the city was razed to the ground. By the turn of the twentieth century Nanjing was a small provincial city, with only its massive brick walls as a reminder of its former power and status. When the leaders of the 1911 Revolution chose it as the new national capital, the choice showed their rejection of the Manchus in favour of a Han nationalism that turned to the Ming as the last racially Han dynasty. However, when Chiang Kaishek chose Nanjing as the new capital in 1928, he did so primarily because it had been the capital during the brief period of Sun Yatsen's presidency in 1912. By choosing Nanjing rather than Beijing as the capital, Chiang seemed to claim that those few months of 1912 were the only true period of republican rule, that the Beijing governments of the intervening period were illegitimate, and that true republican rule was now to start again. Thus the military campaign of the two preceding years, known at the time as the 'great revolution', was depicted as the successor to the revolution of 1911 and Chiang Kaishek, its leader, as the true heir to the revolutionary Sun Yatsen. In line with these ideas the new Nationalist government was inaugurated on the anniversary of the start of the 1911 Revolution.

The institutions of the new government were based on the ideas of Sun Yatsen, and drew their legitimacy from him and his revolutionary heritage. Sun had proposed a government that would follow the separation of the legislature, executive and judiciary commonly endorsed by Western political theorists, but would also include separate bodies in charge of civil service examinations and the impeachment of corrupt officials, which he saw as major functions of the imperial Chinese state. So the Nanjing government was established with five divisions to represent these powers of government. Overseeing the government was a national assembly, which replaced the discredited representative organs of the early republic. It included representatives from all China's provinces and cities as well as representatives of Mongolia, Tibet and Chinese living overseas. Members were chosen not only from these geographical areas but also from organisations that represented various occupations and functional constituencies. Thus peasant associations, labour unions, local chambers of commerce, industrial organisations and educational associations all sent representatives. When it had been selected, the national assembly began the process of drafting a new constitution. The existence of these formal institutions of a modern national government in Nanjing greatly enhanced the Nationalist government's claim to legitimacy both among its Chinese citizens and among foreign governments, who began to negotiate with it over such long-standing sources of contention as extra-territoriality and foreign control of China's customs duties.

The institutions of the Nationalist government spread widely across the country, though in many cases this was the result of local initiative rather than changes in the actual balance of regional and national power. The creation of the Nationalist model of government altered the outer forms and structures of local and provincial government in many places. In Shanxi province the Political Affairs Department became the Secretarial Department, the Justice Department became the Legal Department and the Police Department became the Civil Administration Department, while new departments of Reconstruction and of Agriculture and Labour were created. As a result of this process the Shanxi provincial government came to have structures parallel to and replicating those of the central government. Similarly at village level many commentators have noticed the extension of official government organs into the village during this period. Real political power did not necessarily follow these formal structures. In Shanxi throughout this period all major decisions were made by the provincial governor and military leader Yan Xishan; Chiang Kaishek would have had little hope of enforcing central government policies that Yan was unwilling to accept. Nevertheless, the existence of a set of national political structures did create a sense of a national government that went beyond the actual powers of Chiang Kaishek and the Nanjing administration.

SUN YATSEN

While the new institutions identified the Nanjing government as a national government, other elements emphasised the central role of the party to the new state. In particular the symbol of Sun Yatsen served to emphasise the position of the party at the heart of the state. In promoting Sun as a national hero the party built on the wave of emotion that had swept the country after his death and had identified Sun with the national struggle against war-lordism and imperialism. Since that time party organisations had held regular weekly memorial services at which Sun's political testament was read aloud and the week's work was discussed. In his life Sun had been the party's founder and leader; after his death he became a central symbol linking the party to the nation. In schools throughout the country Sun's portrait was displayed between the crossed national and party flags. Supporters of the Nationalist Party now began to refer to Sun not only as the party leader but also as the father of the nation. Fig. 8.1 is a poster published by the party at the time of Sun's burial in 1929. It is entitled 'Political tutelage according to the party leader's teachings' and shows Sun Yatsen bending forward to lead a small child labelled 'Republic of China' up a flight of steps. The image of the republican state as a child was a common one at the time, but this poster takes that image and links it to the idea of the relationship between the party and the state. At the time that the poster was printed Sun himself was already dead; the poster makes use of Sun's image to legitimise party rule. After his death Sun was widely honoured as an incorruptible leader who had shown genuine dedication to the country; but he was also the founder and throughout his life the central figure of the Nationalist Party, and the party continued to capitalise on his popularity.

Figure 8.1 'Political tutelage according to the party leader's teachings'
Source: The Bodleian Library

The figure of Sun Yatsen was central to both the ideology and the history of the Nationalist government and this was displayed to the population through the huge mausoleum that was built just outside the city to house his body. Sun himself had asked shortly before his death in 1925 that he be buried in the mountains outside Nanjing. This was the resting place of the first Ming emperor, where Sun had paid his respects in 1911 and held sacrifices to report the reestablishment of Han rule. Immediately after Sun's death the Nationalist Party had neither the power nor the finances to ensure the construction of a suitable site and Sun's body was embalmed and left to rest in a temple outside Beijing where he had died. The rise to power of Chiang Kaishek meant that it was essential that Sun's body should be moved. Because of Sun's central position in the party, Chiang's legitimacy depended in part on his claim to be Sun's heir. However, Chiang, unlike many of the Nationalist Party veterans, had in fact had little personal intimacy with Sun. His response was to create that intimacy by acting out the role of a filial son. The construction of a tomb for Sun in the hills outside Nanjing filled this role perfectly, and when Chiang arrived in Nanjing he began to push forward work on the mausoleum.

When it was completed the huge white marble structure high up on the hillside overlooked the city and easily dominated the ancient tomb of the first Ming emperor. A great road was driven from the bank of the Yangzi River through the city and up to the tomb. This new road, which was named after Sun Yatsen, formed the main artery of a new modern city along which the government buildings of the new Nationalist state were constructed. The body of Sun Yatsen was moved to Nanjing from Beijing by train at a time when north China was not really under Nationalist control and it was impossible for Nationalist troops to enter Beijing. Thus the huge procession that escorted Sun's coffin through the streets of Beijing and the train that carried it slowly down to Nanjing were an impressive display of national unity over ideological goals even in a situation of political disunity. When the coffin reached Nanjing it lay in state for several days before being escorted up to the shining new mausoleum by a procession intended to represent the modern nation. This was depicted as consisting of the party, the government, the army and the people. The participants representing the people were chosen from different geographical and occupational groups: the provinces, workers, peasants, commerce, women, merchants, students, overseas Chinese and Mongolia and Tibet. The effect was to depict a nation that was at once ethnically Chinese and based on the boundaries of the Qing empire, but above all one in which the people were led by the party.

The ceremonies organised to commemorate Sun Yatsen's reinterment spread out across the country from Nanjing as a result partly of Nationalist Party orders and partly of the choices made by local authorities. Plans had been made by the Nationalist Party headquarters for ceremonies across China to coincide with the moment of interment at precisely noon. All government offices, military organisations, party units, schools, factories and shops were ordered to close for the day. In the event newspapers reported a variety of commemorative activities ranging from the switching on of all the electric lights in the coastal city of Xiamen to a meeting held by a magistrate for local organisations in the Manchurian country town of Xi'an. As in the case of national institutions, local acceptance of Nationalist Party ideology interacted with the reality of weak political control.

PARTY IDEOLOGY

Following the model of the 'party nation' and Sun Yatsen's idea of a period of political tutelage the Nationalist government also worked to spread party ideology. Laws were issued on the 'partification' of education which would ensure that all schools and colleges conveyed the party's ideas to their pupils. A law issued for Zhejiang province in 1928 required every school to hold a weekly memorial ceremony in honour of Sun Yatsen every Monday morning at which reports would be given on politics and foreign affairs. In addition every school was to hold lectures on party ideology twice a month, set up a party branch and set essay titles that promoted party ideology. National laws were also issued requiring all education to emphasise the Three People's Principles, Sun Yatsen's summary of his ideology. Nationalism was the first of the principles and, for the Nationalist Party of the mid-1920s, the most important. Primary schools were legally required to inculcate the Three People's Principles by songs, lectures and even in science lessons. At university level all students were required to take part in a weekly Sun Yatsen memorial and to commemorate revolutionary anniversaries in order, the regulations stated, to increase their feelings of love for both party and country.

By the 1930s the Japanese had replaced the British as the primary exemplars of imperialism and much of this patriotic education was directed against Japan. Not only did textbooks dealing with the Three People's Principles, history and geography have many lessons dedicated to rousing students' feelings of nationalism and reminding them of past national humiliations, even arithmetic, calligraphy and drawing classes were used to promote patriotic ideas. Pupils had to do sums about the profits made by foreigners at the expense of the Chinese, practise writing patriotic slogans and draw pictures of Japanese atrocities. The compulsory classes on the Three People's Principles dealt with all of the major infringements of China's sovereignty that had resulted from the treaties of the nineteenth century, with particular emphasis on the foreign concessions and the fact that foreigners could not be tried in Chinese courts. They also emphasised China's territorial losses, and especially the loss of Korea and Taiwan to Japan. This kind of patriotic education built on the whole experience of modern education since the 1900s and was practised in schools outside the area of formal Nationalist government control. For many former students recalling their education during this period, the inculcation of patriotic feelings was the most memorable aspect of their years of schooling. From the 1900s nationalism had been central to all state-sponsored modern education and the Nationalist government's regulations and encouragement served to focus that nationalism on the issues of anti-imperialism and party rule.

A whole variety of texts ranging from party guidelines for propaganda to newly published school textbooks began to present a version of China's recent history centred on Sun Yatsen and the Nationalist Party. The history portrayed in these texts was publicised with the declaration of a calendar of national holidays commemorating important historical events. The author of a volume describing these holidays published by the Nationalist Party's military academy explained that all the holidays celebrated were related to Sun. In fact some of the links were tenuous, but it is true that the calendar presented a history focused around Sun, in which the Nationalist Party led the Chinese in a struggle against imperialism. The events commemorated began with the Treaty of Nanjing, the first of the 'unequal treaties', and included the commemoration of occasions on which Chinese demonstrators were killed by warlord armies or foreign police. Events such as the May 4th and May 30th incidents, in which the Nationalist Party was only peripherally involved, were commemorated only by meetings and processions. National holidays were reserved for the anniversaries of the birth of Sun Yatsen, a Nationalist uprising in Guangzhou which shortly preceded the 1911 Revolution, the outbreak of the 1911 Revolution, the establishment of the republic on 1 January 1912, the death of Sun Yatsen and the start of the Northern Expedition. This selection of anniversaries depicts the story of China's modern history as a battle between the imperialist foreign powers and the Nationalist Party.

Celebrations and commemorations were also a noticeable feature of the new Nationalist rule because of the large demonstrations organised to accompany them. The British consul in a southeastern port reacted to the newly arrived Nationalist government by complaining about the 'monster' open-air meetings that were taking place on every possible occasion and the 'ridiculous frequency' with which holidays occurred.[3] In 1929 one Jiangsu county followed central-government instructions on how to commemorate the anniversary of the Twenty-one Demands with particular enthusiasm. This meant that the county branch of the Nationalist Party summoned all government organisations, schools and party-sponsored organisations to a meeting which included speeches and propaganda about the unequal treaties of the nineteenth century, Yuan Shikai's treachery and the Nationalist Party's foreign policy. Despite being sponsored by the government, the commemoration of days of national humiliation often brought the risk of violence and rioting. Some of the riots were the result of local grievances but the fact that they were articulated in terms of nationalist feeling suggests widespread knowledge of the government's support for radical nationalism. By celebrating and commemorating major events in the history of the party as national holidays the Nationalist government was presenting a quite new understanding of the nation and of nationalism. The nation and its history were to be understood through the history and struggles of the party.

Spreading a modern national culture

The continued promotion of the cultural forms of the modern nation accompanied the spread of the new government's ideology. Drawing from its origins among the urban modernising classes, the Nationalist government demanded of all its citizens forms of behaviour that had previously been associated with self-styled citizens of the republic. These included the use of the solar calendar, natural feet for women and short hair for men. There was also a violent campaign against popular religion. Later, faced with communist-led rebellions in certain rural areas, Chiang Kaishek initiated a campaign, known as the New Life Movement, that was intended to create disciplined military citizens. All these campaigns drew from the ideas of the modernisers of the late Qing and early republic with their interest in modern culture and militarism as means of strengthening the nation.

Perhaps the most widespread, and certainly the most widely resented, of these reforms was the imposition of the solar calendar. One of the first actions of Sun Yatsen's government in 1912 had been formally to adopt the solar calendar. Attempts during the 1910s and 1920s to encourage the adoption of the solar calendar had had little effect beyond government circles. As one petition sent in to the Nationalist government in 1927 stated:

> When the PARTY LEADER [Sun Yatsen] established the new national calendar, on the one hand he was strenuously seeking world harmony, and on the other he was stimulating the spirit of the nation. But in the sixteen years between the first year of the republic and today it has been overwhelmed by the old forces and the old customs. Although the new national calendar which the PARTY LEADER established is used in political circles and banks, the people still keep to the lunar calendar and superstitious and immoral customs are as widespread as they were before.[4]

The writer of this petition went on to urge the government to enforce the use of the solar calendar, saying that if people would only use the solar calendar for weddings, trade, monthly receipts and the annual clearance of debts the gods of the old calendar would be forgotten. The government responded positively to initiatives of this kind, with bans on the printing of calendars that included lunar dates alongside the solar ones and laws requiring debts to be settled according to solar rather than lunar dates. Government policies also encouraged New Year celebrations on the solar 1 January and attempted to ban the celebration of the lunar New Year. Measures taken to implement this last ban varied widely but were almost always unpopular: in one country town where the county magistrate had banned sales of incense and images of deities a crowd attacked the government building and beat up several government employees. In rural Shanxi, diarist Liu Dapeng recorded the Nationalist Party's ban on lunar New Year celebrations and visited a local town where people were said not to have had any celebrations at all. He was delighted to find an old man who told him that although people had not been allowed to paste up the customary red paper couplets by the doors of their houses they had in fact kept the holiday in their homes. Like many of the people who wrote petitions that have been preserved in the national archives, Liu Dapeng strongly disapproved of the government's efforts to promote the solar calendar and saw them as going against the people's wishes. Nevertheless, in 1929 his own family recognised the solar New Year for the first time by eating meat dumplings to mark the occasion. Under pressure from the Nationalist government, the solar calendar as a symbol of modern citizenship was gradually being recognised not only in the urban areas of the coastal provinces but also in the rural interior.

Another symbol of modern citizenship that was spread as a result of Nationalist rule was natural feet for women. Foot binding had been banned in 1912 by the republican government, which was deeply concerned with the physical strength of its citizens. As it had done with the solar calendar, the Nationalist government of 1928 renewed the campaign of 1912, though now against a background of considerable popular support for the ending of what had already come to be widely seen as a damaging custom. The government issued a new law banning foot binding, demanding that girls under 14 whose feet were being bound should have them unbound immediately and giving older women three months to complete the painful process. Another law issued and publicised at the same time reiterated the government ban on the wearing of the queue for men. However, the queue had long since ceased to be widespread; foot binding on the other hand was still widely practised and the new government's campaign had a considerable effect. A country girl whose mother had begun to bind her feet in 1928, when she was just 5 years old, and stopped as a result of the campaign, remembered a song that was used for propaganda in her hometown:

> Good ears must not be pierced,
> Good natural feet must not be bound,
> As for the useless hair, quickly cut it.[5]

In Chenliu county in Henan the county magistrate, who was head of the Nationalist Party education office and a keen party member, made himself extremely unpopular by organising tough campaigns against queues and bound feet. These ranged from requiring all primary school-boys to wear armbands declaring 'I swear not to marry a woman with bound feet' to sending groups of armed police round people's homes to investigate the women and girls. The police were required to confiscate the cloths used for footbinding, usually regarded as polluted and unmentionable objects, and publicly burn them. Hardly surprisingly, in many families the women hid and their families stood by terrified as the soldiers searched through chests, beds and woodpiles. Women who did not unbind their feet were threatened with being paraded publicly through the streets. A foreign observer in another part of Henan reported women having the bandages torn off their feet in the streets, which was both extremely painful and deeply shaming. Campaigns like these relied on a combination of fear and propaganda to spread to the rural interior changes that had already occurred in many urban coastal areas.

Prompted by the Nationalist government and party many local authorities also conducted campaigns against popular religious worship, often culminating in the destruction or beheading of statues of deities. Widespread belief in the power of these deities meant that often the magistrate himself would be the only person in the town actually willing to strike the first blow against the statue. In Chenliu groups sent to pull down statues marched through the town shouting 'Down with the gods!' and 'Destroy superstition!', but when they actually came to the temples they recited a rhyme to avert the gods' anger, and put the blame for their actions on the government:

> I don't blame you, don't you blame me,
> Just blame our big brother Feng Yuxiang.[6]

(Feng Yuxiang was the radical warlord allied to the Nationalist Party who had set the campaign in motion in this area.) Local government campaigns of this sort often led to riots. Nevertheless, they did succeed in making clear the new Nationalist government's commitment to a modern nation. People might resist government policy, but if they wanted to manipulate or deal with the government they knew they had to present their case in the new styles. Thus the Nanjing government's self-presentation as a modern nation state gradually came to influence a much broader array of people.

The New Life Movement

In 1934 Chiang Kaishek announced the start of a formal campaign to create a new disciplined and militarised national consciousness. This was the New Life Movement and was initially aimed at the rural areas of Jiangxi where the Communist Party had succeeded in winning power. The movement provided a structured form for spreading cultural change and patriotic education to the villages. Because it was intended to reduce the power of the Communist Party the nationalism that was promoted was strictly tied to devotion to the Nationalist Party. The organisers also tried to distinguish the Nationalist Party from the more radical Communist Party by appealing to certain aspects of a shared cultural past as the foundations for nationalism.

In particular, the New Life Movement promoted the traditional Confucian virtues of propriety, righteousness, integrity and honour. These were chosen to conform with Chiang Kaishek's goal of promoting a disciplined modern nationalism. Filial piety, the primary Confucian virtue, which had been the subject of so much radical attack, was ignored. The promotion of certain selected Confucian virtues was combined with a revival of honours to Confucius in a modern style. The traditional autumn sacrifices to Confucius were renewed in 1929, but were held on a solar date said to be the anniversary of Confucius' birth. A few years later this was made into a national holiday, another entirely modern practice. The Nationalist Party's interest in Confucius suggests the extent to which an expanding portion of the past was now no longer seen as a threat to the modern nation. Although this shared cultural past had provided the foundation for much nationalist feeling, for the modernising Nationalist Party to endorse it was a major change and left many of the party's earlier supporters with a sense of betrayal.

The New Life Movement was much attacked by radicals at the time as a revival of a discredited Confucian past, but it was also seen by many Westerners as an example of a developing Chinese fascism. This view was encouraged by Chiang Kaishek, who made speeches praising militarism in Japan and Germany. A British author who toured rural Jiangxi in 1934 recorded the heavy military influence on primary education at the height of the movement. In one primary school he visited, one of the boys shouted to the other children to stand up as he entered the classroom. Boys and girls 'promptly rose to their feet and stood at soldier-like attention, shoulders thrown back, heads erect. Silence reigned.' When he then asked one of the girls why she came to school she replied, 'I am studying in order to become educated and in order to become a good and true citizen of China, so that I can help my country.'[7] The emphasis on militarism has often been attributed to Chiang Kaishek's personal character and his military background and training. However, as we have seen, the image of the modern Chinese citizen as the citizen-soldier had been a major theme of nationalism since the 1900s. The emphasis on cleanliness, discipline and physical exercise was part of a certain view of nationalist pride being tied to China's military strength that was to continue into the 1960s and 1970s. Like the promotion of the solar calendar and the attacks on foot binding and popular religion, the New Life Movement drew on images of the modern citizen created in the 1900s and attempted to spread them beyond the narrow segment of the population to which they had originally appealed. At the same time the movement tied that heritage of modernity in to the Nationalist Party.

The limits of Nationalist Party rule

The New Life Movement is almost invariably dismissed as a failure because the rules it promoted did not appear either to change people or to strengthen the nation. Indeed the movement is frequently satirised as an example of petty-minded modernity, as in the rules against spitting or those requiring people to button their jackets up to the collar. The image of the movement as a failed attempt to promote a series of petty rules is particularly appealing because it provides a symbol of what is seen as the failure of the whole Nationalist government. In terms of direct control by the Nanjing government and Chiang Kaishek over political decision-making in the provinces this image is certainly true. Up until 1937 only the provinces of Jiangsu and Zhejiang were effectively controlled by the party, and even there large parts of Shanghai were under foreign rule. Other parts of the country were controlled by the major regional power-holders such as Feng Yuxiang and Yan Xishan, who frequently made and broke alliances with Chiang. There were also many areas which were outside the control of the provincial governments let alone the central government. The remote areas of Jiangxi and later Shaanxi occupied by Communist bases were the most politically contentious parts of a much more general problem. During the course of the 1930s Chiang Kaishek's personal control expanded as a result of his campaigns against the Communists, which allowed him to bring large numbers of troops and assert his authority over the regional power-holders. However, despite this expansion of military power, the Nanjing government continued to be troubled by the weakness of its own administrative system. As part of the government's claim to national power, bureaucrats in Nanjing designed plans and worked on a scale that assumed a far greater degree of national control than the party in fact had. In addition the government lacked both the finance and the personnel to carry out many of the plans. The combination of an emphasis on paying for a prestigious, and legitimising, facade of national government with an inability to extract taxes from the regional and local power-holders who collected them meant that direct policy implementation was almost impossible even in the areas the government did control.

However, the failures of the Nanjing government should not blind us to the extent to which many of the processes of nationalism, and indeed of state-building, continued through the first 10 years of Nationalist rule. Nationalist policies, especially those relating to nationalism and cultural change, were in fact implemented in areas entirely outside the direct control of Chiang Kaishek or the Nanjing government. In fact many of the examples of cultural change in this chapter were taken from such areas. The campaign against foot binding led by a Nationalist Party official in Chenliu county Henan took place under the rule of Feng Yuxiang, while calendar reform was only one of a series of new policies promoted by Yan Xishan in Shanxi immediately after the Nationalist Party rise to power. Like several other so-called warlords, Feng Yuxiang and Yan Xishan were active modernisers and shared many of the ideals of the Nationalist Party. A Chinese journalist who visited Feng Yuxiang's troops in 1927 reported that they sang a song called 'Abolish the unequal treaties' before their drill session and another entitled

'Down with imperialism' before their political lecture. In 1928 Feng created rules requiring various forms of commemoration of Sun Yatsen. These included requiring all newspapers to print commemorative materials and all government organisations to mobilise speech-making teams. To some extent enthusiasm for the symbols of the politicised nationalism promoted by the Nationalist Party fluctuated depending on the state of the regional leaders' relations with Chiang Kaishek. However, claims of loyalty to the nation and to the ideas of Sun Yatsen were among the weapons that could be used against the Nanjing government even in times of tension. When the Nationalist government was constructing a series of monumental buildings along the new Zhongshan (Sun Yatsen) Road in Nanjing, Feng Yuxiang had a small mud-brick hut built by the side of the road and went there regularly to drink tea, pointedly referring to Nationalist Party corruption and extravagance.

This sense of the existence of a national government that reached beyond its actual power was very important for the spread of the idea of the modern nation. In 1930 the writer Huang Gongdu conducted a sociological survey of a 100 rickshaw pullers in Beijing. The questions asked included 'What is the Republic of China?' and 'What is revolution?'[8] When asked 'What is the Republic of China?', 50 of the rickshaw pullers replied with phrases such as 'We are' or 'Our country' which suggested that it was something they identified with. Others used phrases Huang Gongdu identified as being drawn from the theatre or tea-house story-tellers: 'The land of the Great Han', 'All within the five lakes and four seas' or 'The descendants of the Yellow Emperor'. Although these terms seemed more traditional to Huang Gongdu, they reflect the changing slogans of nationalism of the early twentieth century, for example the idea of China as the kingdom of the Han rather than the Manchus, and the idea of the Han as a race linked by kinship and descended from the Yellow Emperor. There were also more contemporary political references: 'the five-nation republic' and 'the party state'. When asked 'What is revolution?', many of the rickshaw pullers replied that it was an attack on foreign power in China. The terms used for what was to be attacked ranged from 'imperialism' to 'the Japanese' or 'foreigners', but all suggested an understanding of what the Nationalist Party regarded as one of its main sources of legitimation. Some of the other rickshaw pullers even mentioned Sun Yatsen's doctrine, the Three People's Principles. Beijing was part of an area that Chiang Kaishek himself could not usually enter and the city was certainly outside his control. Nevertheless ordinary people could and did absorb some of the symbols and ideology of the nationalism promoted by the Nationalist government in Nanjing. Thus politicised nationalism came to be common currency not only in the eastern coastal heartland of modern nationalism and indeed of Nationalist Party rule, but also in both rural and urban areas outside Nanjing's control.

Conclusion

The Nationalist Party brought to the Chinese public a new vision of the nation: instead of being beyond and above party politics the nation was redefined as the embodiment of the party. Nationalism was politicised and claims of nationalism were tied in to government policy, a state of affairs that was to continue well into the 1980s. Through the same process the modern urban elite used nationalism to justify their claim to power over the rest of the largely rural population. The political divisions of the country, which continued into the 1930s, meant that resistance to the culture of modern nationalism was often possible. Nevertheless, the culture and ideology promoted by the Nationalist Party were shared by a large proportion of the political elite and were promoted in many areas that were outside the control of the Nanjing government. The new political understanding of the nation was at the heart of this shared ideology even though the different political leaders might disagree about its meaning.

Notes

1 *North China Herald*, 6 November 1926, p. 243.
2 Ou Zhenhua, *Beifa xingjun riji* (Diary of Travelling as a Soldier with the Northern Expedition) (Guangdong yinwuju, 1931), p. 352.
3 PRO FO 228/3272, Swatow Intelligence Reports September 1926 and March 1927.
4 No. 2 Archives 1.1796 18/7/1927.
5 Li Songling, 'Yi fangzu' (Recollections of unbinding my feet), *Nanyang xian wenshi ziliao* (Nanyang County Historical Materials) 4 (1990).
6 Zhang Shifang, 'Ershi niandai Chenliu xian shehui fengqi de gaige' (Reforms in the atmosphere of society in Chenliu county in the 1920s), *Kaifeng xian wenshi ziliao* (Kaifeng County Historical Materials) 1 (1987.
7 C.W.H. Young, *New Life for Kiangsi* (Shanghai: China Publishing Co., 1935), p. 2.
8 Huang Gongdu, 'Duiyu wuchan jieji shehui taidu de yige xiaoxiao ceyan' (A small test of the social attitudes of the proletariat), *Shehui xuejie* (The Sociological World) 4 (1930).

9

War, nationalism and identity

Japanese aggression during the 1930s and 1940s brought to a much larger proportion of the population the issues that had long spurred nationalist ideas in the political elite. In the areas of north and east China that were under Japanese occupation for much of the war nationalism became the dominant issue even in village-level politics. At the same time many of the nationalist modernisers of the urban elite were driven from their homes. Their flight not only provided the opportunity for them to spread the ideas of the resistance, but also made them realise that the fashionable urban culture of modernity could sometimes be a barrier to the spread of nationalism in rural areas.

Responses to Japanese aggression

Manchuria

On 18 September 1931 the Japanese military seized control of the three most northeastern provinces of China, that is the area that had once been the Manchu homeland lying north of the Great Wall and bordering on Korea and Russia. Korea was a Japanese colony and Japan had had interests in the area since the 1890s. In 1904 Japan had fought Russia for dominance over the region. As a result of its victory in that war Japan had gained concessions, the most important of which were the strategically important city of Dalian (then known as Port Arthur) and control over the newly built railway network. Thus, when in 1931 the decision was taken to occupy the whole of Manchuria the Japanese troops were able to move rapidly out from their bases in Korea and around Dalian along a Japanese-controlled railway network. The startling speed of the Japanese conquest was also the result of the fact that Chiang Kaishek had ordered the Chinese forces in the area, which were under the leadership of Zhang Xueliang, not to resist.

Chiang Kaishek's action was motivated by China's internal politics. Zhang Xueliang was the son of Zhang Zuolin, a man who had risen from banditry to become the predominant militarist north of the Great Wall during the 1910s and 1920s. Zhang Zuolin had ruled the area with some concessions to the Japanese, who eventually murdered him, but none to the Beijing government. After his father's death and the rise of the Nationalist government, Zhang Xueliang behaved like many other regional military leaders. He flew the Nationalist shining sun flag, presented himself as a moderniser wearing Western-style suits and encouraging athletic competitions, and paid lip service to the government in Nanjing. In practice, the power politics of the 1920s continued and to stay in even nominal control Chiang Kaishek had to ensure a balance of power between the forces of the various former militarists. In 1930 the most powerful of the remaining militarists, Yan Xishan and Feng Yuxiang, formed an alliance against him. Chiang called on Zhang Xueliang to come to his help. In the war that followed Zhang Xueliang did indeed support Chiang Kaishek, but this meant that when the Japanese invasion came in 1931 many of Zhang Xueliang's troops were engaged south of the Great Wall in north China. Chiang Kaishek knew that if these troops were moved back to Manchuria it was probable that Yan Xishan and Feng Yuxiang would restart the civil war. On the other hand the loss of Manchuria to Japan deprived Zhang Xueliang of a base while not diminishing the territory that Chiang himself controlled.

Chiang Kaishek and Zhang Xueliang's decision to abandon Manchuria was less problematic for most Chinese than it might at first seem, because of the area's ambiguous relationship to the rest of the country. The very fact that it lay outside the Great Wall was of considerable symbolic importance. Moreover, as the original homeland of the Manchus, until the late nineteenth century Manchuria, like Mongolia and Tibet, had been administratively separate from the areas of the former Ming empire. The Qing court had attempted to obstruct the large-scale Han Chinese immigration that began in the eighteenth century with the expansion of agriculture in Manchuria, and particularly the rise in the trade in soya-bean products. However, Qing officials lacked the administrative capacity to control population movements effectively and many Han Chinese provincial officials saw emigration to border regions such as Manchuria as a way of coping with a rapidly expanding agricultural population. By the late nineteenth century, when, in the face of Japanese and Russian expansion, Manchuria was finally absorbed into the system of provincial government used for the rest of China, its population was predominantly Han Chinese. However, a residual sense of a separate identity was encouraged by the fact that from the 1910s the rule of Zhang Zuolin kept Manchuria separate from the rest of the country. After taking control of Manchuria, the Japanese exploited this heritage of ambiguity and mixed identity by setting up a puppet Manchu kingdom, Manchukuo, under the nominal leadership of the last Qing emperor, who had abdicated as a child in 1912.

The establishment of a Manchu kingdom in the Manchu homeland did have a certain amount of legitimacy among at least part of the Chinese population. However, perhaps more importantly, a general sense that Manchuria was a peripheral area weakened the immediate nationalist response to the Japanese invasion. Chinese nationalists who had been driven out of Manchuria by the Japanese invasion and were campaigning for resistance initially found it hard to win popular support in the south. However, the lack of immediate sympathy was eventually outweighed, at least for a large part of the educated elite, by the vigour of the exiles' campaigns. The exiles built up a narrative of Chinese resistance to Japanese invasion through the newspapers and other forms of propaganda. This narrative was centred on the stories of heroes such as Ma Zhanshan, a minor militarist in the remote north of Manchuria who had disobeyed Zhang Xueliang's instructions and fought against the Japanese, forcing them to launch a campaign in order to take the town of Qiqihar. The aim, and to some extent the effect, of these stories of resistance heroes was to redefine what had been Manchuria and was now described by the Japanese as Manchukuo (literally the Manchu country) as the 'three northeastern provinces' of China. Through this process as much as through the earlier Han immigration, Manchuria became part of China in the popular imagination. The result was an outpouring of protest at the Nationalist failure to resist the Japanese. The most striking features of this protest were student demonstrations in Nanjing and a major boycott of Japanese goods that started in Shanghai. Such protests against the Nationalist government began the process of undermining its very legitimacy as a government, which was based on the nationalist and anti-imperialist rhetoric of its rise to power. It was students and the modern educated elite to whom this rhetoric had had the greatest appeal and their support had been crucial to the party; it was these very groups who now began to be disillusioned.

Shanghai

The Japanese conquest of Manchuria was followed the same year by an attack on Shanghai, which was strenuously resisted by soldiers of the Nationalist army but nevertheless further undermined the nationalist credentials of the Nanjing government. Strong anti-Japanese feeling in Shanghai as a result of the crisis in Manchuria had given rise to fights between Chinese workers and Japanese living in the city. Eventually the Japanese admiral based in Shanghai used one of these street fights to give an ultimatum to the city's Chinese mayor demanding the withdrawal of all Chinese troops. When, in response to this, Chinese troops were indeed ordered to withdraw, the troops of the 19th Route Army refused to go and led a successful resistance to the Japanese. The 19th Route Army was from

Guangdong and was affiliated with the Cantonese faction of the Nationalist
Party that opposed Chiang Kaishek. Chiang Kaishek's own troops had been
purged and bullied into cooperation with the policy of non-resistance, but
the leaders of the 19th Route Army had not and their affiliations within the
party meant that they had few qualms about disobeying Chiang's orders.
The fighting that followed their resistance took place in the heart of
Shanghai and resulted in the fire bombing of many buildings and a total of
between 10,000 and 20,000 civilian deaths. Once the resistance had begun
Chiang Kaishek did send reinforcements, but although these troops fought
bravely, the Nationalist government was perceived as having done too little
too late.

The fighting in Shanghai had a huge and immediate impact on public
opinion. This was partly because a lot of what was considered as evidence
of 'public opinion' was in fact created in Shanghai and the surrounding
area. Not only did Shanghai produce several of China's most important and
successful newspapers, but Shanghai people were among the country's
major consumers of newspapers and magazines. With the Japanese attack,
the emerging consumer culture of Shanghai was suddenly turned over to
questions of politics. Thus, for example, *Life Magazine*, which had previously been active in popularising modern lifestyles, now began to publish
explicitly patriotic material. The magazine included articles praising the
Manchurian resistance hero Ma Zhanshan, and others appealing for funds
for the 19th Route Army. Eyewitness accounts of Japanese massacres
brought the violence and fear of the fighting into the imagination of large
numbers of readers at the same time as the magazine was printing attacks on
the Nationalist leaders for their failure to support the 19th Route Army
soldiers. Readers, who had previously written to the magazine with
accounts of their domestic problems, now began to write letters expressing
their outrage at the Japanese attacks and enclosing donations for the
resistance.

As a result of the arousal of public opinion, the leading officers of the
19th Route Army rapidly became heroes. When one of them, Cai Tingkai,
issued a public statement attacking Chiang Kaishek for failing to support
the resistance, it was a direct threat to Nationalist Party legitimacy. Cai
Tingkai, like Ma Zhanshan in Manchuria, became part of an image of a
successful popular resistance defeated only because of the government's
failure to give leadership. The Nationalist Party's legitimacy had been based
on its close ties with the story of modern nationalism and its ability to create
a politicised nationalism focused around the party. The Japanese invasion of
Manchuria and attack on Shanghai at the very beginning of the 1930s began
the process of undermining this politicised nationalism even while the
obvious Japanese threat combined with the modernisation of education and
lifestyles was serving to spread feelings of nationalism to a much larger
proportion of the population.

Nationalist movements in the 1930s

Nationalist feeling among modern-educated elites was kept aflame through the 1930s by continuous Japanese diplomatic and military pressure on the Chinese government. In 1933 Japanese troops moved south through the passes that divided Manchuria from China and towards Beijing, reminding people of stories of the Manchu invasion of the seventeenth century. Negotiations ended in the creation of a demilitarised zone just north of Beijing and Tianjin, which severely limited the government's control over the area. Then in 1935 as the result of further disputes and alleged infringements of earlier agreements the government was pressured into agreeing to remove all 'anti-Japanese' forces from north China. This effectively removed most of the government's own structures as well as its military and police forces. The Japanese also increasingly demanded that the Nationalist government suppress civilian anti-Japanese activities. The government was forced to accept these and other developments because of its fear of superior Japanese military power. However, it was also obvious that Chiang Kaishek was prepared to accept some of the Japanese demands as the price for concentrating his forces on defeating rival claimants to power within the area of Nationalist Party rule. This had been obvious in his decision to use Zhang Xueliang's troops against Feng Yuxiang and Yan Xishan rather than against the Japanese in Manchuria. However, as the decade progressed and the former militarists were weakened by the Japanese attacks, the full force of Chiang's determination to emphasise national unity increasingly fell on the Chinese Communist Party. When the Nationalist government closed down magazines like *Life* that urged resistance, or arrested the editor of the major Shanghai newspaper the *Shenbao*, it seemed to many people that Japanese demands for the suppression of anti-Japanese or Communist activities were being used by Chiang Kaishek as an excuse for suppression of all criticism of his own regime.

Chiang Kaishek's policy of 'first pacification, then resistance' was especially unpopular with the Nationalist Party's own supporters. The core of the party's support had previously come from the modern-educated classes who had been associated with the party during the radical anti-imperialist movements of the 1920s. Along with many others, these people had accepted the Nationalist Party's own dogma that 'warlords' were to be defined as those holders of power who were the tools of the imperialists. This collection of those who had received a modern education and those who had accepted parts of the Nationalist Party's own ideology in the 1920s provided the core of what are often described as the 'student' protests of the 1930s. These began in response to the Japanese attacks on Manchuria and Shanghai in 1931 and included propaganda groups visiting towns around Shanghai where they shouted slogans, made speeches, handed out leaflets and even put on plays. A boycott of Japanese goods was supported by the

Chinese Chamber of Commerce. The protests culminated in a large number of students travelling to Nanjing to petition the government directly. A foreign observer describing the participants and their activities wrote:

> During my twenty-seven years in China I have seen nothing which approximates the present intense though suppressed emotion . . . Students are carrying on an educational campaign in cities and rural districts with cartoons, pamphlets, and lectures; Chambers of Commerce in the cities are concerning themselves with drawing the lines so as to prevent the purchase, sale, and transportation of Japanese goods. Chinese compradores of Japanese firms are resigning their positions ... Committees devoted to the salvation of China, representing merchants and students and all classes, are meeting daily to promote the economic boycott ... Shop windows and vacant walls are covered with slogans [which] declare aggressive action against Japan and command people to boycott the Japanese. We noticed several signs on one shop near this building which read (in Chinese): No Japanese are admitted here.[1]

Although such protests continued intermittently throughout the 1930s, the level of popular participation and enthusiasm rose and fell with the political situation. In 1935 a particularly concentrated round of protests broke out over the government's agreement to remove anti-Japanese forces from much of north China and the arrests in Beijing of several prominent Chinese by the Japanese military police. Student demonstrations in Beijing demanded an end to the war against the Communists and military resistance to Japan. Curiously, the fact that the government had removed its forces from north China in accordance with the agreement meant that it was unable to suppress these demonstrations as it would otherwise probably have done. The protests spread across the country and resulted in the formation of many local and regional National Salvation Associations. These associations put most of their efforts into propaganda designed to arouse nationalist and anti-Japanese feeling. When, about a year later, the protests were beginning to die down they were reinvigorated by a crisis over the Japanese establishment of a puppet state in Inner Mongolia. Nationalist protests flared up across the country, with riots and attacks on Japanese in Chengdu and strikes in Japanese-owned textile mills in Shanghai. The sense of crisis was exacerbated by the Nationalist government's arrest of seven of the most prominent leaders of the National Salvation Movement, and more strikes and labour unrest followed.

As well as creating greater popular awareness of the Japanese threat, the protests threatened the Nationalist Party's remaining legitimacy among its original supporters. For not only had the Nationalist government failed to respond to the calls for resistance against the Japanese, but it had also violently suppressed many of the demonstrations and arrested and even executed their leaders. The result of the government's repression was that the protests came to be more and more closely associated with the Communist Party. The arrest of the leaders of the National Salvation Movement, most of whom were left-leaning intellectuals, increased this sense of links between resistance to Japan and the Communist opposition to the Nationalist Party. The National Salvation protests were also identified with the left because of their leaders' belief in the importance of mobilising the whole population, which was contrasted with Chiang Kaishek's emphasis on discipline as illustrated in the New Life Movement which he was promoting around the same time. Finally, the very fact that the Nationalist government attacked the protesters as 'Communists' had the effect of associating the Communist party with the National Salvation Movement and the student protests. However, for Chiang Kaishek's opponents to use their popular support to oppose the Nationalist government would have opened them to exactly the same accusations of concentrating on internal power struggles in the face of foreign invasion that they were levelling at him. Thus the effect of the Japanese invasion and the popular opposition to it was to strengthen Chiang Kaishek personally as the leader around whom the nation must unite, while at the same time undermining the legitimacy of the Nationalist Party.

At first much of this outpouring of nationalist feeling was expressed in ways that made it quite alien to large sections of the population. At the height of the 1935 protest movement a group of Beijing students decided to walk to the capital Nanjing. They set off across the north China plain distributing propaganda in the villages they passed through. The propaganda was written in the vernacular and designed to be understood by the villagers:

> Men, women, children! Listen to what we say: Have we seen those things, flying overhead every day? Those things are called 'airplanes'. Sitting in them are the devils of the Eastern Sea, the Japanese devils. They speak a foreign tongue, live in the Eastern Sea, and fly their airplanes over here.
>
> Do you know what they are coming to do? . . . They are coming to kill every single man and woman with their guns and knives, and to ravish our daughters and wives.[2]

According to a contemporary observer, the villagers watched the young people with 'frigid curiosity':

> They had heard about Japan – somewhere, indistinctly – but about Manchuria, the nearest point of which [was] barely seventy-five miles distant, most of them knew nothing. The appearance of the column of singing and shouting students was a spectacle to be looked at – like a wedding or a funeral, a break in the day's monotony . . . One of the farmers had countered the patriotic appeal of a student with the words: 'The present government seems all right. Our taxes are lower than before. Why bother us?'[3]

As this remark suggests, the students found that the villagers only really paid attention when the topic of the speeches was changed from the Japanese threat to suggestions that they should refuse to pay unnecessary taxes. On the other hand the students were welcomed by teachers and pupils in village schools, who, despite the large social gap between them and the gilded youth of Beijing's top universities, shared their concern with modern nationalism.

The rural population were not as ignorant of national events as the student protesters tended to assume. In addition to the traditional network of rumour and oral report, circulation of newspapers in the countryside had increased rapidly during the 1920s. Moreover, the area the students marched through was all within a few days' walk of the highly politicised city of Beijing. However, the villagers shared neither the students' attitudes nor their vocabulary. Their primary concern was with matters of such everyday personal importance as taxation, and they evidently did not feel that the recent Japanese manoeuvres posed an immediate threat to their villages. Shortly after war finally broke out the cartoonist Ye Qianyu published a cartoon entitled 'Let's change into new uniform!' showing a heroic young man stripping off a Western-style jacket as he prepares to put on the military uniform and pick up the gun lying before him (Fig. 9.1).

Figure 9.1 'Let's change into new uniform!'
Source: *Tianxia Monthly* 7.4 (Nov. 1938), reproduced in Hung Chang-tai, *War and Popular Culture: Resistance in Modern China, 1937–1945*. Berkeley: University of California Press, 1994

Such a figure suggests the close connection that was perceived to exist between the modern urban population and nationalist feeling, an image that largely excluded the majority of the population.

The outbreak of war and the rhetoric of national unity

The end of Chiang Kaishek's policy of appeasement is usually ascribed to the Xian incident of 1936. Chiang had travelled to the capital of Shaanxi to put pressure on Zhang Xueliang and another regional military leader to participate in his campaign against the Communists in the north of the province. However, when Chiang arrived in Xian the two commanders placed him under house arrest and demanded that he end the civil war against the Communists and turn his attention to resistance to Japan. Chiang remained under house arrest for two weeks, after which time his captors released him either because, as he claimed, they had been moved by the depth of patriotic feeling described in his diary or because he had given in to their demands. The conflicting accounts have meant that the Xian incident has often been depicted as a turning point driven by the personal decisions of the major political actors. However, as Parks Coble points out in his study of nationalism during this period, it is probably better understood as part of a process which included on the one hand the huge growth of the National Salvation Movement and thus of popular demands for resistance and on the other continued conflict over the balance of power between the regional militarists.[4] Ultimately war became inevitable and Chiang Kaishek was forced to accept the demands for resistance. The actual outbreak of war came one night in the summer of 1937 when Japanese forces were taking part in night manoeuvres near Lugouqiao, a strategic railway junction just north of Beijing. Shots were fired in the darkness and a soldier went missing. The Japanese officers demanded that they be allowed to search a nearby town. Chinese troops refused and when the Japanese began to shell the town a battle broke out. Shortly afterwards war was finally declared.

For many of those who had been calling for resistance the outbreak of war was experienced as both exhilarating and unifying. The divisive policy of appeasement was ended and the nation could unite against the Japanese. The writer Ba Jin, who was living in Shanghai, which faced heavy fighting very soon after the declaration of war, had just finished writing a poem entitled 'Freedom weeping in the darkness' about Japanese oppression and China's inability to respond. In a piece published shortly after the outbreak of war he wrote:

> In fact my poem had not yet been published, when the sound of gunfire finally resounded in Jiabei. This sound of gunfire broke through our doubt, discord and despair. This sound of gunfire

brought back our courage, confidence and zeal. This sound of gunfire
united four hundred and fifty million people into a solid single body.
The bloody battle of the front line soldiers, the heroic sacrifice of the
warriors of the air, the ardent service of the masses in the rear . . . one
week of the war of resistance has already placed the flag of Freedom
firmly in the soil of Shanghai.[5]

For many modern intellectuals like Ba Jin the war provided the sense of
national unity and purpose they had been seeking since the 1900s.

Much of the rhetoric through which the war was understood grew out of
these ideas. The emphasis on resistance as the source of national unity
meant that the only alternative to heroic resistance was treachery. The
cartoon 'Let's change into new uniform!' depicts the citizen turned soldier
as hero (Fig. 9.1). The figure of the citizen with his legs spread and his arms
wide dominates the picture and breaks into the title line that runs along the
top of the picture. Even as he strips off his Western-style suit, he displays his
broad muscular chest and the power of his physique. His expression is of
fierce determination. Contrasted to such heroes of the resistance are the
bestial Japanese and their Chinese collaborators. Reports of Japanese atrocities and massacres, such as the Rape of Nanjing, depicted the Japanese
soldiers as scarcely human in their lust for blood. Chinese collaborators
were described as traitors to the Han race and prostitutes without any sense
of shame. Wang Jingwei, once a republican hero and now head of the
Nanjing puppet government, was depicted as the archetype of these shameless traitors.

The other great theme of wartime rhetoric that grew out of the idea that
the war would create national unity was the theory that the commitment of
the masses would be the source of victory. This was not new: an emphasis
on the importance of the spirit of the common people had been at the heart
of the conservative response to the Western threat in the nineteenth century.
The disastrous results of ignoring superior Western armaments and relying
on the people's spirit had, it seemed, been finally demonstrated in the failure
of the Boxer movement. However, the idea, with its origins in the Confucian
emphasis on the importance of the people's support for the upright ruler,
had never entirely died away. It was now taken up again as part of the
socialist emphasis on mass movements. Many intellectuals came to think
that victory in the war required the creation of a mass movement that would
provide support for the government. This was at the heart of the
Communist Party's thinking about the war, but was much less enthusiasti-
cally supported by the Nationalists, who tended to be afraid of the influence
that any such mass movement might give to the Communists. For the
Communists and for many others Japanese weapons would never succeed
when they were pitted against the heroism and determination of the Chinese
common people. Communist Party propaganda materials about the importance of rural militias in the fight against the Japanese illustrate the point

well. One of these describes the resistance in rural Jiangsu, where militia groups formed from the peasantry and operating close to their home villages had caused considerable disruption to the Japanese war effort:

> As a result, the Japanese devils hated them to the bone. They burned down at least 60 houses that belonged to active militiamen. Yet cruelty only deepens the militiaman's resolve. A militiaman, Ts'ai Yun-ho, told his mother that 'the Japanese burned down our house. It only removes any hesitancy I once had. From now on, I will make my home everywhere. While fighting the guerrilla war, I need not worry about my house any longer.' Day and night, the devils looked for the militiamen. But no matter how hard they tried, they could find none because no Chinese would give them a clue. Does silence mean nobody joined the militia? The devils were constantly besieged by sporadic shooting from every direction. The militia was everywhere. The masses treated the militiaman as their own child. An old widow of a billeting house entreated a militiaman to use her only child's bed. A young woman also admonished her husband that 'In a time as tumultuous as this, you had better join the militia. I can take care of the family.'[6]

Such stories of self-sacrificing assistance to the militia draw together the two themes of the heroic resistance of the ordinary Chinese soldiers and the importance of mass support.

It was this rhetoric that was picked up by Chalmers Johnson in *Peasant Nationalism and Communist Power*, his famous account of the origins of Communist power in China.[7] Johnson argued that Japanese brutality during the war and especially the indiscriminate terror of the mop-up campaigns behind Japanese lines meant that collaboration was seen by the rural population as useless. So the peasants realised that they needed to resist the Japanese and that only the Communist Party was prepared to provide them with leadership. The Communist Party was seen as leading the fighting against the Japanese, while the Nationalists were associated both with their earlier policy of appeasement and with the collaborationist forces of Wang Jingwei. Japanese brutality caused the peasants to hate Japan and thus created feelings of nationalism. At the same time these feelings were strengthened by Communist Party propaganda, which emphasised nationalism rather than economic policies such as land reform. This argument takes the wartime rhetoric of national unity and the importance of mass support and develops it into an interpretation of the rise of the Communist Party to power. There is clearly some truth in this, especially in relation to the villages of the north China plain where the Nationalist Party's withdrawal of its forces at the start of the war meant that the Communist Party was indeed able to step in and lead local defence forces. However, the stark contrasts that Johnson depicts between nationalism and collaboration are drawn as much from rhetoric as reality and ignore the complexity of the choices that individuals actually had to make.

Nationalism has sometimes been defined as a feeling that prompts a person to put their loyalty to the nation above all other loyalties. This was certainly an idea that was accepted by some Chinese during the war, as is apparent from a story recounted by a historian in Beijing many years later. During the war this man was a schoolboy living with his parents in Chongqing, the headquarters of the Nationalist government, where his parents had fled from Beijing after pressure had been put on his father to collaborate with the Japanese. When, in the autumn of 1944, the Japanese army was approaching, the boy asked his father what they would do if the Japanese arrived. His father looked out of the window at the Yangzi River and replied in terms that implied that suicide would be the only answer. The boy panicked and asked what would become of him, to which his father replied, 'If such a day really comes, can we still care for you?'[8] But few people could give such a resolute response; indeed many would not have thought such a response right or appropriate. In any case resolute resistance in the face of extreme violence was never an easy choice to make.

In recent years there have been several studies of the war that emphasise the complexities of people's responses to feelings of nationalism. Poshek Fu has described the ambiguity of the nationalist responses of intellectuals in occupied Shanghai.[9] Few dared openly resist in the face of Japanese terror that included bombings, political kidnappings, torture and murder. The offices of newspapers that published material considered to be anti-Japanese were bombed so frequently that they were fortified with iron fences and sandbags. Many journalists were assassinated and kidnapped, leaving others too terrified to speak out. Those who did resist in any way were hesitant and fearful not only for their lives but because if they lost their jobs they and their families would find it hard to survive. Under such pressures there were also many who gave way and cooperated with the Japanese. Such collaborators were not the shameless prostitutes of the resistance rhetoric; many felt deep remorse for their actions while nevertheless justifying them as a patriotic necessity – part of the struggle to save China's heritage and culture from the destructive war. In such a situation all choices were ambiguous and compromise was inevitable.

Chen Yung-fa has described similar responses in the occupied areas of rural Jiangsu. Here the inevitability of a certain degree of compromise with the Japanese was recognised even by the Communist Party in a policy known as 'white skin, red heart'. This policy allowed, and even encouraged, people to give an outward show of submission to Japanese rule as long as they were willing to help the Communist resistance forces in secret. The party assumed that most people would waver and only attacked really notorious collaborators. Participation in the resistance was equally complex. In north China, panic at the moment of Japanese invasion provided an opportunity for leadership by Communist cadres. On the other hand, in central and southern China, the arrival of the Japanese gave rise to local self-defence forces with little or no national commitment. So, for example, in one Jiangsu village, where puppet troops had repeatedly pillaged and burned houses and kidnapped people, the villagers armed themselves to resist, wounded an intruder and rescued several captives. Such a response was not necessarily nationalist but could easily be considered to have arisen from the highly militarised society of the previous years where villages had often had to defend themselves against the depradations of bandits and petty warlords. Villagers were prepared to fight for the safety of their homes and families, but this did not always lead to them joining up with organised resistance forces. Indeed in areas where homes were looted and burnt and villagers raped and beaten, fear of the Japanese forces was also likely to be a driving factor. Fear and localism meant that support for the Communist-led resistance forces had to be carefully built up. At the beginning this was mainly done by young urban-educated cadres motivated by nationalism. They worked to build a resistance out of villagers' need for self-defence and leadership, combined with education in national politics, and the institution of such economic changes as rent reduction. As we look closer the clear distinction between heroic resistance and treacherous collaboration seems to vanish.

The convergence of popular and modern nationalism

As well as drawing an overly simple distinction between resistance and collaboration, Johnson's argument for the role of the Japanese invasion in creating peasant nationalism underestimates the role of existing nationalism in the countryside. I would argue that what the war of resistance saw was not so much the creation of nationalism in a countryside previously characterised by peasant insularity as a change in the nature of both traditional rural and modern urban forms of national identity. This change began with the flight of many members of the elites of the highly modernised east coast cities into the interior at the start of the war. The great cities of Beijing, Tianjin, Shanghai, Guangzhou and Nanjing had all fallen within a year of the outbreak of war, and with them many of the wealthy smaller cities and towns of the Yangzi delta. Meanwhile the National government moved from Nanjing up the Yangzi to Wuhan and then yet further inland to the city of Chongqing, the capital of Sichuan province. Hundreds of thousands of people fled before the Japanese or followed the Nationalist government to the interior. Many of these refugees were members of the educated urban elite. They had seen their homes and their lives destroyed by the fighting and they were determined to arouse the Chinese people to resist Japan.

The refugees tried to convey the importance of nationalism through a whole variety of media ranging from songs and speech-making teams to cartoons and journalism. Drama troupes provide a particularly interesting example since they enabled the participants to observe the audience's response. Spoken drama was a Western art form that had first been imported to China in the 1900s, but had failed to acquire a popular following and was mostly performed by amateurs. However, the fall of Shanghai brought the closure of the thriving cinema industry there, and many of its stars fled the city along with other refugees. When spoken-drama troupes were formed to promote nationalism, the names of these stars proved a powerful attraction for audiences. The dramas they performed laid aside the intellectual concerns that had previously marked the genre in favour of simple, accessible political messages. Plays were informal and short, and were performed in all kinds of public spaces from street corners to tea houses.

One well-known short play that was particularly successful was called *Lay Down Your Whip*. It began with an old man and his daughter, destitute refugees fleeing from the Japanese. They were scraping a living through the girl's acrobatics and singing, and when she performed poorly the old man raised his whip against her. At this point a young man would rush out of the crowd shouting, 'Lay down your whip!' The girl then defended her father, recounting the family's misfortunes, and the young man called on the audience to fight against Japanese oppression. Although there were various different versions of this play the central point was always the same: a call to resistance. This play is said to have been particularly popular and successful, but the symbols of nationalism used by the urban-educated performers were not always so comprehensible to village audiences. One actor recalled his experiences performing in the villages around the south-western city of Guilin:

> We first mounted two shows in a large village: *Little Compatriots in Shanghai* [*Shanghai xiao tongbao*] and *We Have Beaten Back the Enemy* [*Diren datui le*]. Some spectators raised the following questions: 'What are you people doing up there on the stage? How come those young fellows act so recklessly up there? Why aren't there any gongs and drums [as in traditional opera]?' Our conclusion was that the country folk definitely needed a kind of play bustling with noise and excitement . . .
>
> We ran into snags when we staged another show in a different village. The villagers simply did not understand what we were performing. They didn't know what we were talking about and did not understand the play at all. They couldn't even recognize Japanese troops. We had to immediately cut short the dialogue and increase the action scenes, at the same time making it more comical. But all of this still fell on deaf ears: there simply was no response from the audience![10]

According to Hung Chang-tai, who has studied this kind of dramatic propaganda, such complaints were frequently made.

National feeling existed in the Chinese countryside as part of people's sense of identity, but it had not previously been expressed in the same forms as the modern nationalism that had been promoted through the education system and had taken hold in the east coast cities. Although the actors in modern spoken drama might complain of the lack of audience response, the huge propaganda effort that took place during the war was quite successful in bringing the symbols and rhetoric of modern nationalism to a much wider audience. At the same time the circulation of newspapers increased rapidly. Newspaper reading had already expanded during the 1920s and 1930s as the gradual expansion of the railway network made distribution both faster and cheaper. The outbreak of war meant that there was an urgent demand for news. The circulation of the major national newspapers published in the east coast cities increased and many new newspapers were also established, especially as the east coast papers came under increasingly close Japanese control. Newspapers were written almost exclusively by the modern-educated urban elite and their reporting of the war carried with it that elite's perceptions of nationalism.

While urban understandings of nationalism were being spread to the countryside the circumstances of the war also worked to redefine modern nationalism to include elements of traditional culture. From the late nineteenth century and especially during the 1920s modern nationalism had been associated with iconoclastic attacks on Chinese tradition. However Japanese control in occupied areas meant that members of the modern elite there began to express their feelings of patriotism in oblique traditional terms in order to escape Japanese censorship. Thus one former moderniser spent his time in Shanghai during the Japanese occupation making a collection of rare books, which he saw as a contribution to preserving the nation. In addition writers and dramatists began to use traditional forms to try and make their work more accessible to the general population. The writer Lao Xiang composed a *Three Character Classic*, modelled on one of the standard texts of the traditional school curriculum, which began:

> Men at their birth are naturally loyal and persistent.
> Loving their nation is instinctive.
> When the nation falls, the family cannot survive.
> Protecting the nation is the first concern [for everyone].[11]

This piece sold 50,000 copies in addition to being published in a magazine. Patriotic words were also fitted to folk songs and traditional storytelling styles. An old man in a Shanxi village who worked pushing coal carts during the Japanese occupation of the area remembered spreading news of the war heard from travellers by means of a rhyming dialogue performed in the dramatic skits that were a traditional feature of the lunar New Year holidays.

A similar combination of fear of Japanese censorship and the need to appeal to a broad audience meant that dramatists began to produce plays round traditional themes of loyalty, often in the form of historical dramas. Popular subjects included the story of the general Yue Fei, who died because of his determination to fight the northern barbarians, and Hua Mulan, a daughter who took her father's place in the wars against the barbarians. Yue Fei had long been worshipped as a deity, and such subjects fitted modern nationalism into a matrix of traditional values. In particular, writers began to look at nationalism alongside the Confucian discourse on loyalty. The first resistance drama to be a commercial success in Shanghai was a story set in the late Ming about the fidelity of a wife to her husband and of a minister to the emperor. It ended with the hero being executed for refusing to surrender and his mistress committing suicide to preserve her chastity. Attacks on such central Confucian values had been at the heart of the May 4th Movement. For many writers in the 1910s and 1920s loyalty and filial piety were in a sense the antithesis of modern nationalism. But now the novelist Ba Ren could draw the traditional and the modern values together, writing, 'Loyalty is defined not as an ethical obligation to an individual ruler, but rather to the nation. Filial piety is also not defined as an obligation to one's parents, but to the race as a whole.'[12] Such a statement is very different from the traditional view of loyalty with its emphasis on affective bonds between individuals, but it does illustrate the new positive interest in basic Confucian values. Moreover, by picking on these central Confucian values the resistance intellectuals went beyond even the New Life Movement. In so doing they began to speak in terms that were much more in tune with the traditional popular sense of national identity.

It was the intellectuals' conviction of the importance of mass resistance that made these moves towards the popular national identity necessary. And like the nineteenth-century believers in the need for popular determination rather than technology, the intellectuals began to turn to the rural population to act as the core of that resistance. A cartoon entitled 'The people's warriors' (Fig. 9.2) can be used to illustrate this new interest in a more traditional rural nationalism as opposed to the modern urban nationalism depicted in 'Let's change into new uniform!' Here again we see the heroic figure of the common man who has joined the resistance. As in 'Let's change into new uniform!' the massive bulk of the character and the strong vertical and diagonal lines mean that the new soldier completely dominates the picture. Behind him is sketched a crowd of other similarly bulky and determined-looking men. And just as the emphasis has shifted from the individual choice to join the war effort to the resistance of the masses, so the central figure wears not a Western-style suit but a traditional jacket and trousers bound with strips of cloth at the waist and ankles. In his hand he carries not a modern gun but a tasselled spear. The image as a whole is reminiscent of the Boxers, those quintessentially rural fighters against foreign invasion. And yet however different their subjects, both 'Let's change into new uniform!' and 'The people's warriors' place the individual and his determination at the centre of the national resistance. This is characteristic of the reconfiguration of nationalism that allowed peasant militias and urban communists to be seen as working together against a common enemy. While this nationalism was still expressed in the politicised language of the

作雲常趙　　　士戰的間民

Figure 9.2 'The people's warriors'
Source: *Kang dao di* (Resisting to the End), Hankou, Chongqing 10 (16 May
1938), reproduced in Hung Chang-tai, *War and Popular Culture: Resistance in
Modern China, 1937–1945*. Berkeley: University of California Press, 1994

modernising urban elite it now made allowances for the traditions and
cultural identity of the rest of the population.

Civil war

Gradually the war in China was fought to a stalemate in which the Japanese
held the major cities and railway lines but were unable to control effectively
the surrounding countryside except through sporadic raids and terror. In
those areas not controlled by the Japanese the Communist and Nationalist
parties were locked in a contest for power which occasionally broke out into
open warfare despite the declared united front against Japan. When the

Japanese finally surrendered to the allies after the dropping of the atomic bomb there was an immediate race for control over China, and civil war broke out between the Nationalists and Communists. In theory Japan had handed over power to the Nationalists, but the Communist Party's success in building bases during the war, especially in north China, meant that it had good logistical and military support. Meanwhile, land reform meant that it had a core of supporters who had made large investments in the Communist system and had a great deal to lose if the party was not victorious. The Nationalist Party on the other hand had lost the support of its original constituency, the modernising urban elites. That support had been based on its claim to legitimacy as a national and nationalist party. But the appeasement of the 1930s undermined much of this support, as did the party's determination to continue the civil war against the Communists despite the Japanese invasion. Its problems were exacerbated by the mismanagement of the cities that now came under its control. Inflation, extortion by officials, corruption and incompetence alienated what little support was left. By the end of the war it was the Communist Party that could claim to embody the interests of the nation.

Conclusion

The Sino-Japanese war saw the growth of a new and more unified form of nationalism that drew together strands from both the modern nationalism of the early part of the century, which had called for cultural change aimed ultimately at technological superiority, and the earlier traditions of cultural identity. Linking these strands together was the Communist Party, made up of the most radical of the urban elite but dedicated to the promotion of a mass nationalism based on the rural poor. It was this position at the point of convergence between modern and traditional nationalism that allowed the Communist Party to become so closely associated with the resistance movement and ultimately take over the mantle of politicised nationalism from the Nationalist Party.

Notes

1 W.W. Lockwood quoted in John Israel, *Student Nationalism in China, 1927–1937* (Stanford: Stanford University Press, 1966), p. 57.
2 Quoted in ibid., p. 135.
3 Quoted in ibid., p. 136.
4 Parks Coble, *Facing Japan: Chinese Politics and Japanese Imperialism, 1931–1937* (Cambridge, MA: Harvard University, Council on East Asian Studies, 1991).
5 Ba Jin, 'Ziyou kuaile de xiaole' (Freedom has happily smiled) in *Ba Jin wenji* (Collected Works of Ba Jin) (Beijing: Renmin wenxue chubanshe, 1961), vol. 10, p. 278.

6   Quoted in Chen Yung-fa, *Making Revolution: The Communist Movement in Eastern and Central China, 1937–1945* (Berkeley: University of California Press, 1986), p. 287.

7   Chalmers Johnson, *Peasant Nationalism and Communist Power: The Emergence of Revolutionary China, 1937–1945* (Stanford: Stanford University Press, 1962).

8   Perry Link, *Evening Chats in Beijing: Probing China's Predicament* (New York: W.W. Norton, 1992), p. 202.

9   Poshek Fu, *Passivity, Resistance, and Collaboration: Intellectual Choices in Occupied Shanghai, 1937–1945* (Stanford: Stanford University Press, 1993), p. 83.

10 Quoted in Hung Chang-tai, *War and Popular Culture: Resistance in Modern China, 1937–1945* (Berkeley: University of California Press, 1994), p. 53.

11 Quoted in ibid., pp. 205–6.

12 Quoted in Fu, *Passivity, Resistance, and Collaboration*.

10

State-building and nation-building

The Chinese Communist Party had originated among the radical modernisers of the early twentieth century. When it came to power it continued the processes of modernisation and state-building that had been begun under the fragmented governments of the republican period. But although the nationalist goals of the government of the new People's Republic of China may have been similar to those of earlier governments, the new state had an unprecedented ability to impose its will. In this situation many of the projects of the republican period, such as the creation of a national transport network and a national language, came to fruition. The Communist Party also continued the equation of nationalism with support for the party, strengthening the politicisation of nationalism that had begun under the Nationalist Party. Since the version of communism that was promoted by the party was highly moralistic, the effect was to create a politicised nationalism that was reminiscent of the culturalism of the late nineteenth century.

Depicting a Communist China

By the beginning of 1949 it was already clear that the Nationalist Party was losing the civil war. The Communists had controlled much of the north China countryside since the early 1940s. Now the major cities had begun to fall to their armies and then those same armies crossed the Yangzi River and moved rapidly across southern China. As the Communist troops entered each city ceremonies and parades were rapidly organised to welcome them. In Beijing, which the People's Liberation Army entered in February 1949, there was a procession of thousands of students and workers, many of them holding banners welcoming the army or portraits of Mao Zedong, already established as the Communist Party's preeminent leader. Among the marchers were stilt walkers and folk-dance groups who entertained the onlookers but also reminded them of the party's rural bases. Other groups chanted the eight conditions that Mao had laid down for a Nationalist Party surrender. After the marchers came a huge display of military power: tanks, armoured cars, artillery and soldiers. Such scenes were repeated across the country, marking out the central features of the party's power: popular enthusiasm among both urban and rural groups, a leadership centred on Mao Zedong, and huge military strength.

Eight months later, on 1 October 1949, Mao Zedong stood on the Tiananmen Gate, the entrance to the Forbidden City at the heart of Beijing, and declared to the crowds beneath the establishment of the government of the new People's Republic of China. The square was decorated with the new red five-star flags and printed flags had been distributed along with the newspapers that day. Like the earlier shining-sun flag, the five-star flag was a statement of political as well as national allegiance. A competition had been held to design the new flag, with the requirement that the design must represent both China as a nation and the new 'democratic dictatorship' under the leadership of the Communist Party and the proletariat. Three thousand entries were submitted, and 38 selected by the organising committee. From these Mao Zedong picked the winning design, saying that it represented the idea of rallying round the party, and his choice was then ratified by a vote of the members of the National People's Political Consultative Conference. The bright-red ground representing both revolutionary enthusiasm and the red earth of China contrasted with the sky blue of the Nationalist Party's flags and emblems. In the upper left-hand corner four small stars encircled one larger one, said at the time to represent the Communist Party and the four classes of 'the people': the national bourgeoisie, the petty bourgeoisie, the workers and the peasants. Together the stars represented the idea of the people's democratic dictatorship as required by the competition rubric. Although the Communist government had rejected the Nationalist government's national symbols, the flags that decorated the great Tiananmen Square symbolised party rule and showed the continuation of the politicised nationalism that had begun in the 1920s.

The crowd of 30,000 gathered in Tiananmen Square in front of the gate and waving the new red flags along with portraits of Mao Zedong and his chief military commander Zhu De represented the people of this newly reimagined nation. Among them stood the 600 representatives of the Chinese People's Political Consultative Conference who had been meeting to establish the institutions of the new state. They consisted of representatives of the Communist Party and various other political parties which supported the Communists. There were also representatives of the People's Liberation Army; mass organisations, such as the labour unions, the Women's Association, the Communist Youth League and the Student League; the regions; and minority nationalities. Finally there were various prominent individuals who supported the new government. These representatives of the nation formed only a tiny portion of the great crowd, but the rest of the participants repeated the same imagery, with workers representing their factories and enterprises, students and teachers, mass organisations, the defence forces, local city people and also peasants from the area around the city. Despite talk of class analysis, the Communist Party organisers depicted the nation in terms of segments of society (soldiers, workers, peasants, women, students) derived more from the Nationalist Party than from Marxism. Moreover, as at the great ceremonies conducted by the Nationalist Party, the crowd assembled to watch the declaration of the new state represented a politicised nation whose people were, by definition, the supporters of the party.

The leaders of the new state stood together on the Tiananmen Gate. They formed a small group, mostly men dressed in the military-style suits popularised by Sun Yatsen. But it was Mao Zedong whose voice was picked up by the microphones as he read out the formal proclamation announcing the establishment of the new government. As he finished he pressed the switch that caused the new national flag to rise slowly up the great flagpole that had been erected in the centre of the square. Then for three hours the artillery, tanks, cavalry, infantry and military bands of the People's Liberation Army paraded past the leaders, while the spectators marvelled at the smartness of their uniforms, their leather boots, and the quality of their weapons. Aeroplanes flew overhead scattering leaflets. By the time the military review had been completed it was getting dark and the huge procession of political parties, government organisations and others that followed was lit by lanterns. As the marchers passed the reviewing stand they shouted 'Long live the People's Republic!' and 'Long live Chairman Mao!' and Mao replied 'Long life to you, comrades!' In many ways the occasion was similar to the National Day ceremonies of the 1920s and 1930s, except that the older symbols of the nation were now replaced by the symbols of the Communist Party, and above all by the figure of Mao Zedong. During the late 1960s and early 1970s Mao was to become a pervasive symbol of both the revolution and the nation: badges, portraits and statues of Mao were omnipresent and it was claimed that love of Mao was the same as love of China. This was foreshadowed on that first evening of the new state, when a huge portrait of Mao hung on the front of the Tiananmen Gate and was illuminated after dark, while Mao's head had replaced that of Sun Yatsen on postage stamps. Again the symbols of the politicised nation were focused on a single man, but now that man was the living leader of the dominant political party.

On the day of these ceremonies the government organ the *People's Daily* also published the text of the inscription of a memorial to the martyrs of the revolution that was to be erected in the centre of Tiananmen Square. The inscription had been agreed by the People's Political Consultative Conference, and the previous day a ceremony in honour of the martyrs had been held in the square. According to Zhou Enlai's speech, the purpose of the memorial was 'to call upon the people, to commemorate the dead, and to encourage the living'.[1] The didactic aim was typical of republican commemorations of martyrs, and suggests that we should look at the memorial as a monument to those who constructed it, as well as to those who were commemorated. After Zhou Enlai's speech, Mao read out the text of the inscription for the memorial and laid the foundation stone. The inscription proclaimed eternal glory to those who had died in the civil war and revolution of the last three years; those who had died in the wars and revolutions of the last 30 years; and all those who had died fighting either foreign imperialists or domestic forces since 1840. The ideas contained in this text mirror the historical narrative promoted by the Nationalists since the 1920s, except that in this Communist version the Nationalist Party too is depicted as a tool of imperialism. Here again China's modern history is seen as starting with the Opium War of 1840, and as being a battle in which a heroic revolutionary force is pitted against foreign imperialists colluding first with the Qing and then with the warlords.

When the Martyrs' Memorial was completed in 1958, 10 marble reliefs around its base depicted the history implied by the text of the inscription. The scenes begin with the destruction of the foreign opium in Guangzhou, which was the cause of the Opium War, symbolising the battle against imperialism, and the Taiping rebellion symbolising the beginnings of the struggle against the Qing. These are followed by a depiction of the 1911 Revolution. However, the turning point of the struggle comes not with the revolution of 1911, but with the patriotic May 4th Movement of 1919, the start of the 30-year period of war and revolution alluded to by Mao in his inscription. The relief depicting the May 4th Movement occupied the central position on the south side of the monument. It is followed by the May 30th Movement, the creation of the Communist armed forces, and the guerrilla war against Japan. Finally on the centre of the north side of the monument, facing the Tiananmen Gate, came the climax of the story, the soldiers of the People's Liberation Army crossing the Yangzi into south China, symbolising the victory of the Communist Party over the Nationalists. Through the monument with its inscription and reliefs, the history of the Chinese nation and the battle against imperialism and internal enemies was inscribed in stone at the very heart of the nation's capital. For the monument is not only in the centre of Tiananmen Square; it also stands on the central north–south axis around which the city had been built. In imperial times the imperial palace stood at the heart of the city, guarded by the Gate of Heavenly Peace or Tiananmen. Seated on his throne the emperor had looked south along this central axis, a straight route along which his power could radiate out to the rest of his empire. The Martyrs' Memorial blocked this axis and refocused the city on the memorial and on Tiananmen Square in which it stood. Round it were constructed on one side the Great Hall of the People, in which the National People's Congress met, and on the other the twin museums of national and revolutionary history. Much later, in 1976 after Mao's death, the pattern was changed again with the construction of Mao's mausoleum on the south side of the memorial, providing an even stronger emphasis on the centrality of the party and its leaders in the nation's history.

The same national history was depicted in various acts that took place across the country in the wake of the Communist victory. In Guangzhou, on the anniversary of Lin Zexu's destruction of the foreigners' opium in 1840, a huge bonfire was held in which opium and the pipes and lamps used for smoking it were destroyed. In events such as this the establishment of the new state was depicted as the final victory in the battle against imperialism. As Mao famously stated at the time: 'The Chinese people who constitute one quarter of humanity have now stood up.'[2] In a series of deeply symbolic acts, the outer forms of Western influence that had continued since the late nineteenth century were dismantled. Many of the institutions first set up as a result of Western demands had continued to employ foreign staff and conduct much of their business in English. Now customs officers refused to accept documents in English, letters sent through the post office had to be addressed in Chinese, and the foreign-owned Shanghai utility companies were required to send out bills in Chinese only. A foreigner complained to the *North China Daily News* that in the telegraph office, where previously much business had been conducted in English, an official had pushed a sign saying 'Speak Chinese only' towards him and the rest of the staff had laughed. There were also widely reported prosecutions of foreigners for personal violence towards Chinese. A British tram-inspector in Shanghai who refused to extend a Chinese subordinate's sick leave and got into a fight with the man was prosecuted and forced to apologise. Incidents of this sort had long been a source of political tensions and the proceedings were reported as a breakthrough.

In short, the inauguration of communist rule was portrayed as a victory for Chinese nationalism. A song written during the War of Resistance proclaimed 'Without the Communist Party there would be no China.' With simple, memorable words and a catchy tune the song became well known across the country. It was sung on occasions as varied as a meeting of prisoners to urge them to change their ways and a meeting of a Beijing neighbourhood. In 1950, since the Japanese had been defeated and the party had come to power, Mao Zedong ordered that the words should be changed to 'Without the Communist Party there would be no new China'. With the final victory in the battle against imperialism the people of China could now look forward to a period of national construction.

State-building

The territory of the new People's Republic of China was basically the same as that which the Nationalist government had laid claim to in the 1930s: the nineteenth-century Manchu empire except for Taiwan and Mongolia. The island of Taiwan had been ceded to the Japanese in 1895 and handed back to China after Japan's defeat in World War II. In 1949, Chiang Kaishek's Nationalist government retreated to the island, and, after the outbreak of the Korean War in 1950, the island was protected from a communist invasion by the United States navy. Taiwan was thus inaccessible to Communist rule, though both the People's Republic and the Nationalist government on the island agreed that it was rightfully part of China. Mongolia, on the other hand, was now recognised by China as an independent state. A Mongol state had been declared in northern Mongolia at the time of the 1911 Revolution and in the 1920s fighting between Russian forces in central Asia had left northern Mongolia as a satellite of the new Soviet Russian state. The alliance between the Chinese Communist Party and the Soviet Union at the time of the formation of the People's Republic meant that the new government was willing to give up China's claim to northern Mongolia. With these two exceptions, the territorial claims of the People's Republic were the same as those of the Nationalist government.

The crucial difference between the rules of the Nationalist and Communist governments lay in the fact that by the end of the 1950s the People's Republic had succeeded in imposing a unified administration on all the areas to which it laid claim. With the arrival of the Communist government, provinces and regions that had been effectively independent since the early 1910s were incorporated into a centrally administered state. Policies made in Beijing were implemented from Liaoning to Yunnan and the central government could transfer its own personnel to any part of the country. This administrative unification was mirrored in the establishment of a rail and road network. Yan Xishan's building of narrow-gauge railway lines in Shanxi province (when the rest of the country used a wider gauge) had been symbolic of the way in which warlord power had divided China during the Republic. Now, not only were the rail links that had been destroyed in the war rebuilt, but the government embarked on a major program of new construction. Fig. 10.1 shows rail and road links built in the 1950s and 1960s. The motives for this construction were strategic and economic, with the rail line out into northwest China providing access to the oil fields of Xinjiang and the lines to Fuzhou and Xiamen allowing the movement of troops to the frontier with the Nationalists on Taiwan. However, the new road and rail links also greatly increased the central government's access to the outlying provinces. Thus the new railway through Sichuan to the provincial capital, Chengdu, limited the province's long-standing autonomy and regionalism. Even more dramatic was the situation in Tibet, where roads were built for the first time linking the capital, Lhasa, to the Chinese provinces of Sichuan in the east, Qinghai in the north and Xinjiang in the west. In addition to road and railway construction, a radio network was set up across the country and local county or township governments were required to assign someone to copy down news specially broadcast at

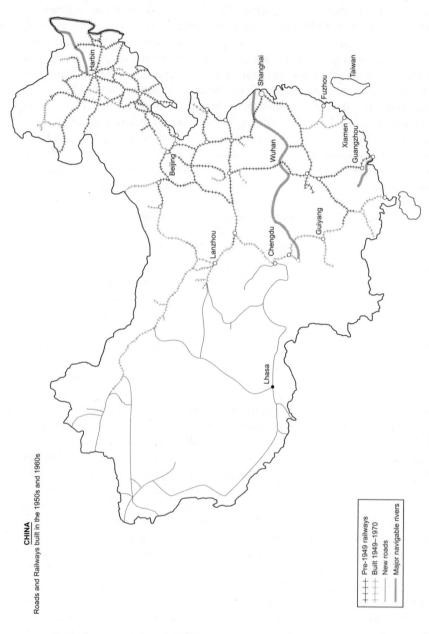

Pre-1949 railways
Built 1949–1970
New roads
Major navigable rivers

Harbin

Shanghai

Fuzhou

Beijing

Wuhan

Xiamen

Guangzhou

Taiwan

Lanzhou

Chengdu

Guiyang

Lhasa

Figure 10.1 Road and rail links built in the 1950s and 1960s

dictation speed. Thus not only could government troops and personnel be rapidly transferred from region to region, but central government policies could reach them immediately wherever they were stationed.

The government used this new infrastructure to carry out policies that radically affected people's everyday lives and the organisation of society. State penetration of local society to ensure modernising goals had begun with the late Qing reforms and continued under the Nationalist government, and indeed under regional rulers such as Yan Xishan and Feng Yuxiang. The difference under the People's Republic was not only the radical nature of the policies, something to which earlier governments had sometimes aspired, but the effectiveness of their implementation. Land reform had been carried out in some Communist-held areas during World War II and the civil war, but now it was imposed on rural areas across the country. Land was confiscated from schools, lineages and temples, and redistributed to the poor. Wealthy individuals were labelled landlords and subjected to meetings in which they were accused of exploiting their neighbours and retribution was demanded. Thus, as well as losing their land, they lost the prestige that had been central to their power. Land reform destroyed both the corporate structures of rural society and the power of local elites. Communist activists, who mainly came from poor backgrounds, were placed in positions of power, but remained heavily dependent on the Communist Party and local officials. Thus traditional rural power structures were replaced by a structure that was effectively controlled by the central government. In the cities a series of campaigns in the early 1950s achieved a similar result. These campaigns concentrated on government officials and businessmen to dismantle the network of connections that had linked them together into a structure that had long prevented state control. Officials and businessmen were ordered to attend 'study groups' where they were subjected to considerable pressure to reveal both the connections between them and the various semi-legal or illegal practices that had been used to resist government regulation and taxation. When the businessmen returned to their companies they found their workforce unionised under government control and themselves labelled as capitalists. Again government cadres and party activists formed a new power structure responsive to central government control. A Thought Reform campaign directed at academics and teachers to restrict their teaching to ideas compatible with Marxism demonstrated the power of the state over education. By these means the party was able to take control of local society to a much greater degree than any previous Chinese government.

Intertwined with the campaigns of the early 1950s was the impact of the Korean War. War broke out in 1950 when Communist North Korea launched an attack on South Korea. United Nations, and specifically American, troops supporting South Korea then marched northwards into North Korea and towards the Chinese border. In the face of this threat to its own security, the People's Republic of China sent soldiers as volunteers to assist the North Koreans. The war was portrayed in China as an act of resistance to American imperialism. A campaign urging people to 'Resist America, aid Korea' was launched and people were organised through their work to attend meetings and make donations. Through its soldiers' participation in the war the Communist government was able to reaffirm the link between patriotism and support for the government. The identification of patriotism with support for the government had been central to the politicised nationalism of the republic. In the early 1950s the government not only replaced the power structures of local society, but also began a period when government policies were implemented by campaigns in which the population was mobilised to achieve particular goals. State penetration and the government's claims for patriotic support were increased at the same time.

The development of a national language

Administrative unification created an urgent need for a single language of government. Not only did the country now have a unified administration for the first time since the fall of the Qing, but the modern state's demands for greater control over society meant that for the first time a large proportion of the population was expected to need to come into contact with state organisations.

On the occasion of a conference on language reform held in 1955, a government statement explained that a national language was necessary in order to 'increase the political and economic unity of the Han people' and aid socialist construction.[3] This was especially important because the establishment of the new state, with its administrative unification and new communications system, had resulted in many people being transferred around the country. The government posted technical personnel to wherever they were needed, and it was soon obvious that highly trained people found it very hard to operate outside their home areas because of the language barriers. Even in north China, where dialects differed much less than in the south, government employees posted away from their home areas had problems: newly qualified doctors could neither understand nor speak to their patients and education officials could not understand the meetings they attended. Moreover, the institutions of government itself found their operations impeded by language barriers. In Guangdong the provincial People's Congress had to be interpreted into the Cantonese, Hakka and Chaozhou dialects as well as Mandarin. The army too needed a common language. The People's Liberation Army had in practice developed a common language based on the north China dialect and recruits were expected to pick this up after at most a year. However, the army also had to communicate with the local people. One soldier, writing in 1955, reported that his unit had already been stationed in 10 different provinces from the far northeast to Guangdong. Clearly it was impossible for officers and men to learn local dialects if they were transferred as often as this. A common national language was essential to administrative efficiency.

A national language was also seen as a way to increase nationalism. A single language that could be used over the whole country would provide a sense of national unity and counteract traditional regionalism and localism. State officials would no longer need an interpreter in their contacts with local people and this would weaken the power of local officialdom in favour of the central government. Differences in local dialects and regionally based hiring practices meant that it was often difficult for a meeting of all the workers in one factory to understand the same speech. The Guangxi local radio station found it necessary to repeat all its broadcasts in Cantonese and the Liuzhou dialect as well as Mandarin. Moreover, since some dialects varied greatly over very short distances, even this kind of repetition was not always sufficient. On the southeast coast the Wenzhou local radio station claimed that its broadcasts in the Wenzhou dialect could not be understood in places only 50 kilometres from the city. Thus the promotion of a national language was intended to give the state direct access, both through officials and through the media, to the whole population.

The form of national language that was chosen was much the same as that promoted by the Nationalist government, which had adopted a phonetic syllabary based on Beijing pronunciation and encouraged the use of a written vernacular corresponding to the north China dialect. Since the time of the May 4th Movement a considerably quantity of literature had also been written in this new style. The Communist Party, on the other hand, had supported increased use of dialect speech during its years in opposition and had criticised the new written vernacular for its excessive use of Western and Japanese phrases. The inaccessibility of the written vernacular was a particular concern because it made the language a poor tool to communicate with the working classes. Consequently, the Communists had formally adopted a romanisation scheme that provided different romanisations for the eight major dialects. There was also considerable enthusiasm within the party for the abolition of Chinese characters altogether in favour of a romanised language that would be easier for the people to learn. The party's sudden transition in the 1950s to the promotion of the Beijing dialect as a national vernacular is thus surprising. The justification was provided by the publication of Stalin's *Marxism and Problems of Linguistics* in 1950 in which Stalin claimed that language was not tied to class interests, and therefore the creation of a single national language was a natural development and not an expression of power. This view of the development of national languages fitted well with the needs of the new Chinese state for mobility of its personnel, a national media and a national education system. As in the Qing, the choice of the Beijing dialect as a common language reflected Beijing's position as the centre of power within the country. Language might not reflect class interests, but the new national language was certainly the expression of political power.

During the late 1950s and early 1960s Mandarin was actively promoted by the government. Radio was used to spread the new 'common speech' and Beijing Radio became an informal standard. In order to make its broadcasts more widely understood it omitted some unusual features of the Beijing accent and avoided vocabulary that was only used in the local area. Where more than one pronunciation of a word was current or pronunciations were disputed, letters written to the station by members of the public were used to provide an audience consensus. The outcome was a spoken language that was not only standardised, but was also more accessible to a national audience than the pure Beijing dialect, and thus more acceptable as a national language. Government regulations also required that all People's Liberation Army cultural organisations should use Mandarin and that staff working for national institutions such as the post office or the railway network should study it. Beginning in 1956 all primary schools and teacher-training colleges were required to hold Mandarin classes, and from 1960 they were required to use Mandarin as the language of instruction. The difficulty of implementing such policies is suggested by the fact that the central government issued an identical demand in 2000 and it was still seen as requiring several years to achieve. Nevertheless, most people educated from the 1950s onwards did learn to speak some Mandarin in school even if not all their classes were conducted in Mandarin.

Nevertheless, dialects continued to be the major means of communication in many areas. Radio stations admitted the popularity of dialect broadcasting even while they bemoaned the waste of time and equipment. In Guangdong in the 1950s people are said to have claimed that they would rather sell their ancestral halls than abandon their ancestral language. The prestige of Cantonese and Shanghainese has continued. In the 1980s a couple living in Wuxi, which has a dialect related to Shanghainese (though the two are not mutually comprehensible), were asked why they spoke Shanghainese at home although only the wife came from Shanghai and the husband came from a Mandarin speaking area. The wife explained, 'Anyone can learn to speak Mandarin, but when people who are not from Shanghai speak Shanghainese it does not sound right. Wuxi people all want to learn Shanghainese.'[4]

However, the association of Mandarin with the power and prestige of the central government meant that as early as the 1950s it had become necessary for a successful career. This had, in fact, been apparent to many people even before the government began actively to promote Mandarin in 1955. It was reported in Hangzhou, where the first northern cadres to arrive in 1949 needed interpreters, that by 1955 village cadres and activists were using the northern dialect for their meetings. From 1960 some level of Mandarin became virtually mandatory for anyone in a position of responsibility even in country villages: youth leaders, brigade cadres and militia leaders were all required to be able to speak some Mandarin. A natural result of this was an increase in the prestige of Mandarin. This was intensified by the reliance of an increasingly competitive education system on Mandarin, which meant that parents anxious to improve their children's educational chances often encouraged them to speak Mandarin at home. A study several generations of a large family conducted in Fujian in the 1980s found that while the grandparents born in the 1920s spoke only the local dialect, the father who was educated in the 1950s spoke the local dialect at home but Mandarin outside the home. Both father and mother spoke Mandarin to their children with the result that the children spoke the local dialect very poorly and used it only to their grandparents, communicating with everyone else only in Mandarin. This example suggests the complexity of language use patterns and the persistence of dialects, but above all the growing importance of Mandarin.

Defining the nation

The party

Nationalism continued to be linked to support for the ruling party. This had begun with the new national symbols adopted by the People's Republic in 1949, but was expanded during the years that followed and especially during the Cultural Revolution that began in 1966. Fig. 10.2 shows the way in which nationalism was linked to images of the party. It comes from an illustrated story of a type sold in large numbers during this period. This particular volume tells the story of Feng Fusheng, who is described in the title as an enthusiast for studying the works of Chairman Mao. The picture shows Feng Fusheng holding Mao's *Selected Works*. Behind him a giant image of Mao with the rays of the sun radiating out behind it rises above a scene of students and soldiers who move across the picture in the direction indicated by his arm. The iconography of the soldiers and students makes them instantly recognisable as the figures who adorn the base of the Martyrs' Memorial in Tiananmen Square. The narrative of nationalism and liberation depicted on the monument has been transformed by the imposition of Mao. Where the figures on the monument were heroic it is now the superhuman figure of Mao that dominates the scene and the historical characters lose not only their individuality but also their stature. During this period Mao became the embodiment of both the party and the nation in a way that illustrated the near total identification of the two.

The centrality of the Communist Party to the self-definition of the People's Republic of China meant that class distinctions were central to defining the nation. In a famous speech 'On people's democratic dictatorship', made shortly before the party took power, Mao Zedong explained

Figure 10.2 'The more he studied with class feelings the more warmly he loved
Mao Zedong and the more he loved to read Mao Zedong's works'
Source: Liu Shifeng et al., *Xuexi Mao Zhuxi zhuzuo jijifenzi Feng Fusheng* (Feng
Fusheng: An Enthusiast for Studying Chairman Mao's Works). Beijing: Renmin
meishu chubanshe, 1966, p. 10

that in a people's democratic dictatorship only 'the people' would have the
right to voice their opinions and influence the state. He went on to explain
that the people consisted of the working class, the peasantry, the petty bourgeoisie and the national bourgeoisie united under the leadership of the
working class and the Communist Party. This was the view of the state that
was embodied in the design of the new national flag with its four stars representing the four classes of the people clustered round the larger star that
represented the Communist Party. The people, Mao went on to explain,
would conduct their dictatorship over the landlord class, the bureaucratic
capitalist class, and the Nationalist Party, which represented those two
classes. Thus from the very start of the new state some parts of the population were declared enemies of the people and excluded from the nation. The
practice of government by a series of political campaigns, many of which
involved attacks on particular groups, meant that as time went on the
number of people who were excluded from the nation increased. Those who
were excluded were no longer treated as members of 'the people' and this
was dramatically acted out through 'struggle sessions' in which the 'class
enemy' was forced to stand separate from the people and facing them and
was publicly ill-treated and humiliated. Such exclusion was particularly
widespread during the Cultural Revolution, when groups of students were
authorised by the government to overthrow members of the bureaucracy

thought to be leaning towards capitalism. The fluidity of the definition of 'capitalist roaders' was combined with extreme violence towards those who were accused on the grounds that they were no longer members of the people. This was a logical outcome of the way in which nationalism had been tied to the party and left widespread terror. In a time of such chaos and factional fighting there were few people who did not fear that they too could be excluded from the people.

People who were accused of failure to support the party and thus the nation were often also accused of being supporters of the Nationalist Party. Since the period of the Civil War, the politicisation of nationalism had meant that supporters of the opposing political party were depicted as traitors to the nation. Thus the new Chinese nation was also defined in opposition to the Nationalist regime that had preceded it. Since the Nationalists continued to rule the island of Taiwan, this process of definition through opposition was constantly renewed. Nationalist rule in Taiwan was depicted as a continuation of Western imperialism in China. The rhetoric of opposition to American imperialism that had begun with American support for the Nationalist regime and had been reinforced by the Korean War continued through the 1960s and 1970s. Throughout this period Nationalist spies from Taiwan backed by American money were the villains of children's stories and much government propaganda. Fig. 10.3

Figure 10.3 'A Nationalist Party spy dines with an American'
Source: Zhang Wei and Gao Shimin, *Minbing de gushi* (A Story of the Militia).
Tianjin: Tianjin meishu chubanshe, 1966, p. 2

illustrates how depictions of the Nationalist Party as traitors continued to be used to create a sense of identity between the Communist Party and the nation. The illustration shows a Nationalist spy, standing, at a banquet that is being given before he departs for his work on the Chinese mainland. Immediately in front of him and the focus of the gaze of all the other characters is an American. From the text the reader knows that the other figures are Chiang Kaishek's son Jiang Jingguo and other leaders of the Nationalist Party in Taiwan. By depicting the Nationalist Party leaders and the spy dining with the American the picture reinforces the message of the story that the Nationalist spy is a traitor to his country. The rest of the story tells how his wicked mission is foiled after he parachutes into the mainland, where he is caught by some enthusiastic and watchful rural militia members. In this story, as in countless others, China is portrayed as a country still threatened by expansionist imperialist powers. The Nationalist Party in Taiwan provided the personification of this threat, for it was the means through which national identity was linked to a story of nationalism which depicted the Communist Party as the vanguard of nationalism and excluded all those who could be considered the enemies of communism.

Meanwhile the Nationalist regime in Taiwan was promoting a very similar model of national identity. Chinese identity was still politicised though it was defined in opposition to Soviet rather than American imperialism. Fig. 10.4 is a design for a patriotic wall-poster issued in 1980. The Communist and Nationalist regimes are symbolised by their flags. The flag of the Nationalist government in Taiwan is the shining sun on a red ground which the party had inherited from Sun Yatsen. Rays of light shine out from it and illuminate the island. The Communist government is symbolised by a

Figure 10.4 Taiwan propaganda poster
Source: Liang Yangyuan, *Zuixin bibao fanben* (New Models for Wall-Posters).
Tainan: Zhuangjia, 1980, p. 60

tattered flag on which the circle of small stars surrounding a larger star is clearly visible. Under a sign saying 'People's communes' sit a woman and child dressed in rags and emaciated by hunger. In the foreground are two skulls and the coastline is guarded with rolls of barbed wire. Here the Communist Party is depicted as the evil enemy, but the emphasis on politics is the same. There were, in fact, close similarities between the promotion of nationalism in the People's Republic and the Republic of China on Taiwan. Both states placed the revolutionaries' struggle against the Qing and the patriotic movements of the 1910s and 1920s, especially the May 4th Movement, at the centre of their historical narratives. Like the Communists, the Nationalist regime in Taiwan implemented a land reform policy that gave it much greater control over local society. In addition the relatively large size of the administration compared to the population of Taiwan and the modernising legacy of Japanese rule made it possible for the Nationalists to impose policies that had previously been little more than paper outlines. This included the imposition of a national language based on the north China dialect as spoken in Beijing. Though this was referred to as 'national language' in Taiwan and 'common speech' on the mainland, it was in fact very much the same language. Schools in Taiwan were required to conduct all education in Mandarin, and the enforcement of Mandarin use went well beyond that achieved on the mainland, with much-resented humiliation for children who spoke the local dialect in school. As on the mainland, Mandarin became a language associated with education and status and was used for almost all formal and public occasions, while local dialects continued to be used within the family and in more informal situations. Thus, like the People's Republic, the Nationalist government in Taiwan emphasised a model of national identity tied to the politicised modern state. The opening lines of a poem written by an elder of the Nationalist Party as he lay dying in Taiwan and quoted in a book of teaching materials on nationalism published in Beijing in the 1980s sum up the similarity of the two regimes' views of the nation and their place in it:

Bury me on the top of a high mountain
Looking towards my mainland.
The mainland cannot be returned to
I can only weep in pain!

Bury me on the top of a high mountain
Looking towards my home town.
My home town cannot be seen
I can never look on it . . .[5]

This poem could be quoted in a mainland textbook not only because its author was a well-known patriot of the early twentieth century, but also because he shared with the mainland educators a feeling of deep sadness at what he saw as a nation divided. Both on the mainland and in Taiwan official nationalism, widely promoted by the state, looked towards the same model of China in terms of its territory as well as its politicised modernity.

This identification of the party, and thus a particular political system, with the nation can also be seen as a restatement of traditional culturalism. For both on the mainland and in Taiwan morality was placed at the intersection between the party and the nation. On the mainland a large part of Communist propaganda was devoted to promoting a moral system based on self-sacrifice for the revolution. This system was embodied in some of the most frequently reproduced essays of Mao Zedong, which told of hard work, courage, struggle and self-sacrifice. These were also described as being valid beyond the Chinese nation. In his essay 'In memory of Norman Bethune', a Canadian doctor who had worked for the communists during the anti-Japanese war, Mao asked 'What kind of spirit is this that makes a foreigner selflessly adopt the cause of the Chinese people's liberation as his own? It is the spirit of internationalism, the spirit of communism, from which every Chinese communist must learn.' Following this spirit he urged his readers not only to liberate 'our nation and people' but also 'to liberate the other nations and peoples of the world'.[6] Many people, especially those who were educated during the 1950s and 1960s, accepted these values and their relationship to the nation state. School-children were constantly reminded that, in the words of the song, 'Without the Communist Party there would be no new China'. They were taught to respect revolutionary heroes and martyrs who embodied these morals. Many of those who were most successful at school became members of the Young Pioneers and wore a distinctive red scarf that symbolised both the national flag and the blood of the revolutionary martyrs. Thus communism and especially communist internationalism filled a gap left by the collapse of Confucian moral values as a defining feature of Chinese identity. China was being defined as a model for the world, but a model of a new revolutionary society. The content of the culture that was being promoted had been transformed from Confucian to socialist civilisation, but the idea that the nation was defined by its promotion of a central ideology had been recreated.

Race

As in the past, this model of identity based on a central ideology interacted with other forms of Han identity. The introduction and popularisation of ideas of race in the early twentieth century and the promotion of practices that contradicted traditional markers of Chinese ethnicity caused a further shift of emphasis from customs to heredity as a marker of Chinese identity. This shift was intensified by the attitude of the Communist state towards non-Han groups within its boundaries. In the 1950s the various non-Han peoples of the People's Republic were not under the same administrative system as the rest of the population. Following a national survey certain groups were identified as 'minority nationalities'. The criteria used to make this identification were taken from the writings of Stalin and were based on the group having a common language, territory, economic life and psychology. Areas with large populations of minorities were then provided with an autonomous administration. This ensured that the leaders of minority communities would have a certain degree of power within local, regional and national government. During the 1950s autonomous districts and regions were also encouraged to preserve some aspects of their separate culture, so that in Inner Mongolia, for example, there were Mongol-language schools and a separate Mongolian publishing industry. On the surface, this model of equality between the nationalities living in autonomous areas was similar to the separation of China from Manchuria, Mongolia and Tibet under the Qing.

In practice, however, the minority regions were much more closely integrated into the Chinese state than they had been under the Qing. The justification for this was the Communist Party's policy that since all the different peoples within the national boundaries were equal, it was the party's duty to assist in their liberation. The party claimed that the most important power relationship for the minority nationalities was not the ethnic difference between themselves and the Han, but class differences within the minority groups. Among the minority peoples themselves there was considerable resistance to this model. A 1948 speech by Gao Gang, then a leading party official, on policy in the province of Inner Mongolia criticised Mongol cadres for putting ethnic struggle above class struggle and claiming that the Chinese Communist Party was a Han party. Meanwhile, Han cadres were criticised for Han chauvinism: during land reform one local Han official, acting on the assumption that Mongols were unable to farm, had given good land to the Han and poor land to the Mongols. However, despite occasional admissions of problems like these, the party continued to hold to the primacy of class struggle. This meant that, although minority areas were separately administered, they were nevertheless expected to take part in the government's political campaigns and in the collectivisation of agriculture. Tibet was the only exception to this. When, in 1956, the government called for constructive criticism and ideas in the Hundred Flowers Movement, many criticisms were received from minority areas, including some about Han chauvinism. The Hundred Flowers Movement was rapidly followed by the Anti-rightist Campaign, in which those who had criticised the government, and many others who had not, were attacked as Rightists. In many minority areas the Anti-rightist Campaign emphasised the evils of local nationalism and its potential for harming the socialist cause. In Yanbian Korean Autonomous County on the Korean border, the Anti-rightist Campaign involved attacks on Korean cadres for thinking themselves superior to the Han and for complaining that Han monopolised the top positions. At the same time Korean children were required to study Chinese from the first year of primary school. There was also criticism of cadres who could not speak Chinese, in which the ability to speak Chinese was identified with loyalty to the government.

Attacks on ethnic difference on the ground that it prevented the achievement of national goals became even more common during the period from the late 1950s to the 1970s. It was during this period that the moral definition of the nation, which promoted a radically new set of beliefs and practices for the individual and claimed to be universal rather than culturally specific, was at its height. The result for many ethnic minority areas was forcible assimilation. During the early years of the Cultural Revolution minority customs, which had previously been seen as markers of identity, were attacked as examples of undesirable traditions. Schools and colleges for minorities were disbanded and all privileges for minorities were ended. In Yanbian radicals attacked Korean-language schooling and forced Korean and Chinese schools to integrate. At the same time the United Front institutions through which the separate administrative structures for minorities operated were destroyed and their leaders attacked. Those involved in minority administration were particularly severely attacked in border regions where it was feared that there was a threat of separation. In Mongolia hundreds of thousands of people were accused of having formed a Revolutionary People's Party of Inner Mongolia, which was said to want to split off from the rest of the country. Tibet, which had not been included in the earlier campaigns, was suddenly incorporated into the national political system in 1959 after the crushing of a major revolt and the flight of the Dalai Lama to India. Land reform was imposed and was soon followed by agricultural collectives. In Tibet ethnic identity was a particular point of strife during the Cultural Revolution. People were attacked in the streets for wearing Tibetan dress and there was a ban on Tibetan songs and dances. A refugee later remembered her life at the time:

> In the Red Flag Commune, the Cultural Revolution began at the end of 1966 . . . They showed contempt for the Tibetan script and banned Tibetan songs and dances. Tibetans were made to sing Chinese songs, wear Chinese dress and practice Chinese customs. We were also asked to speak in 'Tibetan-Chinese Friendship Language', which was a mixture of Tibetan and Chinese.[7]

Throughout the country the 1960s and 1970s brought intense pressure for assimilation to the normative forms of modern national identity promoted by the state.

The practices and lifestyles promoted during the Cultural Revolution were, of course, extremely oppressive for many Han Chinese, whose religious and cultural practices were also the subject of violent attacks. Nevertheless, the behaviour that was being promoted was clearly derived from the modern Chinese identity that had grown out of the late Qing reforms and the May 4th Movement, and it was perceived and promoted as Han. A book on the Korean minority explained:

> In our big united family of nationalities Han Chinese are the central nationality because they have a large population, a long history, and relatively rapid development in political, economic, and cultural areas. This is a result of our historical development.[8]

The model of the relationship between the different peoples of China as that between brothers, with the Han as the eldest brother, had been a feature of republican texts. However, the Communist government's effective rule over the minority areas transformed the theory into practice. The Chinese Communist Party, which sprang out of the urban Chinese radicalism of the 1910s and 1920s, was indeed a primarily Han organisation. Modernity provided the legitimation for its rule over the non-Han minorities, and thus demanded that the minorities and all others should be assimilated to the new modern Chinese customs.

Memory

The Cultural Revolution tore apart the idea of a politicised nation and opened the way for new definitions of identity, but it also provided a fund of shared memories and experience that united the People's Republic and separated it from areas such as Taiwan and Tibet, which had not gone through the same trauma or had experienced it in a different way. Indeed the whole experiment in government by campaign, with its violence and extreme, but erratic, state penetration, created a fund of national collective memories. In the city of Xian today both the Han Chinese and the large Muslim Hui community remember their past in terms of the differences before and after liberation in 1949, and can tell similar stories of hunger and food rationing during the famine that followed the Great Leap Forward in 1958. Indeed, there are few communities throughout the People's Republic that do not relate their experiences in similar terms. All this combined with the collective trauma of the Cultural Revolution unites those people who have been ruled by the People's Republic since 1949 and divides them from those who have different memories.

Tibet was not affected by the campaigns of the 1950s, and the beginning of Communist Party reforms at the time of the Great Leap Forward in 1958 led to a widespread popular revolt and the flight of the Dalai Lama to India. Subsequent political campaigns, and indeed the administrative system, continued to be perceived as the result of foreign invasion. This was to make Tibetans' experience of identity very different from that of the majority of Chinese. Taiwan, like Tibet, had been excluded by and large from the shared experiences of the rest of the country during the Republican era, in this case because it was a Japanese colony. This was followed almost immediately by the separation of the island from the mainland under Nationalist Party rule. Between 1949, when the Nationalist government retreated to Taiwan, and 1986, when under pressure from its ageing veterans it allowed visits to relatives on the mainland, there was a strict ban on all contact with the mainland. Not only were there no direct transport links, but even letters between family members had to be sent via a third country. In addition there was extreme political pressure to avoid all contact. At the same time the political system on the island, whose government claimed to be the government of all of China, effectively discriminated against the native population in favour of the mainlanders who had arrived in 1949 and could claim to represent the rest of China. The result was that instead of sharing the experiences of the mainland Chinese, the majority of the island's population, who had been there before the arrival of the Nationalist government in 1949, began to develop a sense of their own identity as 'Taiwanese' in opposition to the 'mainlanders' who had arrived in 1949.

Conclusion

During the period of Mao Zedong's rule from 1949 to 1976, the Communist government pushed the idea of a politicised national identity to its logical extreme. The existence, for the first time since 1911, of a unified and effective administration began the process of creating a strong national identity within the area ruled by the People's Republic. However, the violence of campaigns as a system of government undermined the idea of politicised nationalism even while it strengthened feelings of shared experiences, collective memory and a common identity. Moreover, the strength of the shared experience within the People's Republic also had the effect of excluding and alienating the populations of areas that the People's Republic claimed but did not effectively rule.

Notes

1 *Dagongbao*, 1 October 1949, p. 1.1.
2 Mao Zedong, *Jianguo yilai Mao Zedong wengao* (The Writings of Mao Zedong since the Establishment of the People's Republic) (Beijing: Zhongyang wenxian chubanshe, 1987), vol. 1, p. 6.
3 Xiandai Hanyu guifan wenti xueshu huiyi mishuchu, ed., *Xiandai Hanyu guifan wenti xueshu huiyi wenjian huibian* (Collected Documents from the Conference on the Question of Regularising Modern Chinese) (Beijing: Kexue chubanshe, 1956), p. 167.
4 Shen Xiaolong, *Shequ wenhua yu yuyan bianyi: shehui yuyanxue zongheng tan* (Local Culture and Language Change: Free Talks on Socio-linguistics) (Jilin jiaoyu chubanshe, 1991), p. 236.
5 Yu Youren quoted in Qi Zhenhai et al., *Aiguozhuyi jiaoyu gailun* (Outline of Patriotic Education) (Beijing: Beijing shifan daxue chubanshe, 1985), p. 147.

6 Mao Tse-tung, *Selected Works of Mao Tse-tung* (Peking: Foreign Languages Press, 1965), vol. 2, p. 337.
7 A. Tom Gronfeld, *The Making of Modern Tibet* (London: Zed Books, 1987), p. 181.
8 Quoted in Chai-Jin Lee, *China's Korean Minority: The Politics of Ethnic Education* (Boulder, CO: Westview Press, 1986), p. 81.

PART

IV

CHINESE NATIONAL IDENTITY TODAY

11

The emergence of alternative nationalisms

The opening up of China economically in the 1980s led to a crisis of cultural identity. After the death of Mao Zedong in 1976, policies shifted back in favour of those members of the Communist Party elite who wanted a more predictable form of government and it was announced that government goals were no longer to be achieved by campaigns. Instead of the moral pressure campaigns had applied, material incentives could now be used to motivate the workforce. Beginning with agriculture, state planning and intervention were gradually reduced and the economy was opened up to the forces of market competition. The so-called 'socialist market economy' retained elements of state control, for example in the pricing of certain essential items, but nevertheless the changes did greatly reduce the role of the state in everyday life. It was obvious that the socialist market economy was a major change from the moralistic forms of socialism promoted by the Communist Party in the 1960s and 1970s. During that period, arguments for the legitimacy of Communist Party rule had rested on socialism and class struggle. Clearly, the reforms undermined this source of legitimacy. Members of the government in search of an alternative legitimating ideology now turned back to the nationalism that had been central to the party's popularity during its rise to power.

However, it was not only the government that was in search of alternative ideologies during the 1980s and 1990s. Much of the population, especially those born since the start of Communist rule, had been committed to socialism as a personal as well as a national ideal. That ideal had been shaken by the violence of the Cultural Revolution and was now collapsing under the pressure of the new economic system. The 1980s saw a rise in interest in a whole variety of alternative ideologies ranging from religions, like Christianity and Islam, to alternative political systems, like democracy. Nationalism was one of these ideologies and held a particular appeal for both the government and the population. Ideas of nationalism had been central to China's modern history and had been heavily promoted by the government, whose foundation myth lay in the story of the battle against imperialism and Japanese invasion. However, the nationalism people now espoused was not necessarily the politicised nationalism promoted by the Communist Party. As both the legitimacy and the coercive power of the party declined, a variety of new types and interpretations of nationalism emerged. Alongside politicised nationalism, there was now talk of ethnic Han identity and of culturalist pride in China's traditions. Moreover, many people began to look beyond definitions of Chinese identity limited to citizens of the People's Republic, and to think about how Chinese nationalism was to be related to the people of Hong Kong or Taiwan or to the many people of ethnic Chinese origin living elsewhere in the world.

Politicised nationalism

During the 1980s and 1990s state leaders consciously promoted nationalism, or patriotism as they preferred to call it, in an attempt to strengthen their own position. From government statements in newspapers to television dramas, the official media emphasised the role of the Communist Party as the leading patriotic force in the country. Such patriotism was strictly tied to conformity with the party-state. Thus, for example, when Ulanfu, a lonstanding Communist Party leader from Inner Mongolia, gave a speech to students and young people in 1983, he asked his audience:

> In the present state of historical development, what is the content of the patriotism of the people of each of the nationalities of our country? It is simply to complete the three great tasks which Comrade Deng Xiaoping has promoted on behalf of the party centre: to intensify socialist modernising construction, to obtain the real unification of our ancestral land including Taiwan, to oppose [US] hegemonism and to protect world peace.[1]

Here patriotism is simply and specifically identified with adherence to party policy. Patriotism, in other words, was the emotion that was expected to motivate people to work towards government goals as laid down by Deng Xiaoping. A very similar line was taken in less formal contexts. Thus in a preface to a book of patriotic stories for young people the author claims that the purpose of the book is to counter the idea that because of government mistakes such as the Cultural Revolution, the ancestral land is not worthy of love. Instead, he argues that patriotism and love of socialism (that is the ideology of the Communist Party) are closely linked together.

Many people experience this type of nationalism through the mass media and through the symbolism of the government's propaganda activities. In recent years the anniversaries of World War II have provided important

occasions for government promotion of nationalism. The fortieth and fifti-
eth anniversaries of the Japanese defeat, in 1985 and 1995 respectively, were
both occasions for major official commemorations designed to promote
nationalist feeling. In 1985 commemorations included a long television
series about the sufferings of a Chinese family during the Japanese occupation and newspapers were full of reminiscences about the war. In Beijing
10,000 children attended a widely reported ceremony at the Martyrs'
Memorial in Tiananmen Square. There was also much media attention given
to a museum of the Nanjing massacre as a symbol of Japanese aggression
against China. Commemorations in 1995 were similar, with a particular
emphasis on the construction of a museum and memorial hall in Beijing.

At the same time the social changes that have accompanied the economic
reforms have had the effect of spreading a single nation-wide popular
culture. This is particularly well illustrated by the ever-increasing use of
Mandarin in ordinary social contacts. In the 1950s Mandarin was the
language of officials; today it is a necessity for the everyday lives of a large
proportion of the population. Increasing wealth has brought television into
the homes of the vast majority of Chinese families and with it a national
popular culture articulated in Mandarin. Economic development has also
caused migration, especially from rural areas to the cities and from the relatively impoverished western part of the country to the richer south and east
coast areas. For migrants Mandarin, or 'common speech' as it is known, is
essential for everyday life in their new place of residence. Perhaps the development of Mandarin as a truly popular language is best illustrated by
official complaints that since the reforms it has become westernised, coarse
and feudal. Western loan words such as *dishi*, which comes from a translit-
eration of taxi into Cantonese, rather than the official *chuzuqiche* or 'hire
car', are widely used despite official disapproval. Obscenities too have been
adopted, though this time mainly from local or regional dialects. The term
'feudal' refers to the vocabulary that has been incorporated from the traditional written language, often to add a sense of elegance and stylistic range
to writing or speech. In the last 20 years Mandarin has finally become a
truly national language used not only by politicians and modernisers, but by
ordinary people across the country.

The extent of popular nationalism compatible with state ideals can also
be seen in responses to China's international position. International sports
events have a huge television audience. In 1981, in what was seen as a
particularly symbolic event, China's women's volleyball team won the
world cup, defeating Japan in the final match. More than 30,000 letters
were sent to women on the team, including several written in blood, a traditional way of expressing deep emotion that is widely associated with
patriotic feeling. The final match was broadcast live and people across the
country came out onto the streets after it finished. A rural sports cadre
reported that in his Hebei village people let off fire crackers and 'some
people even cried. Some people were so agitated they were unable to eat and

skipped several meals.' He went on to point out the nationalist moral of all this, saying, 'The team won glory for China and showed the world that China is also good. Peasants also care about China's world reputation.'[2] Nationalist feeling is presented here as something that the rural population might well be excluded from and to which they aspire as a source of status and respect. The interaction between state and popular nationalism can also be seen in responses to the bombing of the Chinese embassy in Yugoslavia in 1999. Scenes of state leaders meeting the distraught families of those who had died during the bombing were repeatedly shown on television and police looked on as demonstrators threw stones and pieces of concrete at the British and American embassies. The reactions demonstrated genuine popular emotion, but were at the same time influenced by the state-run media's depiction of the incident and by the fact of government support. Combining popular feeling with official orchestration, they were fully compatible with the diplomatic and political aims of the government.

Politicised nationalism has also been used against the government. In 1985 commemorations of the anniversary of the end of World War II were part of the official promotion of nationalism. However, demonstrators went on to attack the role of Japan in the contemporary Chinese economy, an attack which used the nationalist narrative of China's modern history to criticise government policy. Thousands of students from universities in Beijing gathered for mass meetings at which anti-Japanese speeches were made and slogans shouted. Students from Beijing University self-consciously mirrored the anti-Japanese demonstrations of the 1920s and 1930s by going to Tiananmen Square and shouting slogans that included both 'Down with Japanese militarism!' and 'Down with the second occupation!', the latter using nationalist history to criticise the government's policy of encouraging Japanese investment in China. Similar demonstrations two weeks later in the city of Xian included calls to boycott Japanese goods, which again combined references to the 1920s and 1930s with contemporary criticism. In this case the official narrative of politicised nationalism was being used to shield protests against government policies: the demonstrators' publicity materials included attacks on official corruption and calls for liberalisation and democracy. The combination of government promotion of nationalist feelings with people's perception of nationalism as a potential tool against the government meant that both the government and its critics tended to take a strongly nationalist line during the 1980s and 1990s.

It is a testimony to the power of nationalism as a crucial source of legiti-mation for the government that there were some controversial cases in which the narrative of official nationalism was questioned. These involved both outright dissent and cases in which the criticisms grew out of factional differences within the government and consequently received a certain amount of official support. In the early 1980s there was considerable interest in the idea that Chinese culture was holding the country back from modernity and development. Phrasing these criticisms in terms of attacks on

the 'Confucian tradition' or 'feudal thought' made them outwardly acceptable to a socialist government that had grown out of a radical criticism of
China's past. However, with the government's new emphasis on nationalism as a source of legitimacy, such criticisms were also problematic.

Public expression of these criticisms culminated in the huge debate that
surrounded a television series called *River Elegy* put out by China's Central
Television in 1988. The series began with the story of an American who
wanted to be the first person to raft down the Yangzi River. To the Chinese
such an ambition immediately called to mind the foreign gunboats that had
steamed up and down the Yangzi from the 1840s to the 1950s and the
whole history of imperialism at the heart of politicised nationalism. Two
Chinese teams were formed to challenge the American and were tragically
drowned in the attempt. After telling the story, the announcer asked,
'Should we praise them for their patriotism or should we criticize them for
their blind love for their country?'[3] This set the tone for the series which
went on to criticise many of the symbols of nationalism: the dragon, the
Great Wall, the Yellow River and the yellow earth of north China. Much of
the impact came from the dramatic juxtaposition of highly symbolic images:
pictures of carved and painted dragons were combined with footage of
people bowing and clips from film of the 1960s and 1970s to suggest that a
specifically Chinese reverence for charismatic authority lay behind both the
symbol of the dragon and some of the disasters of Mao's rule. Beneath these
criticisms of popular symbols of China's traditional culture lay an attack on
the whole narrative of politicised nationalism. The series implied that
China's decline since the greatness was not due to imperialism but to its
traditional culture, which had made it unable to assimilate Western indus-
trialisation. Particular criticism of the poverty and traditionalism of the
rural areas of north China, which were the heartland of the Communist
Party before 1949, implicitly linked the critique of Chinese culture to a
critique of the party. Thus the series denied two key elements of the narrative of politicised nationalism: the wicked imperialists and the heroic
revolutionary party. Such a controversial series on a national television
channel was only possible because of high-level support within the government and party from those who favoured radical economic reform, which
the series had depicted very positively, contrasting gleaming towerblocks in
Shanghai with rural poverty in the traditional Communist heartland of
Yan'an. However, even with this support, it was apparent that the series
was criticising ideas that were at the heart of the Communist Party's claim
to power. Public interest was intense, the script of the series was published
both in book form and in the newspapers, Central Television received
around 1,000 letters in response to the first episode, and the series was soon
repeated. Many of those who responded wanted to defend patriotism,
Chinese culture and Communist rule. The public debate raged for several
months and illustrated the centrality of nationalism to the way in which the
Chinese state was being constructed and viewed during the 1980s.

The debate that surrounded *River Elegy* reflected the factional disputes within the government that were eventually to lead to the Tiananmen protests of 1989 and the crackdown that followed. The protests had grown out of the anniversary of the May 4th Movement, which both students and government saw as a patriotic movement. The government used the rhetoric of nationalism against the protestors and in the aftermath of the massacre the arguments over politicised nationalism hardened on both sides. For the first time since Chen Duxiu's famous attack on patriotism in 1919, the debate over China's future shifted so that it was possible for some of the government's opponents to state openly that patriotism was a problem. The dissident physicist Fang Lizhi blamed patriotism for the disasters of the 1950s and 1960s, saying that people had been so preoccupied with 'saving China' that they froze their critical judgement. He also questioned the whole idea of politicised nationalism. While love of one's homeland and family was a natural and praiseworthy emotion, love of the nation state was something different and far more problematic. To illustrate his point he told a story that reflected both the intensity of the politicised nationalism of the 1960s and his rejection of it:

> I remember in my younger days joining in on the criticism of our poor old teachers, who would always defend themselves by saying 'At least I'm patriotic; at least I love my country.' Our standard reply was 'But what country do you love? A communist country? Or a Kuomintang [Nationalist Party] country?' Of course what we were implying was that they weren't really patriotic at all. In this context, patriotism obviously does not mean loving your native place, your rivers, your soil, your cities, your kin; it means loving the state.[4]

The tone of this passage, with its obvious sympathy for his teachers and the positive repetition of native place, rivers, soil, cities and kin, carries with it the condemnation of politicised nationalism.

But such criticisms of patriotism were neither frequent nor necessarily popular. Since the late nineteenth century intellectuals had indeed been preoccupied with 'saving China' and patriotism had become a highly valued emotion. Many voices were raised to defend politicised nationalism. The debate that had followed *River Elegy* was played out again, but with the lines now more clearly drawn. So, for example, the author of a book on late Qing and republican patriotism published in 1991 drew attention in his preface to the recent questioning of patriotism. He was particularly concerned with the much debated issue of how far it was appropriate to love a country that had caused suffering to its people. In response to this he argued that a distinction should be made between one's ancestral land and culture on the one hand and the state on the other hand. Nevertheless, the tone of his argument was to reinforce the politicised nationalism promoted by the government. In using traditional culture in support of politicised nationalism, he suggests how the debate had moved on to incorporate the kinds of criticisms made by the authors of *River Elegy* and Fang Lizhi. After the events of 1989, nationalism was still central to the Communist government's claim to legitimacy, but the nature of nationalism was no longer unquestioned, but had come to be at the heart of the debate over Communist power.

Redefinitions

However, while the government and its opponents debated the narrative of politicised nationalism that had developed through the course of the twentieth century, other forms of identity were emerging. The 1980s saw a revival of thinking about the nation outside the mould of politicised nationalism, and a variety of new ways of understanding what the nation might consist of.

Regional cultures

Many of these new forms of identity grew out of changes sparked by the economic reforms. The success of the reforms in southeast China, and the consequent influence of Hong Kong and Taiwan culture, meant that a southern regional culture began to emerge as an alternative to Beijing. The great cities of Hong Kong, Guangzhou and Shanghai had long exerted a powerful cultural influence on their hinterlands, with their local dialects, for example, being spoken or understood beyond their immediate area. Regional dialects came to be more openly used in official contexts, so for example when a Shanghai cadre had spoken in Shanghai dialect at a major state meeting it was widely reported in the media that he had done so. Regional cadres unable to speak Mandarin had existed since the 1950s, but for this to be emphasised on the national media was new. As the state gradually became more responsive to public demand, there were obvious advantages for officials in speaking local dialects. In Guangdong even the top provincial leaders were often unwilling to speak Mandarin. In the late 1990s the fact that the Guangzhou mayor Li Ziliu had begun to use Mandarin for his daily work was worthy of considerable press comment. A test of Shandong officials in 1995 found that only 15 per cent of them were unable to speak Mandarin but less than half of them used Mandarin for their daily work. One of the reasons for this continued use of dialect was suggested by a 1990s survey of Fujian students at teaching universities who were asked to listen to the same speeches read in their local dialect and in Mandarin. When the students were tested it was found that they thought that the speakers using the local dialect were considerably more reliable, honest and warm hearted. With these kinds of attitudes among trainee teachers it is also not surprising that dialect use continues to be common in schools.

The economic reforms and increasing wealth of the southeast also created a sense that the kind of traditional folk culture that had been promoted by the Communist Party was not the only possible Chinese culture. This can be seen in *River Elegy* with its positive depictions of the coastal cities and its contrast between these cities and the rural areas of the north. People began to see the Chinese culture promoted by the national government as being specific to the poverty-stricken north, and there was a new emphasis on regional variation. This led to an interest in the whole question of the origins of Chinese culture, long depicted as being in the basin of the Yellow River, that is the areas of north China that were also the heartland of the Communist Party. Now academic studies of the ancient southern kingdom of Chu became popular. Archaeological evidence showed that this kingdom had had a culture with many elements that now seemed 'un-Chinese'. These studies were used to suggest that Chinese culture did not have a single line of descent from the culture of the Yellow River basin, but had merged elements from several ancient regional cultures. The new regionalism did not directly threaten the narrative of politicised nationalism, but it did undermine it by shifting the centre of attention away from Beijing and the Communist Party and towards the cities of the southeast coast. It also undermined the role of imperialism in the narrative of the nation state, since especially in the case of Shanghai it was argued that the city's development had been largely due to the Western powers, and it became clear that regional leaders were hoping to recapture Shanghai's former international position. Finally the increasing stress on regional identity shifted the balance between regional and national identity that had been heavily dominated by the nation during the 1950s and 1960s back in favour of the regions. For many people native place again became central to their sense of public identity.

Ethnicity and race

Economic reforms and the consequent reduction of the coercive power of the state also led to increased expressions of identity among some of China's ethnic minorities. The reforms brought about a revival of traditional culture across the county and in particular there was less interference in religious practices, which had previously been labelled as superstitious and wasteful. This allowed a much greater degree of expression of local identity and ethnic difference. In Tibet altars were set up again in people's homes, the holidays of the Tibetan calendar were widely and publicly celebrated and many monasteries were rebuilt. The end of the Cultural Revolution also saw a rejection of policies that explicitly promoted assimilation. At first this was largely symbolic: in 1983 ballots for the fifth National People's Congress were printed in Korean, Mongolian, Tibetan, Uyghur and Kazakh as well as Chinese. But separate administration for minority areas was also reestablished and gradually benefits were given to minority areas, many of which were among the poorest in the country. These included development aid, more lenient application of population control and affirmative action policies for education, which allowed minority students to enter university with lower scores than those required for Han Chinese. Members of ethnic minorities found that they could manipulate these policies to their own advantage and some highly acculturated groups began to reemphasise their cultural differences from the Han Chinese.

However, in other ways pressure for assimilation continued. Government administration at anything other than the lowest levels continued to be primarily conducted in, and usually by, Han Chinese. Thus in Tibet, although Tibetan was supposed to have become the primary language in legal matters in 1979 and the primary official language in 1990, Chinese continued to be the working language of government offices. In fact economic development created a demand for technical staff, usually Han Chinese brought into the region on short-term contracts, which exacerbated the problem. At the same time the economic reforms and the increase in wealth in rural areas were changing the lifestyles of many members of minority groups. Like their Han Chinese neighbours, members of ethnic minorities aspired to be seen as modern and 'civilised'. As they watched national television with its advertisements for a modern consumer culture, bought fashionable clothes and ate new Western-style foods they became less and less distinctively different from their Han Chinese neighbours.

The government procedure for identifying ethnic minorities interacted in a variety of ways with these pressures for assimilation. The criteria used to identify a group as an ethnic minority were subjective and hard to define, nor was any allowance made for self-identification. Consequently groups had often been recognised for reasons of size or historic importance. Moreover, in the years that followed the original survey no attention had been given to the actual degree of assimilation of these minorities to the Han majority. Consequently, once the groups had been established genealogy became ever more important in assigning minority identity to individuals. Children born of parents both of whom were members of a given nationality were automatically registered as members of that nationality. If children were born to a marriage where the parents were of different nationalities, the parents could choose the nationality under which they registered the child. This was extended so that the requirement for registration was by ancestry from either parent three generations back. Thus members of many minorities could not be distinguished from the majority unless the observer knew their official status. Minority identity became something whose choice was limited by the state and registered in state documents relating to the individual. However, because of official discrimination in favour of minorities in the education system and birth control policies, there were considerable advantages to being registered as an ethnic minority. The result was that many parents chose to register their children as members of ethnic minorities even though the children were culturally no different from the Han majority. These young people certainly could not have been defined by the Stalinist criteria originally used to identify minority groups. The most extreme example of this is provided by the Manchus. The majority of those labelled Manchu had lost most cultural markers by the nineteenth century and after the 1911 Revolution the former Manchus rapidly assimilated into the local Han Chinese communities. The Manchu language dwindled until it was spoken only by a few hundred elderly people in the far north of the country. However, in the 1982 census there were more than 4 million registered Manchus. For these people, and for many others like them, ethnic identity was a state-imposed category and was created not by cultural practices but by genealogy.

This increasingly racial view of identity also affected the way that the Han Chinese identified themselves. During the 1980s the cult of the Yellow Emperor was revived. During the late nineteenth and early twentieth centuries the Yellow Emperor had been invoked by revolutionaries as the ancestor of the Chinese race. Sun Yatsen sacrificed to him when he became president in 1911 and the term 'sons and grandsons of the Yellow Emperor' became a common way of referring to the Chinese people. The vision of Chinese as descendants of the Yellow Emperor became increasingly popular in the 1980s and the state revived the official rituals at the Yellow Emperor's tomb. In 1993 10,000 people attended a grave-sweeping ceremony at the tomb and large sums of money were donated to rebuild the site. The interaction of the state with explicitly racial images of Chinese identity of this sort suggests that the traditional cultural models of identity were under threat as much from a new emphasis on genealogy as from the political ideologies of the Communist state.

Identity and modernity

The economic reforms also made problematic the idea that governments had espoused since the 1920s that the culture of the state was equivalent to modernity and could be based on the culture of the more developed Han Chinese majority. In many minority areas during the 1950s and 1960s government policies had been seen as requiring strict conformity with Han practices, but this had been hidden by the rhetoric of class struggle. Now with the new emphasis on modernity and nationalism the idea that minority cultures were in themselves an impediment to progress became more visible. Thus an article printed in the *Tibet Daily* asserted that:

> The influence of religion in Tibet is profound and broad. Religion permeates all fields of social activity, and religious culture is integrated with ethnic culture. Although the masses have fine traditions, such as hard work, bravery, wisdom and patriotism, their level of modern

culture and education is low, many know nothing about science, and the proportion of illiterates is high; they have little concept of a commodity economy and a weak idea of competition.[5]

In the face of ideas of this kind, members of ethnic minorities began to question the equation between Han Chinese culture and modernity. Instead of looking to the centre of the Chinese state, they began to look outwards to other models of modernity: the Western democracies in the case of Tibet, and the Islamic Arab states in the case of the Chinese Muslims. In northwest China Muslims began to build mosques in Arab styles, learn modern standard Arabic rather than traditional Chinese-based systems for reciting the Koran, and even adopt Arab styles of clothing such as long skirts for women.

Increasing ethnic assertion, economic change and a questioning of the superiority of Han Chinese culture led to ethnic tensions. In 1989 there were riots in Lhasa during which the contents of Chinese shops were burned and rocks were thrown at Chinese cyclists. Ethnic violence also occurred repeatedly in Xinjiang. Economic change and the relaxation of political controls created tensions in minority areas while the government's emphasis on nationalism instead of class struggle made minority nationalisms harder to criticise. Government campaigns against 'splittism' were unable to change the underlying cultural trends. Thus the government's use of nationalism during the 1980s and 1990s led directly to the creation of alternative minority nationalisms not necessarily so much by its oppression as by the culture of nationalism it helped to create.

Tension between popular culture and the state's definition of Han Chinese modernity has also been created by the continued existence of communities outside China which identify themselves as ethnically Chinese. Since the early twentieth century all governments of China have asserted some degree of interest over these communities. The Nationalist government, which had had close links with Southeast Asian Chinese since Sun Yatsen's early fundraising journeys, established a ministry for overseas Chinese affairs and had representatives of the overseas Chinese in its National Assembly. The People's Republic took over the same pattern with a commission for overseas Chinese affairs and overseas Chinese representatives in the National People's Congress. From the 1950s to the 1970s the free traffic between many ethnically Chinese communities and the Chinese nation state, which had characterised the earlier period, became impossible for political reasons. However, the reforms of the 1980s led to efforts to strengthen the links between overseas Chinese and their homeland in order to encourage investment by rich overseas Chinese in their ancestral homeland. However, in the countries of Southeast Asia those whom the Chinese state defines as 'overseas Chinese' have developed their own identities tied not only to their cultural heritage, but also to the political situations within which they and their communities live and work. Many of the Chinese in

Southeast Asia have been very successful in commerce and business since at least the nineteenth century and their communities are often perceived as wealthy compared to the indigenous populations among whom they live. Partly as a result of this and partly because of the pressures of indigenous nationalism, they have developed a concept of Chineseness which is closely linked to modernity and transcends the need for allegiance to any particular nation state.

In the People's Republic traditional Chinese culture was criticised in the 1980s as being a barrier to modernity, but in much of Southeast Asia the presence of elements of traditional Chinese culture, often labelled Confucianism, is used to explain the business and commercial success of the Chinese community. Thus in Singapore the idea of Chinese values includes an emphasis on the family, education, high savings and hard work, which could be seen as universal values associated with capitalist modernity. In Thailand, where the Chinese community previously aspired to aristocratic Thai images of wealth and status, there was a fashion in the 1980s for what were seen as Chinese images of modernity. Transnational Chinese identities of this kind are imported into China through films and television. This is partly because of the increasing commercialisation of the Chinese media as a result of the economic reforms. In addition, advances in technology mean that satellite and cable television are now available in China, especially in the southeast of the country, and many families can watch television broadcast from Hong Kong and Taiwan. The availability of this type of commercialised transnational identity which transcends political boundaries and is no longer controlled by the political centre in Beijing is the product of the economic reforms and in itself brings into question the simple and increasingly old-fashioned narrative of politicised nationalism.

Taiwan

A changing sense of national and ethnic identity in Taiwan is also undermining the politicised nationalism of both the Nationalist and Communist Chinese states. When the Nationalist government retreated to Taiwan in 1949 it saw the island as a base for the recapture of the mainland. Even in the early 1990s cinemas in Taiwan started each show by playing the national anthem. The images that accompanied this, mostly footage of former Nationalist leaders, ended with a map of China on which Taiwan was coloured with the blue of the Nationalist flag and the mainland was red. As the anthem reached its dramatic conclusion rays of blue spread out from Taiwan and entirely covered the mainland. It was inevitable that running what was intended to be a future national government from one island would result in discrimination against the local population. In 1949 the representative organs of the national government, which had been elected in 1947, were removed from the mainland and installed in Taiwan. As time went on and the mainland was not retaken those who died or retired were replaced by others from the same province. Occasional 'supplementary' elections were held to elect members of the local Taiwanese population, but these never came close to breaking the political control of the small minority of the population who had come from the mainland between 1945 and 1949. The result was the formation of a distinct Taiwanese identity with which the local population distinguished themselves from the 'mainlanders' who had come to the island with the Nationalist government and whom they now saw as a dominant political class.

When in 1986 martial law was lifted, a new political party emerged to challenge the Nationalists. This was the Democratic Progressive Party, which drew its support almost entirely from the local Taiwanese population and campaigned for greater representation for them. Tied in with the campaign for greater democracy and representation for the majority population was a critique of the structures of the Nationalist government that laid claim to mainland China. With the election of Li Denghui, a native Taiwanese, to the presidency, it became apparent that neither the government nor the general population had any real enthusiasm for reunification, and that the islanders were seeking a form of independence, while finding it necessary to ensure that this did not provoke the People's Republic into an invasion. Then in 2000 the Nationalist Party finally lost power to a presidential candidate from the Democratic Progressive Party. The Democratic Progressive Party cautiously abandoned its demand for Taiwan independence in order to achieve this goal. Nevertheless, the party's roots in opposition to Taiwan's position as a base for Chinese reunification meant that the politicised Chinese nationalism of both the Nationalist Party and the Communist Party had been decisively rejected.

Throughout this period, both the mainlander and the Taiwanese communities in Taiwan have shared a sense of their Han Chinese ethnic identity and their Chinese cultural heritage. However, they have distinguished this from loyalty to either the People's Republic of China or the Republic of China as a nation state. This was particularly apparent during the 1990s when many Taiwanese visited the mainland for the first time after the lifting of the long-standing ban on travel to communist-controlled areas in 1987. The visitors were shocked both by the poverty of the mainland and by the very different society they found. Many who had been educated to believe themselves to be Chinese now began to look for the first time at the influence of the period of Japanese colonial rule in Taiwan. The problems were exemplified by a pair of Taiwanese cousins studying at Nanjing University on the mainland in 1994 who were asked one day in a shop 'Are you Chinese?' They replied immediately, one yes and the other no. Both girls denied that the question of not being Chinese had ever even crossed their minds before their arrival on the mainland and both were deeply disturbed by the encounter. The separation of governments and political systems had worked to create division between the two territories even while both governments promoted a very similar form of modern Chinese nationalism.

Thus the economic reforms of the 1980s and increased contacts with Han Chinese communities that had not been under the control of the government of the People's Republic brought up a series of different views of identity that were no longer linked to the narrative of politicised nationalism. These included ethnic nationalisms in opposition to the government, but also ideas of Chineseness that dismissed the link between nation and state and emphasised instead either a transnational Chinese identity, as in the case of Southeast Asian Chinese, or a local Chinese identity as has been the case on Taiwan.

The end of empire?

This book has told the story of a Chinese nationalism forged by two empires: the great Manchu Qing empire that was formed in the seventeenth century and the expansive British empire of the nineteenth century. The traditional narrative of Chinese history has defined Chinese nationalism in opposition to these two empires, but in fact the ideologies of imperialism were also important in shaping the Chinese nation state. The return of Hong Kong to China in 1997 illustrates both the power of the continuing historical narrative of opposition to foreign imperialism and the equally powerful legacy of Qing imperialism that can be seen in the practices of the contemporary Chinese state.

Hong Kong, ceded by the Qing as a result of the first Opium War, stands at the beginning of the story of Western imperialism in China. Its early prosperity grew from the favourable provisions of the unequal treaties. Later it became the home of innumerable refugees from China who felt themselves to be protected by its imperialist government. In the last two decades of the twentieth century much of its wealth was built on its access to and yet separation from Guangdong during that province's rapid growth as a result of the economic reforms. When Hong Kong was handed back to China this history of imperialism was brought to an end and the politicised nationalism of the Chinese state was shown triumphant. However, the ceremonies of the handover demonstrated not only the symbols of the modern Chinese nation and the story of imperialism and politicised nationalism, but also the imperial origins of the Chinese state and the popular emotions that could be aroused by a nationalism that was so closely tied to the idea of empire.

The actual transfer of power took place at the moment of midnight on 30 June 1997 with the lowering of the British flag and the raising of the Chinese flag at a ceremony in Hong Kong itself. Throughout the media coverage of the event the raising of the Chinese national flag was taken as being the central point of the ceremonies. A national public holiday was also announced to mark the occasion. Both the use of the flag and the declaration of a public holiday were modern symbols of the nation state that had come to China as a result of that same imperialism that had created the city of Hong Kong. Indeed the formal part of the ceremonies had an old-fashioned air amid the internationalism and commercialism of contemporary Hong Kong. But the nineteenth-century symbols of nationhood still have a powerful hold over the imagination: it was the raising of the Chinese flag that attracted a huge television audience all over China as being the actual moment of the transfer of power, rather than the various celebrations and displays that followed it.

The story of China's battle against imperialism also played a central role in the image of the nation that was put forward. This seems natural given Hong Kong's role in that story, but it was also part of a continuing government campaign to promote an official politicised version of nationalism. Ceremonies that accompanied the handover in Beijing laid a particular emphasis on this aspect. In Tiananmen Square 100,000 people watched a giant clock that counted down the final minutes and seconds until the handover. Performances put on in the square used the Martyrs' Memorial, with its resonances of the battle against imperialism, as a backdrop. The next day a huge pageant was laid on in the Workers' Stadium displaying the history of China since the Opium War. Hong Kong pop stars sang patriotic songs, and speakers intoned Sun Yatsen's promise to abolish the unequal treaties, Mao Zedong's claim that the Chinese people had stood up, and Deng Xiaoping's determination not to discuss the issue of sovereignty over Hong Kong. Jiang Zemin's speech covered the same territory, dealing with China's hundred years of humiliation, a standard narrative of China's modern history as a nationalist battle against imperialism, and the contribution of revolutionary leaders and martyrs. Jiang Zemin also spoke of the desire to extend national reunification to include not only Hong Kong but also Taiwan. The story of imperialism and China's battle against it under the leadership of a heroic revolutionary party was at the heart of the nationalism of the 1920s and 1930s. This was a narrative that the Communists shared, in its general outline, with the Nationalist government in Taiwan and it thus led directly to the issue of a national reunification that would include Taiwan. The narrative of politicised nationalism was still at the heart of the Chinese government's approach to the question of nationhood.

The symbols of the nation and the story of the battle against imperialism also had the power to move many ordinary people, whether they were the crowds in Beijing watching the great clock as it ticked down the seconds to midnight, or a villager whose family had lived in the rural hinterland of Hong Kong since before the area was ceded to the British. This man told a reporter that he had bought a Chinese flag and had a flagpole erected on his roof so that he could raise the flag at midnight:

'I climbed onto the roof when the clock struck 12 and raised the flag as planned. It was an emotional moment when I saw the flag flying on our own soil. I will remember it for the rest of my life.

'I have deeply inherited patriotic feelings from my family and my ancestors. And I have been looking forward to this moment since I was a child.'[6]

For this man, as for many others, nationalism and the story of imperialism had been internalised and accepted at a very personal level.

But there were also many people within the People's Republic of China for whom the legacy of the Qing empire and the politicised nationalism of the Chinese state made the nationalist displays of the handover highly problematic. In Tibet and Xinjiang government leaders were warned in advance that the occasion might be seen as a potential flashpoint for separatists. To guard against this the governments of both areas used the occasion as an opportunity to reinforce messages of national unity. A report in the *Xinjiang Daily* explained that the handover proved 'that ethnic unity and the unification of the motherland are irreversible tendencies'[7] Fig. 11.1 is a propaganda poster entitled 'Warmly celebrate the return of Hong Kong', which was printed and distributed in the People's Republic. It shows a woman in a red dress, representing the motherland, holding in her arms a

Figure 11.1 'Warmly celebrate the return of Hong Kong'

smiling child who holds aloft the flag of the new autonomous region of Hong Kong. Behind the woman and child are doves, balloons and the smiling faces of members of China's ethnic minorities, instantly identifiable by their elaborate headdresses. In Tibet a huge ceremony was held in front of the Potala Palace in Lhasa at which doves and balloons were released. In Hong Kong itself 3,000 people gathered in the central district to count down the seconds to the handover with shouts of 'Long live democracy!' and 'Fight for democracy!' Many people in Hong Kong also used the publicity created by the occasion and the opportunity generated by the rhetoric of nationalism for their own ends. On the night of the handover there were street protests not only against human rights abuses in the People's Republic, but also against the behaviour of the Hong Kong police and the Hong Kong and British governments. Other protestors demanded the immediate right of abode for the children of mainland parents living illegally in Hong Kong. Yet another group represented buyers of properties in a tower block in the Guangdong town of Zhuhai demanding that they be given their money back.

Nationalism has never been merely a simple allegiance to nation or nation state. Ever since the late nineteenth century Chinese nationalism has been a means by which people made claims for political power at both the lowest and the highest levels of Chinese politics. The complaints of a Beijing taxi driver that the ceremonies had been a waste of money and the shouts of the protestors on the streets of Hong Kong reflect the ways in which ordinary people have used the rhetoric and occasions of nationalism to make their own political demands. A few days after the handover the *South China Morning Post* announced that the clock used to count down the seconds to the handover in Tiananmen Square was to be moved to the Great Wall, where it would stand beside a statue of Lin Zexu, whose dramatic attempt to suppress the opium trade was the cause of the first Opium War. This would bring together the Great Wall, a symbol of China's imperial rule and ancient culture, with Lin Zexu, a symbol of the narrative of politicised nationalism and the clock with its resonances of the success of the contemporary national leadership in its negotiations with Britain and effective orchestration of the handover. The combination suggests the many ways in which China's leaders too have continued to make use of the symbols of nationalism for their own political ends.

Notes

1   Li Fan (ed.) *Zai xin de lishi tiaojian xia jicheng he fayang aiguo zhuyi chuantong* (Building and Developing a Tradition of Nationalism in New Historical Circumstances) (Beijing: Hongqi chubanshe, 1990), p. 109.
2   Quoted in Susan Brownell, *Training the Body for China: Sports in the Moral Order of the People's Republic* (Chicago: University of Chicago Press, 1995), p. 80.

3 Su Xiaokang and Wang Luxiang, *Deathsong of the River,* introduced, translated and annotated by Richard W. Bodman and Pin P. Wan (Ithaca: Cornell University East Asia Program, 1991), p. 102.
4 Fang Lizhi, 'Prologue: On Patriotism and Global Citizenship' in George Hicks, ed., *The Broken Mirror: China after Tiananmen* (Harlow: Longman, 1990), p. xxi.
5 Quoted in Ronald D. Schwartz, *Circle of Protest: Political Ritual in the Tibetan Uprising* (London: Hurst, 1994), p. 5.
6 *South China Morning Post,* 1 July 1997, p. 18.
7 *South China Morning Post,* 1 July 1997, p. 12.

Bibliography

Introduction

Benedict Anderson, *Imagined Communities: Reflections on the Origin and Spread of Nationalism*. London: Verso, 1983.

Ernest Gellner, *Nations and Nationalism*. Oxford: Blackwell, 1983.

E.J. Hobsbawm, *Nations and Nationalism since 1780: Programme, Myth, Reality*. Cambridge: Cambridge University Press, 1990.

Joseph R. Levenson, *Confucian China and its Modern Fate*. 3 vols. London: Routledge and Kegan Paul, 1958–65.

Chapter 1

Myron Cohen, 'Being Chinese: the Peripheralization of Traditional Identity'. In Tu Wei-ming ed., *The Living Tree: The Changing Meaning of Being Chinese Today*. Stanford: Stanford University Press, 1994.

Benjamin A. Elman, 'Political, Social, and Cultural Reproduction via Civil Service Examinations in Late Imperial China' *Journal of Asian Studies* 50.1 (1991).

Benjamin A. Elman and Alexander Woodside eds, *Education and Society in Late Imperial China, 1600–1900*. Berkeley: University of California Press, 1994.

David Faure, 'The Lineage as Cultural Invention: The Case of the Pearl River Delta' *Modern China* 15.1 (1989).

Daniel K. Gardner, *Chu Hsi and the Ta-hsueh: Neo-Confucian Reflection on the Confucian Canon*. Cambridge, MA: Council on East Asian Studies, Harvard University, 1986.

Evelyn Sakakida Rawski, *Education and Popular Literacy in Ch'ing China*. Ann Arbor: University of Michigan Press, 1979.

John R. Shepherd, *Statecraft and Political Economy on the Taiwan Frontier, 1600–1800*. Stanford: Stanford University Press, 1993.

Helen F. Siu, 'Who were the Women? Rethinking Marriage Resistance and Regional Culture in South China' *Late Imperial China* 11.2 (1990).

James Watson, 'The Structure of Chinese Funerary Rites: Elementary Forms, Ritual Sequence, and the Primacy of Performance'. In Evelyn Rawski and James Watson eds, *Death Ritual in Late Imperial and Modern China*. Berkeley: University of California Press, 1988.

Madeleine Zelin, *The Magistrate's Tael: Rationalizing Fiscal Reform in Eighteenth-Century China*. Berkeley: University of California Press, 1984.

Chapter 2

Michael Aris, *Hidden Treasures and Secret Lives: A Study of Pemalinga (1450–1521) and the Sixth Dalai Lama (1683–1706)*. Shimla: Indian Institute of Advanced Study, 1988.

C.R. Bawden, *The Modern History of Mongolia*. London: Weidenfeld and Nicolson, 1968.

Pamela Kyle Crossley, '*Manzhou yuanliu kao* and the Formalization of the Manchu Heritage' *Journal of Asian Studies* 46.4 (1987).

___, *Orphan Warriors: Three Manchu Generations and the End of the Qing World*. Princeton: Princeton University Press, 1990.

___, *A Translucent Mirror: History and Identity in Qing Imperial Ideology*. Berkeley: University of California Press, 1999.

David M. Farquhar, 'Emperor as Bodhisattva in the Governance of the Ch'ing Empire' *Harvard Journal of Asiatic Studies* 38.1 (1978).

Antoinette K. Gordon, *Tibetan Religious Art*. New York: Columbia University Press, 1952.

Dorothea Heuschert, 'Legal Pluralism in the Qing Empire: Manchu Legislation for the Mongols' *International History Review* 20.2 (1998).

James Hevia, *Cherishing Men From Afar: Qing Guest Ritual and the Macartney Embassy of 1793*. Durham, NC: Duke University, 1995.

John D. Langlois, 'Chinese Culturalism and the Yuan Analogy: Seventeenth-Century Perspectives' *Harvard Journal of Asiatic Studies* 40.2 (1980).

Dian H. Murray and Qin Baoqi, *The Origins of the Tiandihui: The Chinese Triads in Legend and History*. Stanford: Stanford University Press, 1994.

Peter C. Perdue, 'Boundaries, Maps, and Movements: Chinese, Russian, and Mongolian Empires in Early Modern Central Eurasia' *International History Review* 20.2 (1998).

L. Petech, *China and Tibet in the Early 18th Century*. Leiden: E.J. Brill, 1950.

Evelyn S. Rawski, *The Last Emperors: A Social History of Qing Imperial Institutions*. Berkeley: University of California Press, 1998.

Eliot Sperling, 'Awe and Submission: A Tibetan Aristocrat at the Court of Qianlong' *International History Review* 20.2 (1998).

Rolf Trauzettel, 'Song Patriotism as a First Step toward Chinese Nationalism'. In John W. Haeger ed., *Crisis and Prosperity in Sung China*. Tucson: University of Arizona Press, 1975.

Rudolf Wagner, *Reenacting the Heavenly Vision: The Role of Religion in the Taiping Rebellion*. Berkeley: Institute of East Asian Studies, University of California, 1982.

Chapter 3

Paul Cohen, *Between Tradition and Modernity: Wang T'ao and Reform in Late Ch'ing China*. Cambridge, MA: Harvard University Press, 1974.

____, *History in Three Keys: The Boxers as Event, Experience, and Myth*. New York: Columbia University Press, 1997.

Prasenjit Duara, *Culture, Power and the State in Rural North China, 1900–1942*. Stanford: Stanford University Press, 1988.

Joseph W. Esherick, *The Origins of the Boxer Uprising*. Berkeley: University of California Press, 1987.

John K. Fairbank, *Trade and Diplomacy on the China Coast: The Opening of the Treaty Ports 1842–1854*. Cambridge, MA: Harvard University Press, 1953.

____, *The Chinese World Order: Traditional China's Foreign Relations*. Cambridge, MA: Harvard University Press, 1968.

Luke S. Kwong, *A Mosaic of the Hundred Days: Personalities, Politics, and Ideas of 1898*. Cambridge, MA: Council on East Asian Studies, Harvard University, 1984.

James M. Polachek, *The Inner Opium War*. Cambridge, MA: Council on East Asian Studies, Harvard University, 1992.

Benjamin Schwartz, *In Search of Wealth and Power: Yen Fu and the West*. Cambridge, MA: Harvard University Press, 1964.

Frederic Wakeman, *Strangers at the Gate: Social Disorder in South China, 1839–1861*. Berkeley: University of California Press, 1966.

Mary Clabaugh Wright, *The Last Stand of Chinese Conservatism: The T'ung-chih Restoration, 1862–1874*. Stanford: Stanford University Press, 1957.

Chapter 4

Sally Borthwick, *Education and Social Change in China: The Beginnings of the Modern Era*. Stanford: Hoover Institution Press, 1983.

Roswell S. Britton, *The Chinese Periodical Press, 1800–1912*. 1933. (Repr.) Taipei: Ch'eng-wen Publishing Company, 1966.

Susan Brownell, *Training the Body for China: Sports in the Moral Order of the People's Republic*. Chicago: University of Chicago Press, 1995.

Meribeth E. Cameron, *The Reform Movement in China 1898–1912*. London: Humphrey Milford, 1931.

Frank Dikotter, *The Discourse of Race in Modern China*. Stanford: Stanford University Press, 1992.

Paula Harrell, *Sowing the Seeds of Change: Chinese Students, Japanese Teachers, 1895–1905*. Stanford: Stanford University Press, 1992.

Joan Judge, *Print and Politics: 'Shibao' and the Culture of Reform in Late Qing China*. Stanford: Stanford University Press, 1996.

Joseph Levenson, *Liang Ch'i-ch'ao and the Mind of Modern China*. Cambridge, MA: Harvard University Press, 1959.

Li Boyuan, *Modern Times: A Brief History of Enlightenment* (trans. Douglas Lancashire). Hong Kong: Research Centre for Translation, Chinese University of Hong Kong, 1996.

Edward A. McCord, *The Power of the Gun: The Emergence of Modern Chinese Warlordism*. Berkeley: University of California Press, 1993.

Mary Backus Rankin, *Early Chinese Revolutionaries: Radical Intellectuals in Shanghai and Chekiang, 1902–1911*. Cambridge, MA: Harvard University Press, 1971.

Hans van de Ven, 'The Military in the Republic' *China Quarterly* 150 (1997).

Rudolf G. Wagner, 'The Role of the Foreign Community in the Chinese Public Sphere' *China Quarterly* 142 (1995).

Chapter 5

Edwin J. Dingle, *China's Revolution, 1911–1912: A Historical and Political Record of the Civil War*. New York: McBride, Nast & Co., 1912.

Joseph W. Esherick, *Reform and Revolution in China: The 1911 Revolution in Hunan and Hubei*. Berkeley: University of California Press, 1976.

_____, 'Founding a Republic, Electing a President: How Sun Yatsen became *Guofu*'. In Eto Shinkichi and Harold Z. Schriffin eds, *China's Republican Revolution*. Tokyo: University of Tokyo Press, 1994.

Thomas E. Ewing, *Between the Hammer and the Anvil? Chinese and Russian Policies in Outer Mongolia, 1911–1921*. Bloomington: Research Institute for Inner Asian Studies, Indiana University, 1980.

A. Tom Gronfeld, *The Making of Modern Tibet*. London: Zed Books, 1987.

Urgunge Onon and Derrick Pritchatt, *Asia's First Modern Revolution: Mongolia Proclaims its Independence in 1911*. Leiden: E.J. Brill, 1989.

Ono Shinji, 'A Deliberate Rumour: National Anxiety in China on the Eve of the Xinhai Revolution'. In Eto Shinkichi and Harold Z. Schriffin eds, *China's Republican Revolution*. Tokyo: University of Tokyo Press, 1994.

Nakami Tatsuo, 'A Protest against the Concept of the "Middle Kingdom": The Mongols and the 1911 Revolution'. In Eto Shinkichi and Harold Z. Schriffin eds, *The 1911 Revolution in China: Interpretive Essays*. Tokyo: University of Tokyo Press, 1984.

Chapter 6

John Fitzgerald, *Awakening China: Politics, Culture and Class in the Nationalist Revolution*. Stanford: Stanford University Press, 1996.

Valery M. Garrett, *Chinese Clothing, an Illustrated Guide*. Hong Kong: Oxford University Press, 1994.

Henrietta Harrison, *The Making of the Republican Citizen: Political Ceremonies and Symbols in China, 1911–1929*. Oxford: Oxford University Press, 2000.

Claire Roberts, *Evolution and Revolution in Chinese Dress, 1700s-1990s*. Sydney: Powerhouse Publishing, 1997.

Peter Zarrow and Joshua A. Fogel eds, *Imagining the Chinese People: Chinese Intellectuals and the Concept of Citizenship, 1890–1920*. New York: M.E. Sharpe, 1997.

Chapter 7

Chow Tse-tung, *The May Fourth Movement: Intellectual Revolution in Modern China*. Cambridge, MA: Harvard University Press, 1964.

Emily Honig, *Sisters and Strangers: Women in the Shanghai Cotton Mills, 1919–1949*. Stanford: Stanford University Press, 1986.

E. Perry Link, *Mandarin Ducks and Butterflies: Popular Fiction in Early Twentieth-Century Chinese Cities*. Berkeley: University of California Press, 1981.

Hanchao Lu, *Beyond the Neon Lights: Everyday Shanghai in the Early Twentieth Century*. Berkeley: University of California Press, 1999.

Elizabeth J. Perry, *Shanghai on Strike: The Politics of Chinese Labour*. Stanford: Stanford University Press, 1993.

Lucian W. Pye, 'How China's Nationalism was Shanghaied'. In Jonathan Unger ed., *Chinese Nationalism*. New York: M.E. Sharpe, 1996.

S. Robert Ramsey, *The Languages of China*. Princeton: Princeton University Press, 1987.

Benjamin I. Schwartz ed., *Reflections on the May Fourth Movement: A Symposium*. Cambridge, MA: East Asian Research Centre, Harvard University, 1972.

Wen-hsin Yeh, 'Shanghai Modernity: Commerce and Culture in a Republican City' *China Quarterly* 150 (1997).

Chapter 8

Stephanie Po-yin Chung, *Chinese Business Groups in Hong Kong and Political Change in South China, 1900–25*. Basingstoke: Macmillan, 1998.

Prasenjit Duara, *Rescuing History from the Nation: Questioning Narratives of Modern China*. Chicago: University of Chicago Press, 1995.

Lloyd E. Eastman, *The Abortive Revolution: China under Nationalist Rule, 1927–1937*. Cambridge, MA: Harvard University Press, 1974.

James C. Thomson, *While China Faced West: American Reformers in Nationalist China, 1928–1937*. Cambridge, MA: Harvard University Press, 1969.

Arthur Waldron, 'The Warlord: Twentieth-Century Chinese Understandings of Violence, Militarism and Imperialism' *American Historical Review* 96.4 (1991).

____, *From War to Nationalism: China's Turning Point, 1924–1925*. Cambridge: Cambridge University Press, 1995.

Chapter 9

Yung-fa Chen, *Making Revolution: The Communist Movement in Eastern and Central China, 1937–1945*. Berkeley: University of California Press, 1986.

Parks M. Coble, *Facing Japan: Chinese Politics and Japanese Imperialism, 1931–1937*. Cambridge, MA: Harvard University, Council on East Asian Studies, 1991.

Poshek Fu, *Passivity, Resistance and Collaboration: Intellectual Choices in Occupied Shanghai, 1937–1945*. Stanford: Stanford University Press, 1993.

Chang-tai, Hung, *War and Popular Culture: Resistance in Modern China, 1937–1945*. Berkeley: University of California Press, 1994.

John Israel, *Student Nationalism in China, 1927–1937*. Stanford: Stanford University Press, 1966.

Chalmers A. Johnson, *Peasant Nationalism and Communist Power: The Emergence of Revolutionary China, 1937–1945*. Stanford: Stanford University Press, 1962.

Steven I. Levine, *Anvil of Victory: The Communist Revolution in Manchuria*. New York: Columbia University Press, 1987.

Rana Mitter, *The Manchurian Myth: Nationalism, Resistance and Collaboration during the Manchurian Crisis, 1931–33*. Berkeley: University of California Press, 2000.

Wen-hsin Yeh, 'Progressive Journalism and Shanghai's Petty Urbanites: Zou Taofen and the Shenghuo enterprise, 1926–1945'. In Frederic Wakeman and Wen-hsin Yeh eds, *Shanghai Sojourners*. Berkeley: Institute of East Asian Studies, University of California, 1992.

Chapter 10

Frank Dikotter ed., *The Construction of Racial Identities in China and Japan*. London: Hurst, 1997.

June Teufel Dreyer, *China's Forty Millions: Nationalities and National Integration in the People's Republic of China*. Cambridge, MA: Harvard University Press, 1976.

Stevan Harrell, 'Ethnicity, Local Interests, and the State: Yi Communities in Southwest China' *Comparative Studies in Society and History* 32 (1990).

Thomas Heberer, *China and its National Minorities: Autonomy or Assimilation*. New York: M.E. Sharpe, 1989.

Beverly Hooper, *China Stands Up: Ending the Western Presence 1948–1950*. Sydney: Allen and Unwin, 1986.

Chae-Jin Lee, *China's Korean Minority: The Politics of Ethnic Education*. Boulder: Westview Press, 1986.

Kenneth G. Lieberthal, *Revolution and Tradition in Tientsin, 1949–1952*. Stanford: Stanford University Press, 1980.

Perry Link, 'China's "Core" Problem' *Daedalus* 122.2 (1993).

Richard Madsen, *Morality and Power in a Chinese Village*. Berkeley: University of California Press, 1984.

Glen Peterson, *The Power of Words: Literacy and Revolution in South China, 1949–95*. Vancouver: UBC Press, 1997.

Michael Schoenhals, ' "Non-people" in the People's Republic of China: A Chronicle of Terminological Ambiguity' *Indiana East Asian Working Paper Series on Language and Politics in Modern China* 4 (1994).

David Y.H. Wu, 'Chinese Minority Policy and the Meaning of Minority Culture: The Example of the Bai in Yunnan, China' *Human Organisation* 49.1 (1990).

Wu Hung, 'Tiananmen Square: A Political History of Monuments' *Representations* 35 (1991).

Chapter 11

Kjeld Erik Brodsgaard and David Strand eds, *Reconstructing Twentieth-Century China: State Control, Civil Society and National Identity*. Oxford: Oxford University Press, 1998.

Edward Friedman, *National Identity and Democratic Prospects in Socialist China*. Armonk: M.E. Sharpe, 1995.

Maris Boyd Gillette, *Between Mecca and Beijing: Modernization and Consumption among Urban Chinese Muslims*. Stanford: Stanford University Press, 2000.

Dru C. Gladney, *Muslim Chinese: Ethnic Nationalism in the People's Republic*. Cambridge, MA: Council on East Asian Studies, Harvard University, 1991.

Christopher Hughes, *Taiwan and Chinese Nationalism: National Identity and Status in International Society*. London: Routledge, 1997.

Perry Link, *Evening Chats in Beijing: Probing China's Predicament*. New York: Norton, 1992.

Aihwa Ong and Donald M. Nonini eds, *Ungrounded Empires: The Cultural Politics of Modern Chinese Transnationalism*. London: Routledge, 1997.

Ronald D. Schwartz, *Circle of Protest: Political Ritual in the Tibetan Uprising*. London: Hurst, 1994.

Su Xiaokang and Wang Luxiang, *Deathsong of the River* (intro., trans. and annotated by Richard W. Bodman and Pin P. Wan). Ithaca: Cornell University East Asia Program, 1991.

Jonathan Unger ed., *Chinese Nationalism*. Armonk: M.E. Sharpe, 1996.

Allen S. Whiting, *China Eyes Japan*. Berkeley: University of California Press, 1989.

Mayfair Mei-hui Yang, *Gifts, Favors and Banquets: The Art of Social Relationships in China*. Ithaca: Cornell University Press, 1994.

Index